William Paterson
and
Frank Candy

An illustrated history of two pioneers in water treatment and the companies they founded

M.H.Goss

Paterson Candy Ltd

Text copyright M.H.Goss 1999

Published in England by Paterson Candy Ltd, 632/652 London Rd, Isleworth, Middx. TW7 4EY

ISBN 0/9537696/0/7

All rights reserved. No part of this book may be reproduced or transmitted in any form without the permission of the publishers.

Printed and bound by Bookcraft, Midsomer Norton, Somerset, England.

Contents

"Those who cannot remember the past are condemned to repeat it."
Gordon Maskew Fair, Professor of Sanitary Engineering at Harvard.

Preface		5
Historical overview		9
Chapter 1	Frank Candy, 1886-1906	21
Chapter 2	The Bell Brothers, William Boby, the Lassen-Hjort Partnership	35
Chapter 3	The Candy Filter Company, 1906-1918	49
Chapter 4	William Paterson, 1902-1955	67
Chapter 5	The Candy Filter Company, Technical Expansion, 1918-1940	83
Chapter 6	Paterson takes over Candy's	109
Chapter 7	Permutit	115
Chapter 8	The Second World War	137
Chapter 9	Recovery and the move to Portals, 1945-1960	143
Chapter 10	Paterson Candy International, 1960-1970	163
Chapter 11	The Big Contracts, 1970-1988	183
Chapter 12	Epilogue, 1988-1996	199
Appendices		
A.	Extract from Bob Williams' final notes	207
B.	Chapter notes	209
C.	Conversion factors	215
D.	Glossary of technical terms	215
E.	Sources	218
F.	List of illustrations	221
Index		231
The Family Tree		235

Portsmouth Water Company, River Itchen Scheme, built by Paterson Candy Holst. 1970s. Capacity 7 mgd, later extended to 14.

Preface

This is the story of two late Victorian entrepreneurs, Frank Candy and William Paterson who founded their businesses at the turn of the century. For the next seventy years, they and their successors more or less dominated the water treatment market in those parts of the world under British influence, and were responsible for much of the progress in drinking water quality. Although their companies were relatively small by comparison with the better known giants of engineering, their contribution to public health in much of the world was out of all proportion to their size and their legacy will be with us for years to come. Such firms employed few people but generally retained a core of long serving and often very competent staff who generated and passed on the company's knowledge to their successors, and provided the continuity necessary for this essentially long term industry.

W.G.(Bob)Williams joined Candy's in the drawing office and retired some 40 years later in 1971 as Contracts Director and deputy MD, intending to record the company's story. With his breadth of experience he was well placed to tackle the project and clearly had a great affection for the firm. He spent four years researching the history, but for various reasons, wrote only an initial draft before he died in 1985, with the work still incomplete.

When I retired after thirty-two years with Candy's in its various guises, I felt that Willams' text was worth resurrecting and turning into a book. I have extended his account and include some notes on Bell Brothers, Permutit and William Boby Ltd, but the story is mainly about Paterson and Candy.

Bob Williams, 1906 to 1985
Photo taken in the late 1960s

The two were very different personalities; Frank Candy was essentially an engineer who generally preferred to design the equipment he sold, an approach that continued through his son Pullen to the present times. William Paterson took a more pragmatic view. He was very willing to licence technology, and his company continued with this approach until the amalgamation with Candy's which Paterson then controlled. The combined company, Paterson Candy International, reflected the Candy approach, with its emphasis on in-house technology and expertise, although temporary neglect of this brought the firm close to disaster in the early 1970s; but that is a later story.

Preface

Inevitably, I have taken a personal view of the relative value of many of the firm's achievements, and I freely accept that their importance in the wider context may be much less than I have claimed here. It is also probable that some of the developments credited to the founders were based on others' ideas. The brief overview of the technology skates over the events and does not do justice to the subject but this book is primarily about the company.

What is not in contention is that Frank Candy, his son Frank Pullen Candy, and William Paterson, were exceptional men whose early work is now standard water treatment practice, and their efforts improved the health of much of the world's population through the provision of clean water. Despite the ups and downs of the industry over the last hundred years, the company which they founded is still held in high esteem and has a long and proud record of achievement.

The chapters covering the last twenty years or so are deliberately brief as the opinions expressed are primarily mine and much of the detail might be very contentious. For that reason, I have chosen not to refer to any staff members still alive, even though many of them have made significant contributions to the company's fortunes.

Conventions

I have used the country names applicable at the time rather than the current name,

A Reeves patent "Compound" pressure filter at Ilkeston, Derbyshire. Capacity 0.5 mgd. 1899

which is given in brackets. Similarly, Imperial units are used throughout, e.g. million gallons per day, "mgd", as these were in use in the industry until the 1970s. The few conversion factors which are relevant are included in an appendix.

It seems logical to use the name given to the company at the time. The Candy Filter Company became Paterson Candy International, "PCI", as did the Paterson Engineering Company. In turn, PCI became PWT Projects Ltd and recently reverted to the name

Preface

Paterson Candy Ltd. Similar confusion surrounds The Permutit Company, which started life as United Water Softeners Ltd and used a variety of names. In this story, after 1937 I have stuck to "Permutit" which was a well respected name throughout the world.

Appendices

Much of this story is about the technology of water treatment. In Appendix D I have included a brief, layman's glossary of some of the technical terms used.

MHG
September 1999.

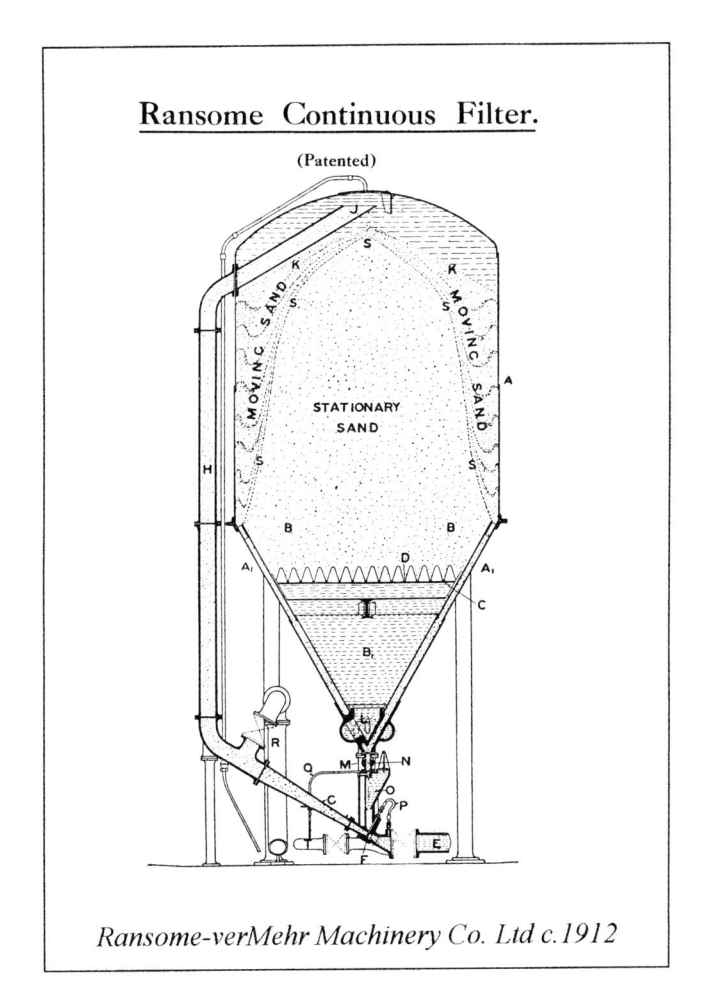

Ransome Continuous Filter.
(Patented)

Ransome-verMehr Machinery Co. Ltd c.1912

Preface

Historical Overview

Water and sewage treatment in the UK in the late 1880s

Frank Candy started his professional career in about 1858 but did not specialise in water treatment until 1887. At the time, typhoid was distributed periodically by the public drinking water supply and still killed numbers of people each year. The concept of disinfection with chlorine was in its infancy and not routinely practised.

The major towns that depended on a surface water source used slow sand filters as their means of treatment, but generally the public supply relied for its purity on the quality of the source, and wells and upland impoundment were generally used. Treatment of surface water for the smaller communities consisted of rudimentary brick chambers filled with limestone chippings and coarse sand which was skimmed periodically. Contamination was frequent and there were no means for dealing with iron or acidic, peaty waters. Virtually universal chlorination of the water supply began only in the period immediately prior to the second war, implementation having been accelerated following the Croydon typhoid outbreak in 1937.

Candy's display to celebrate the inauguration of a 1 mgd treatment plant for Standerton, South Africa, in 1911

In 1870 only forty-one towns in England and Wales had any form of sewage treatment works, and sewage disposal relied on untreated discharge to a river or water course, or more generally outside the major towns, the use of septic tanks. The great Victorian engineers had started to construct the sewers in our major cities (many of these are still in service) but the effluent was mostly channelled untreated, to a disposal point. Industry did no better and industrial effluents were discharged to pollute the rivers, until the second half of this century.

The next 100 years

Until the mid-1940s the water supply was a municipal responsibility, via over one thousand statutory water companies or city councils. By then, virtually all towns in England and Wales had piped water and main drainage, whereas much of the rural area did not. There were few standards other than a need to provide "pure and wholesome" water, and there was little or no regulation on the control of pollution. Sewage disposal was the responsibility of the local and district councils and again, the countryside had few services.

There are three landmarks in the administration of water supply and pollution control in the United Kingdom. The first was the 1945 Water Act which led to the re-grouping of many of the small statutory companies and local authority suppliers, and the formation in 1946 of the River Boards, determined by the catchment areas of the major rivers in England and Wales. They had responsibility for the management of the rivers from source to mouth, as well as the discharges to the rivers. In practice their powers were limited, although subsequent legislation strengthened the requirements and standards. The 1973 Act formed the Regional Water Authorities, and incorporated the River Boards into the new Water Supply and Sewage Disposal Authorities whose boundaries followed those of the old River

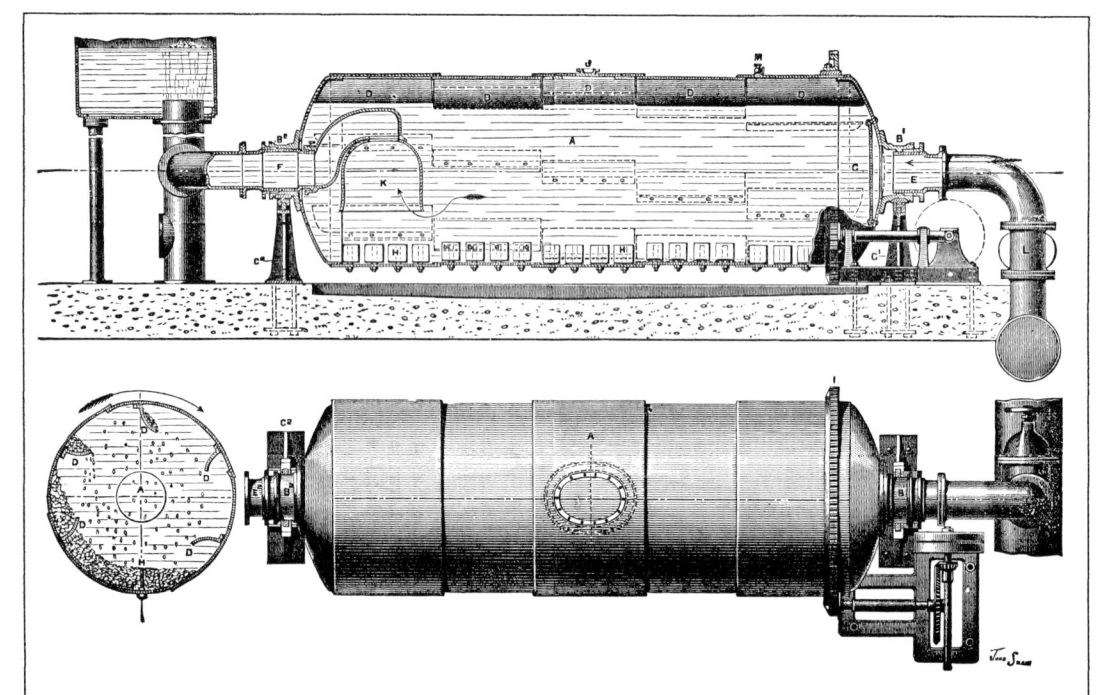

The Revolving Purifier, Anderson's patent. This device from 1890 consisted of a tank with internal trays, partly filled with metallic iron particles of about 3/8 inch size. It was driven by an external engine which caused the particles to "shower" through the water with a contact time of about 3.5 minutes. Presumably the corrosion products from the iron particles acted as a coagulant and the water then had to be filtered. It was installed in a number of major European cities.

Boards. Then in 1989, the water and sewage utilities in England and Wales were privatised. Each stage brought about a major change in the way the industry was run. The incorporation of the River Boards into the Water Authorities had largely emasculated them, and it was not until the separation of the policing duties at privatisation that the National Rivers Authority (NRA) achieved real power of enforcement. This was a long overdue reform and it is worth noting that the NRA remains a public body and has not been privatised.

During these changes the water side was energetic in re-structuring itself, and by 1973 the number of statutory organisations had been reduced to about 187, whereas sewage disposal administration remained in the hands of local government which usually had other financial priorities, and had made little effort to improve itself. (In 1946 there were 1,393 Sewerage and Disposal Authorities as well as the 29 River Boards).

The period of the late 1940s and early 50s saw the extension of water supply and main drainage to most of the UK. Then the Privatisation Act led to the formation of today's water companies, and consolidated responsibility for both water and sewage disposal in the common organisations which the 1973 act had created. (In passing, we might note that the trading surplus of the superseded Statutory Water Companies had by law to be ploughed back into the business, and their water charges were generally substantially lower than those of other water providers).

The fundamental reason for the difference in the development of water and sewage administration arises from the desirability of treating sewage near the source, to avoid pumping. By contrast, water is easily pumped for long distances. This difference has meant that there remain thousands of small sewage works whereas the water suppliers have re-grouped to take advantage of accessible bulk sources.

Technology - drinking water

Frank Candy did not live to see the fundamental move from relatively unpolluted sources to the use of most of our rivers for drinking water, but he would have well understood how this would affect the treatment needs. At the start of this story, with some notable exceptions such as the Metropolitan Water Board, water supplies were not treated except by simple filtration or straining, and chlorination was not used except as an emergency treatment. Frank Candy altered this with his Polarite filter for Reading in 1892 and his Declor filters, also for Reading, in 1909. However, these processes had declined by the late 1920s when Wallace and Tiernan introduced first, marginal chlorination and then break-point treatment. The 1930s and 40s saw the construction of increasingly large and complex plant and the widespread use of gravity filters. By the 1950s, we see the establishment of the modern treatment plant, combining the use of coagulation, settlement and filtration, although the pattern varied across the country with the north generally preferring pressure filters to open gravity filters.

Paterson and Candy continued to build the bulk of the municipal plants during this period, not only in the UK but throughout the then Empire, together with some notable plants in Europe and South America. Bell Brothers who had dominated the raked filter market for much of the period began to decline, having failed to modernise their technology.

The 1960s brought a surge in plant construction in the UK as the demand for water increased rapidly in response to the changes in the prosperity of the country. This necessitated the widespread use of more polluted and turbid surface sources, and as a consequence, the introduction of more complex treatment coupled with new river balancing reservoirs, constructed on the upper reaches of our major rivers, to regulate flow and provide flood control, as well as improving the quality and supply reliability. Many of the reservoirs were opened to the public for fishing, boating etc.

These more polluted surface waters needed several stages of treatment and clarifiers became widely used. In particular, precipitation softening was adopted for many major works with the dual purpose of reducing hardness and assisting purification. Pressure filters, sometimes with in-line coagulation, gave way to very complex plants employing large quantities of chemicals and demanding much more control.

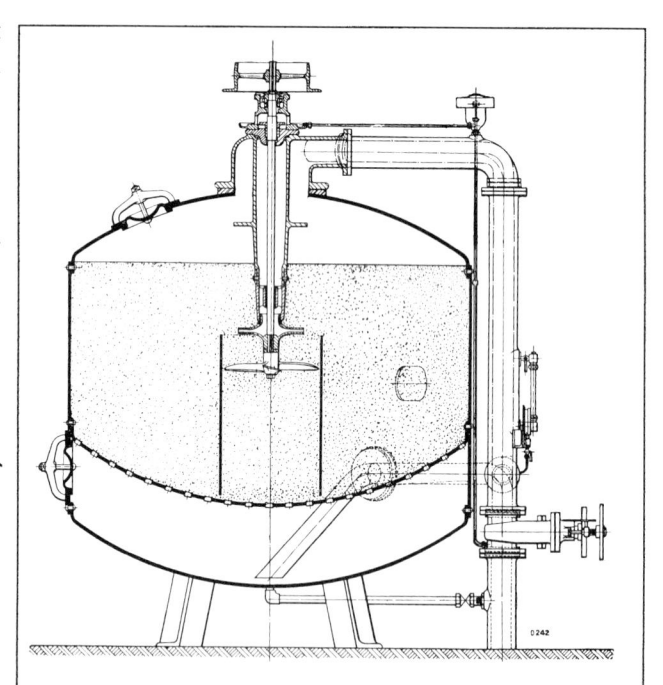

An illustration from an early Bell's catalogue showing the Mather and Platt patent filter which used an impeller to agitate the sand during backwash. Presumably the impeller mechanism was less satisfactory than rakes as the concept disappeared quite early.

Widespread automation to manage the handling of the chemicals and cleaning of the filters appeared in the 1960s, based initially upon somewhat unreliable Post Office relay technology. Nonetheless, the big plants of the 60s were very similar in automation terms to modern plants, with the exception of regional telemetry which was then not possible. The Candy Filter Co and Paterson Engineering were in the forefront of these developments and they built the first plants to handle chemicals in bulk. Plants such as Pitsford (Mid-Northants WB) and Elvington, for the supply to Sheffield, were as advanced in terms of chemical handling, automation and control as any being built in the 1990s, although the technology was perhaps pushed further than the reliability of the equipment justified.

The heart disease scare in the 1960s implicated the softening of water and led to the end of construction of the big precipitation softening plants. Few were built after the early 1970s. Paradoxically, the next generation of treatment plants is likely to use Nanofiltration and so partially soften the water.

The 1990s have seen settlement give way in the UK to floatation and the widespread introduction of Ozone, long used in Europe, and prompted by our current concerns over micro-pollutants which chlorination either exacerbates or doesn't deal with. Again, PWT Projects, as Paterson Candy had become, played an important part in developing the use of these modern treatment methods.

Sewage treatment

The development of sewage treatment was to be much slower, reflecting perhaps the fundamental need for simple and very robust processes. Trickling filters and activated sludge processes were in use long before the 1940s and they continued to dominate the industry until the 1980s when a variety of processes appeared with the aim of reducing land needs and costs.

Bell filters at Clarkston paper mill. Pre-WW1

It is important to recognise the part that Frank Candy and his son Pullen played in the development of sewage treatment through their patents for rotary and travelling distributors for trickling filters at the turn of the century. These resulted in the first sensible sewage plants, and continued to be supplied by Candy's until after the 1920s. In more recent times, the company has played only a minor part in the sewage market with a few notable exceptions, including the introduction of coarse media gravity filters for "tertiary" treatment of sewage effluent.

The changes of fortune - the companies

Frank Candy preceded William Paterson by about fifteen years and the two were in competition until a dispute in 1934 when Paterson, having the larger business, bought Candy's, although they continued to trade separately until the early 1960s.

Historical overview

By then, Portals Holdings owned the company and they decided to rationalise the activities and reduce duplicated tendering.

The next landmark came in 1965 when the two companies were amalgamated as Paterson Candy International with the municipal activities transferred to the Candy side and Paterson's staff concentrating on industrial work. In the ensuing power struggle, the ex-Candy senior management took over and effectively reversed the position of the previous thirty years.

Paterson Candy International continued to thrive, although less important in the world context, off-setting the investment cycles of the UK market with overseas work. Then in 1988 PCI was merged with The Permutit Co Ltd which had been purchased by Portals in 1970. The new company was renamed PWT Projects Ltd (Portals Water Treatment). This nondescript name wasted much of the value inherent in the great names of Candy, Paterson and Permutit, and led to a period under ownership by Thames Water (perhaps the wilderness years) when the company rather lost direction in the maelstrom that the UK market became after privatisation.

On the way, William Paterson bought Bell Brothers, British Berkefeld, Jewell Filters and the Metafiltration Co. Subsequently, Portals bought (through Permutit) William Boby Ltd, a company as old as Candy Filters. There were also some others, but none of these has had the impact that Candy, Paterson and Permutit brought to the world water treatment business. Then in 1997 Black and Veatch of Kansas City, Missouri, itself an old and well respected firm, bought the successors of Candy's, restored the names of Candy and Paterson, and re-launched the company as Paterson Candy Ltd. Unfortunately, Permutit which once dominated the world industrial market has not survived as a major specialist contractor in the UK.

The design and supply engineers

Because the intimate relationship between the purchasers and the plant designers and suppliers altered radically from the mid-60s onwards, it is worthwhile to look at how the changes to the structure of the water and sewage utilities affected the engineers and contractors.

The period saw the development of two influences which fundamentally altered the industry. Firstly, a number of consulting engineers started to take a much stronger role in defining the treatment and plant details, and secondly, the formation of the Water Authorities in 1973 brought in many new people with little knowledge of the water industry but who were much more aggressive commercially. This further moved the relationship away from the traditional co-operation between the contractor and the water company, resulting in an arms-length and for a few years, confrontational, supplier-purchaser position.

These developments brought with them profound changes to the relationship between the specialist contractors and the utilities, which although they occurred gradually and unevenly, were to the detriment of the long established plant suppliers.

BEWARE! UNFILTERED WATER

Water is a sure and swift vehicle of
DEADLY DISEASES
Reliable Authority tells us
IT IS POSITIVELY ESSENTIAL
to the safety of the health of all men, women and particularly infants,
THAT EVERY DROP OF DRINKING WATER
supplied from cisterns of any type, or from wells, streams and other such sources
MUST BE FILTERED BEFORE DRINKING
Even when the water comes from a Corporation main supply it is advisable, and safer, to
FILTER BEFORE DRINKING

A Metafilter advertisement from the early 1920s

The consulting engineers

British consulting engineers have long held a proud position in the international and domestic markets, and for most of this century they provided the designs for much of the infrastructure. In the water and sewage fields, however, the overall scheme design has often been done in-house by the utility's new works engineer and his staff. In such cases, consultants usually provided the design of dams, tunnels, conduits and the civil engineering structures. The process and hydraulic design and the layout of the treatment plant and its ancillaries were often the responsibility of the specialist contractors such as Candy's and Paterson's (in conjunction with the client's engineers). This appears logical as the specialist contractors built many more works than any single utility or consultant, although there have always been some water providers who designed their own treatment plants. The accumulated experience was put to good use in the UK and throughout the world and contributed to the company's success for a long period.

Towards the late 60s this pattern began to change when some consultants targeted the detailed engineering of the treatment plants, offering a total design service which was notionally independent of the specialist water treatment contractors. Whilst this brought some benefits, it was often at the cost of over-elaborate specifications. Companies like PCI who were particularly successful in working to such designs found themselves increasingly uncompetitive in overseas markets and had to develop dual standards to cope with the conflicting needs.

In the 90s, with the advent of privatisation in England and Wales, the consultant's role changed once again, as the utilities built strong in-house design teams, although these were run down fairly quickly once the bulk of the treatment plant construction was complete.

The civil engineering contractors

It is important to say a few words about the civil contractors and their impact on the market. In general, the civil contractors built to consultants' (or the clients') designs, and few had their own design teams. There were exceptions such as Holst's with whom PCI formed an alliance, Paterson Candy Holst, in the mid-60s to bid for and execute turn-key work, but there was almost no overlap with the treatment specialists and relatively few of the civil contractors were comfortable with building the type of watertight structures that were needed.

The formation of Degremont-Laing in the late 60s turned this comfortable arrangement on its head, as they offered a complete turn-key service for treatment plants from a single company, and took several substantial contracts from traditional PCI customers. This turn-key approach did not become widespread (apart from PC-Holst) until Biwater entered the market a few years later. In the 90s privatisation turned the UK market on its head, and many of the civil contractors entered the treatment plant market as direct competitors to the treatment specialists.

The impact on the specialist contractors

Companies like Candy's and Paterson's had traditionally made a major contribution to the design of waterworks, and until the late 60s they commonly provided the treatment concept as well as the detailed plant design for many of the new plants. This strength served them well in the UK and overseas. The huge surge in demand at the start of the 1960s required an overall design capability to provide chemical storage, handling and automation on a scale never dreamt of in the UK public supply industry. At the time Candy Filters were better equipped than perhaps any other supplier to meet the requirements, and they produced some spectacular designs and innovative contracting ideas which enabled the company to respond to the construction needs at a rate out of all proportion to the size of the organisation.

The market changes reflected those taking place throughout industry in Britain, but by the time the water supply industry was privatised the traditional specialist contractors were in a parlous state and very short of worthwhile business. Most of them were quickly absorbed by the newly privatised water companies, and just as quickly disposed of. Privatisation brought its own problems. The by now in-house firms were given much captive work but the honeymoon was very short and the transfer of effort to the UK market to meet the demand meant that little effort was available for overseas work. The brief glut of UK work also brought in many hungry civil contractors. Within about five years, there was little left to do in the UK, but by then most of the specialist contractors were no longer able to hold their own in other markets. None of this should have been beyond the normal requirements of competent management but the fact remains that few of the companies recognised the fundamental changes which had occurred in the marketplace, and British water treatment expertise no longer enjoys the dominant position it once had.

Duplicate oil engines, driving Turnover filters, c.1900

Historical overview

The acquisition of PWT Projects by Black and Veatch in 1997 has brought about another major change in the company's fortunes, and Paterson Candy Limited, as the organisation has become, is once more flourishing and is re-building its long standing position in the market

Paterson's supplied a treatment plant for Omdurman (Sudan) in 1929. The view is looking north to where the famous battle occurred. This fine photo is from the plant archive of the time.

Chapter 1

Frank Candy (right) in front of the filter for Chippenham, 1914

1 - FRANK CANDY, 1886-1906

One of the few remaining photos of Frank Candy shows the company's founder in 1914, standing majestically in front of the pressure filter for Chippenham, formally dressed in the style of the time, and complete with buttonhole and spats. But this imposing, rather stern image does not do justice to the open minded and very practical entrepreneur. Totally confident in himself and his ideas, he was a pioneer in water treatment at a time when the technology was in its infancy and much of the water distributed as potable would have sent the present generation to hospital. Candy was not afraid to make claims that sound boastful today, but he was essentially a technical man who revelled in his ability to innovate.

Frank Candy was born at Styrtingale Farm on the outskirts of Bath in 1842, one of four sons and two daughters of a family that had farmed in the south west for several generations. He went to the King Edward IV Grammar School in Bath but left little to record any achievements there. When he finished school, he joined a firm of auctioneers and surveyors in Bath, and by 1866 was working in Islington. In the same year, then aged 24, he married Elizabeth Pullen. They were to have three children, May, Frank Pullen and Edgar Ralph.

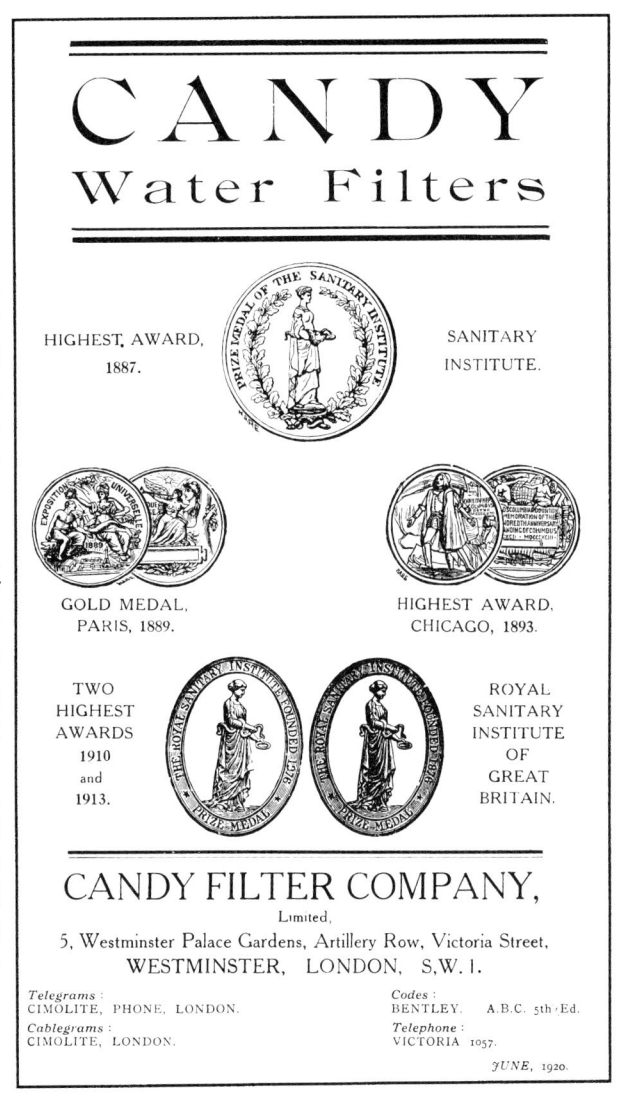

Early patents

Over the next few years, Candy devoted his energy to improving road surfaces, and in 1871 he was granted his first patent for the invention "Improvement in Making Roads, Ways, and Floors." The patented product was made from granite particles extracted from china clay waste, plus ironstone and mineral tar, mixed into hot asphalt, which sounds very much like tarmacadam. The material was claimed to be *"economical, durable under great traffic, and to present a sufficiently rough surface to furnish a good foothold for horses and other beasts of burden."* It was used in some districts although we have no record of how widespread this was.

Candy and Company

The roads venture cannot have been a major success, because Candy was soon looking at other ideas. During his geological surveys in the early 1870s, he found large deposits of clays near Chudleigh in South Devon, situated near the main Great Western Railway and Newton Abbot. He believed that the clays were suitable for making high grade tiles, bricks and other clayware, so he raised the money to form a company and moved to Chudleigh and later, to Newton Abbot where his young son went to school.

He went into partnership with a Mr Ludlum and the company, Candy & Company Limited, was formed in 1874 with a share capital of £10,000 subscribed equally by the two partners. The site chosen for the works was alongside the railway near Heathfield, and was named "The Great Western Pottery and Patent Brick Works."

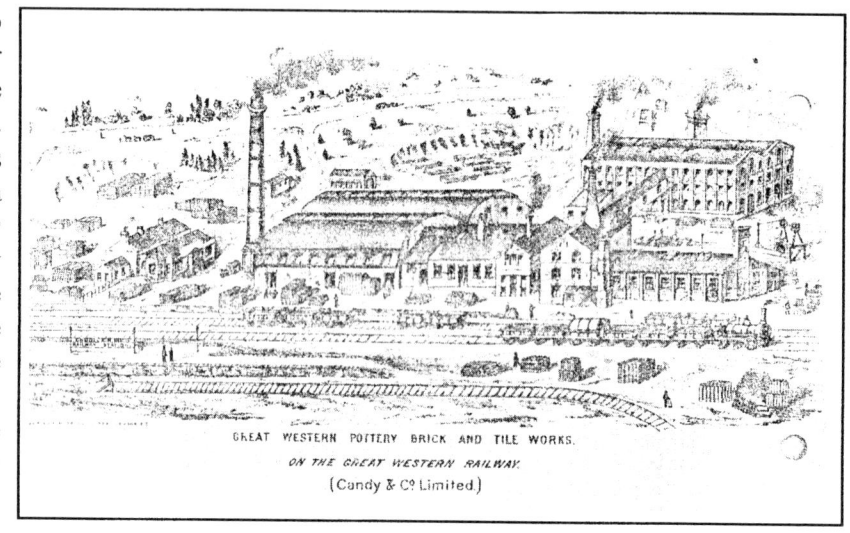

GREAT WESTERN POTTERY BRICK AND TILE WORKS.
ON THE GREAT WESTERN RAILWAY.
(Candy & Co Limited.)

The works appears to have started active operations quickly, and by 1880 it was supplying a wide range of products, with a brick machine in constant use, turning out 4,000 bricks an hour. Candy obtained a number of patents related to making clay products but he also widened his interest to improving fertilisers made from sewage works effluent, as well as clarification aids for the food and drinks industry, and for water and sewage treatment.

In 1882, clearly still restless, he sold his interest in Candy and Company to his partner, and the company (now BCT) continues to manufacture ceramic products in 1999.

Shortly afterwards Candy and his family returned to London, this time settling down at Bexley in Surrey, and there decided to form a new company to concentrate on water and sewage purification.

The Partnership

Between 1883 and 1887 Candy's various activities brought him into contact with engineers and chemists who had a common interest in improving methods of clarifying sugar syrups and brewing liquors. As it seemed probable that their developments might also be useful to the water supply and sewage industry, they formed a partnership to exploit the developments. The Partners had facilities for experimental work at a factory in Whitechapel. There, two important products, Polarite and Ferrozone, were invented, which were to have a significant impact on water and sewage treatment in the future.

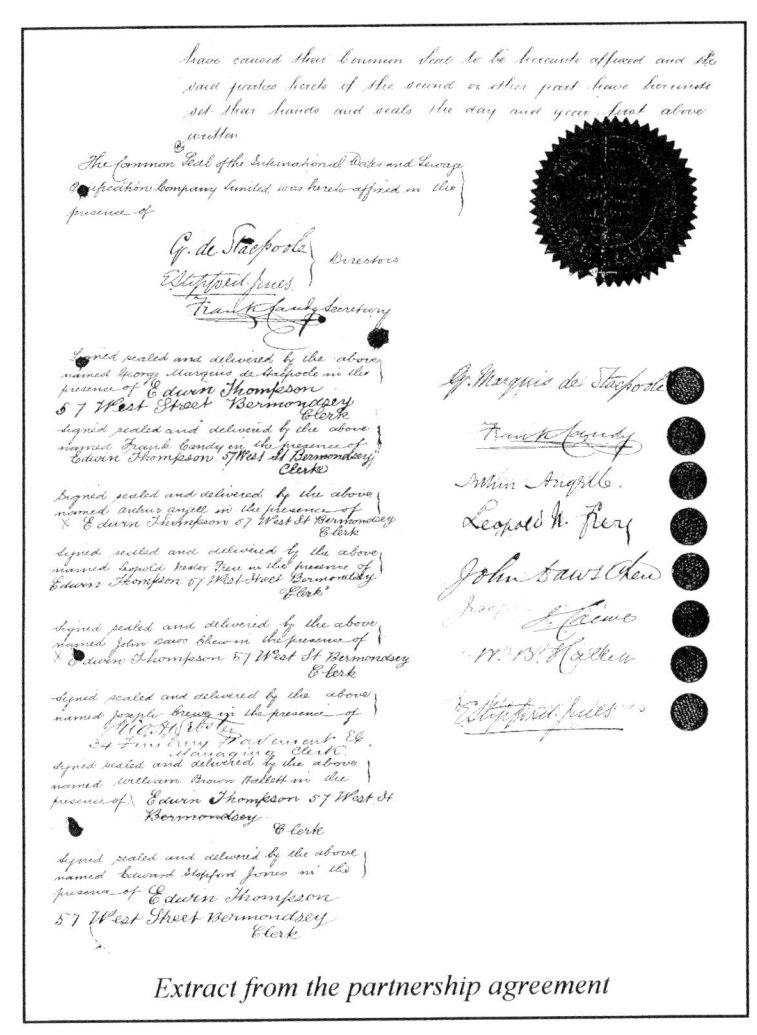

The commercial success of the venture depended on being able to control the sources of the raw materials as well as the manufacture and distribution, so, on the 28th September 1886 Candy took a licence for twelve months, *"to dig, search, win and try for Ironstone, Blackband, Fireclay and Coal, lying and being under the farm and lands called Tio Maur, Glyn Elyn and Cae Hopkin, in the Parish of Ystradgwynlais in the County of Brecon, with option to lease."* Through this agreement, the partners secured a source of their raw materials that was close to the Abercrave railway station.

Extract from the partnership agreement

At the time, the area was rather remote, and it appears that Candy was in the habit of carrying a handgun while visiting.

Chapter 1

Polarite

When Candy took out his patents for filter materials in 1886, the normal method of treating water was by slow sand filtration and coagulants such as alum (aluminium sulphate) were little used. However, some suppliers used animal charcoal, coarse sand or other granular media, and there was considerable activity to find improved filtering materials to replace them. Towards this end and based on his geological experience, Candy developed Polarite, a porous oxide of iron with a high silica content that was free from phosphates. The material was made by controlled heating, followed by anaerobic cooling, of granulated South Wales ironstone. The process burned off much of the carbon and vented trapped gases, to produce a very porous structure which functioned as a filter material by what we now call biological filtration. However, Candy's development was not original and Thomas Spencer had used "magnetic oxide of iron" as a filter material at Wakefield for the previous twenty-five years.

A leading analytical chemist, Sir Henry Roscoe, analysed Polarite as follows:

Magnetic oxide of iron	*53.85*
Silica	*25.50*
Lime	*2.01*
Alumina	*5.68*
Magnesia	*7.55*
Carbonaceous matter and moisture	*5.41*
	100.00 %

Candy's material was an instant success and the sale to the town of Reading of the first substantial plant for treating the public water supply using Polarite launched his future. Polarite was to become an important filter medium, and with a later, improved variant called Oxidium, was widely used by Candy in the UK and abroad. The product was effective in removing colour from water, although it was later found that this was mainly by adsorption rather than oxidation, so the service life was limited and it was gradually dropped for this purpose. However, the initial application as a purifying filter medium at Reading was followed by its use for iron removal at Hastings with spectacular success, and it is for this that we now know Polarite. A further development was for sewage treatment, and Pullen Candy supplied thousands of tons of Polarite as the medium for his newly-developed trickling filters during the sewage works construction boom around the turn of the century. The material was described as being graded to *"about the size of a walnut."*

The original Polarite source at Abercrave in South Wales disappeared from the record in the early 1920s and it is probable that the plant was sold when Frank Candy retired. By then, the material was wanted in much smaller quantities and it was used only as a catalyst for iron removal.

It is not clear at what stage the specification changed but the material we now know as Polarite is quite different from Candy's, and is based on a processed manganese ore imported from South Africa and elsewhere. In whatever form, Polarite played an important part in water treatment for over fifty years, even so legend has it, being supplied in a Candy plant to remove iron from the water supply for the atomic bomb project in the United States during the war.

Chapter 1

Ferrozone

Frank Candy's patents Nos. 1792 and 2517 both describe materials suitable for filtering water and sewage effluent as well as for use as precipitants. Two variants of Ferrozone were produced, one for use with acids in processing alkaline effluents, the other using a caustic lime and tar distillate mixture for treating acid effluents. The material was essentially ferrous sulphate with a high proportion of insoluble weighting agents, and it was used as a coagulant for treating sewage effluent, a process that was revived in the 1970s for nutrient removal.

Sir Henry Roscoe gave the analysis of the Acton Works Ferrozone as follows:
Soluble constituents

Ferrous Sulphate	26.64
Aluminium Sulphate	2.19
Calcium Sulphate	3.30
Magnesium Sulphate	5.17
Combined Water	8.20
Moisture	24.14
Insolubles, Silica	11.35
Magnetic Oxide of Iron	<u>19.01</u>
	100.00 %

The insoluble material in addition to being a weighting agent also reduced odour.

The raw material was carbonised anaerobically in the same way as Polarite, and the fines screened from the Polarite manufacture added, presumably as a weighting agent. Ferrozone with the caustic lime and tar distillate mixture was apparently also a good black mortar mixture for use in the building trade.

FOR PUBLIC WATERWORKS, INSTITUTIONS, &c.
AUTOMATIC COMPRESSED AIR AND OXIDISING
WATERWORKS FILTERS
ARE THE
CHEAPEST AND MOST EFFICIENT.

This form of **POLARITE OXIDISING FILTER** is specially useful for removing Iron and Peat and all Organic Impurities in solution.

Extremely simple in operation, and MORE ECONOMICAL THAN SAND OR ANY OTHER KIND OF FILTER.

Adopted by the Corporations of Hastings, Bedford, Newport, and many other public authorities.

The illustration shows two of a Battery of Six Filters for purifying one million gallons a day.

Of all the large towns, the two with the LOWEST death rates from waterborne diseases (ENTERIC or TYPHOID) are Reading and Hastings, where the public water supplies are purified by Polarite.

CANDY'S PATENT.
For Reports, Analyses, Estimates, and Particulars, apply to:—
FRANK CANDY, 5, Westminster Palace Gardens, Westminster, London, S.W.

An advert in "Water", April 1904. Note the early claim to remove peat and organic matter, probably by coagulation by the oxidised iron, as a separate coagulant was not used.

Chapter 1

NEW INVENTIONS.
IMPROVED DISINFECTING AND DEODORISING COVER FOR CLOSETS AND PANS.

This excellent little appliance, of which we append illustrations in section and elevation, is the invention of Mr. Frank Candy, the managing director of the International Water and Sewage Purification Company, Limited, of Mansion House Chambers, 11 Queen Victoria Street, E.C., and Mr. Nestor Frere, engineer. It is designed as a cover or lid for any kind of closet or other receptacle used to receive human excreta, and to discharge automatically a certain quantity of disinfecting powder every time the vessel is used. It can be made of any metallic substance; plain tin, or tin japanned, being the most inexpensive, and sufficiently good for all purposes, excepting where the appliance is exposed to much damp when copper would be preferable. It consists of a circular vessel with a suitable discharge orifice at the bottom controlled by a double valve or valves, carried on a spindle, which passes upwards through the cover of the vessel and terminates in a convenient handle.

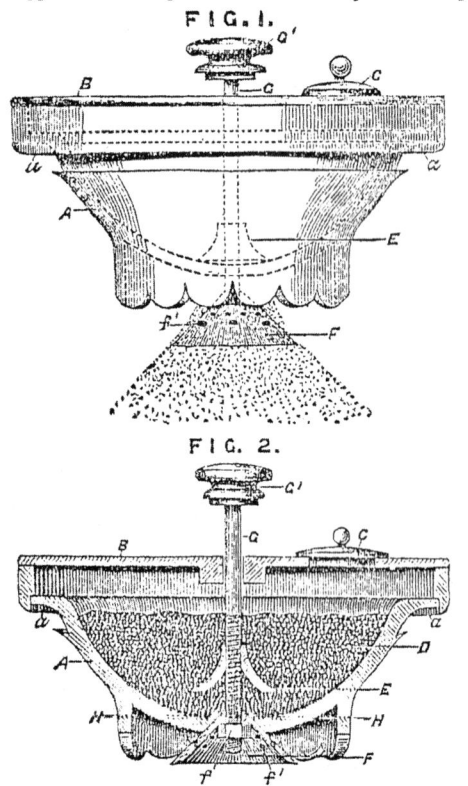

Extract from The Sanitary Record Nov. 15 1887, describing an early Candy invention for adding "aromatic disinfectant powder" - which contained oil of pine, eucalyptus and camphor - to the lavatory pan after use.

The International Water and Sewage Purification Company Ltd

In August 1887, the partners established a new company to continue the work, and named it the International Water and Sewage Purification Company, Ltd. (See Appendix B).

Until then, the small works at Whitechapel had manufactured the products although the raw materials came from Abercrave in South Wales. Business must have been good as the company purchased the mine and installed crushing and grading machinery and furnaces, as well as facilities for storage, weighing and packing the products for distribution. The first advertisements were soon appearing in exhibition literature, and the Sanitary Institute exhibition at Bolton gave the company an opportunity to show its products, which included a variety of filters and filter materials in addition to disinfection powders and some special paints.

The early records give an idea of the considerable amount of work already in progress at the birth of the company in 1887. The new Acton Sewage Works, the first to operate with Ferrozone as the coagulant and Polarite for the filter medium, was already in use in 1886 and had established Candy's reputation. In the same year he supplied a Polarite filter to Balmoral Castle, and after extensive tests with Polarite, the Sanitary Institute awarded the company its highest award, the Silver Medal.

However, the most important event for the company at the time was a report by The Royal Commissioners on Metropolitan Sewage Discharge. Their brief was to discover the best method of sewage disposal, and in their report of 27 November 1884 they recommended precipitation followed by filtration. This was exactly what Candy and his partners had concentrated on and Ferrozone and Polarite reached the market at just the right time. It was then a logical step from the manufacture of specialised filtering materials to the development of an improved filtering apparatus, and so the first Candy mechanical filters appeared in the 1890s.

The Acton Sewage Works

The Acton plant is of interest as although it was very small, it appears to have been the first of its kind. It attracted substantial attention (as well as scepticism and criticism of the costs) and the many visitors to the works were surprised to see fish swimming in the clear effluent. Candy had produced a works that resembled in many ways a present day water treatment plant, with inlet screens, settling tanks, coagulation and chemical plant, followed by sand and Polarite filters and it was a big leap forward compared to existing sewage plants.

A paper given by Henry Cadell to the Royal Scottish Society of Arts (see Appendix B) was awarded a silver medal in 1891, and gives a valuable insight to the state of sewage and water treatment at the time. Cadell describes the various methods then in use for treating sewage, including land irrigation, precipitation with various agents and an oxidation process called the Webster Process, which used electrolysis to generate oxygen in situ.

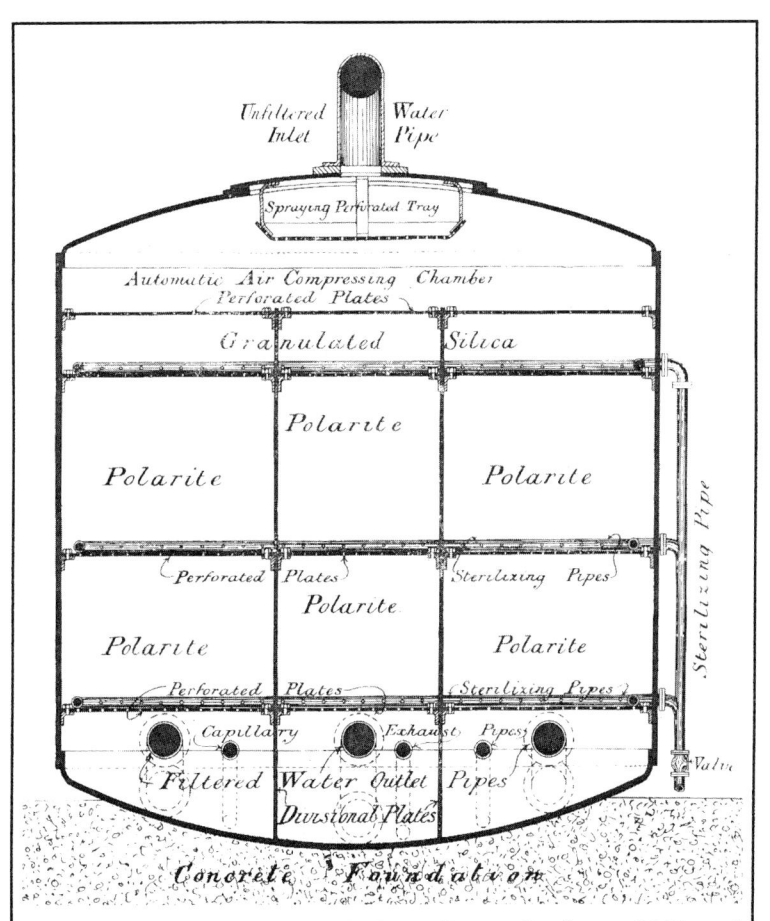

Section drawing reprinted from "Water" about 1910, of Candy's patent oxidising filter. The design is remarkably similar to Polarite filters made in the 1970s. Note the provision of steam sterilisation pipes as well as the very early appearance of the airspace to provide oxygen for the process.

The precipitation methods used alum, blood and clay, the "ABC" process, and produced large quantities of sludge; or lime, which produced a clear effluent but caused major smell problems as well as an alkaline effluent. Cadell indicates that none of these processes was satisfactory and he goes on to laud the merits of "The International System of Sewage Purification" as Candy and his colleagues were marketing their process. He says, *"After one of the most exhaustive enquiries... the*

Chapter 1

Royal Commissioners on Metropolitan Sewage Disposal... unanimously recommend... the system of precipitation and filtration... I am convinced that the 'International' is by far the best method of sewage purification that has yet been devised."

The Acton plant was designed to treat the sewage from 22,000 people and it had previously used the ABC process. The conversion to Candy's process replaced the coagulant with Ferrozone, the average dose being 11 ppm with the supernatant liquid filtered through Polarite. As Cadell said, *"The suspended matter was reduced from 240 to 80 parts per 100,000 of effluent whilst the effluent from the filter was... clear and transparent."* No doubt Candy made full use of Mr Cadell's paper. Later, reference can be found of similar works at Huddersfield, Larbert, Forfar and Mangotsfield and it appears that about twelve of these plants were either built or the existing apparatus was converted to Candy's system.

However, the real significance of the Acton works was the realisation by one of the original partners, Dr Angell, of the biological effect of the filters: although the Ferrozone process was a landmark at the time, it would be shortlived. At a meeting of municipal engineers at Acton in 1890 Angell remarked, *"as to the activity of these beds... I can say they are more active now than when they were started... I am strongly of the belief ...that it becomes a biological bed as well as a filter bed."* This observation led Angell and his associates to develop circular filters using Polarite as the filter medium. This was to alter the future of sewage treatment, leading to the development of the trickling filter for which Candy and others designed a range of sprinkler mechanisms.

Reading

Reading was to be a valuable contact for Candy, and through his long association with the town, he pioneered processes which are in widespread use today. In 1892 after some trials, Candy supplied the first Polarite plant for the town's water supply which, with the second plant he

---

POLARITE FILTER CHAMBERS
at the
READING CORPORATION WATERWORKS.
Quantity filtered, as taken from the
REPORT of the WATERWORKS' ENGINEER,
Mr A.T.Walker, Associate, M.I.C.E.
Town Hall, Reading, September, 1894

The first two sets of these Chambers were started at the Works in November, 1892. Each Polarite Chamber measures 40ft. by 9ft., and has a depth of $2\frac{1}{2}$ ft. of Polarite, giving an Area of 40 yards super each Chamber, or a total of 160 yards super for the two sets. By adding the $2\frac{1}{2}$ ft. of Polarite in each set it gives a thickness of 5 ft. to each set of Chambers, and an Area of 80 yards super per set.

From December, 1892, to August, 1893, there had passed through these two sets a total quantity of 409,880,000 gallons of water, giving an average of **18,848 gallons per yard super per day,** a quantity considerably in excess of that intended.

Two additional sets were finished and started in August, 1893. These are of the same dimensions as the above, giving a total Area of 160 yards super, with a depth of 5 ft. for each set of Chambers. These have filtered on average 12,500 gallons per yard super per day.

From January 1st, 1894, to August 31st, 1894 upwards of 541 million Gallons of Water have been effectually purified by means of Polarite in these special Polarite Chambers, being an average of **2,226,878 gallons per 24 hours, equal to 13,917 gallons per square yard, or 579.8 gallons per yard super per hour.**

Since the introduction of Polarite we have had no complaints as to the quality of the Reading water, previously they were of an everyday occurrence.

supplied a year later, had a combined a capacity of about 2.2 mgd, a substantial works for the time. The first plant consisted of a series of open concrete chambers fed with water from the River Kennet. It was claimed that the plant operated at a rate about six times faster than slow sand filters, that the chemical and bacteriological results were very good, and the performance remained constant over time.

Typical results showed average bacterial counts of 47,000 per cc in the river, reducing to 45 per cc in the filtrate. Since the plant did not employ any chemical treatment, the filters must have operated in a biological mode, and the claim was that the high porosity of the Polarite stored oxygen and released it to the water. Whatever the real mechanism or reliability of these figures, the Reading Corporation was delighted with the works.

The Reading plants led to a number of developments based on the use of the material but attention then turned towards treating irony waters from underground sources, using pressure filters charged with Polarite.

Hastings 1895

In the late 1880s Candy was joined by his son Pullen, with Candy concentrating on water purification and Pullen on sewage treatment. The wide interest in Polarite resulted in a number of towns experimenting with its use to remove dissolved iron, and the first air-space pressure filter order came from the Hastings Corporation. There the water was being treated by slow sand filters which blocked quickly due to the very high level of iron and Candy supplied new pressure filters which were placed at the end of the twelve-inch pumping main from Filsham. The plant consisted of six 7'6" diameter vessels 8'6" high,

Hastings, Brede, 1902. 1.92 mgd Iron removal filters.

arranged to work in pairs, with one pair acting as standby. The diagram p.27 shows the patented construction of the filters and indicates a remarkable similarity to many modern designs. The filter rating was 169 gph/ft^2 and shows how right Candy had got the design. The Filsham plant was followed by a much larger works at Brede (near Hastings) and others followed shortly afterwards. Although the Hastings concept was viewed with suspicion at the time, the plants worked extremely well and Polarite became established as a practical means of treating dissolved iron. The company took part in the Paris Universal Exhibition of 1889 and the Chicago World Fair in 1893, at both of which Polarite gained "Highest Awards". The name has since become a generic term for iron removal catalysts.

In 1895 Pullen left to set up his own company. By then his father was exploiting a number of patents for water and sewage treatment, and leaflets he published at the time refer to "plumbism", an early term for plumbo-solvency, for which he introduced a treatment about ten years later. He also mentioned the growing practice of "filming" - the use of aluminium sulphate as a filter conditioner for a short period after backwashing.

However, trouble was looming. The work in hand, coupled with the developments Candy was working on, meant that the company needed to raise additional capital by issuing public shares. The take-up of the share offer was poor, and it appears that Candy himself did not take his full salary for some time, a problem familiar to many private owners. The precarious finances led to bankruptcy and the eventual dissolution of the company in 1900.

Filters for Paignton en-route by steam lorry, 1909

In the meantime, enough money was raised to keep going, probably from the Candy family's own sources, and in 1898 the International Purification Syndicate was formed with Frank Candy as general manager.

The International Purification Syndicate 1898-1906

In practice, the Syndicate appears to have been a continuation of the partnership, with Candy and Angell as the active members but whether any of the others were involved is not recorded. The Syndicate built on the successes of the previous few years, promoted Polarite filtration to a number of towns, and progressively modified the original Reading design.

The Reading Corporation was well pleased with their 1892 and 1893 Polarite chamber pre-filters, and commissioned another works at Fobney, where the water passed through a series of chambers (tanks) instead of single chambers. The first filter chamber contained coarse coke, the second coarse sand, and finally, a chamber with combined sand and Polarite completed the purification process. The whole chamber system was in a building, to prevent algal and icing problems.

Chapter 1

At about the same time the South West Suburban Water company at Staines also installed similar, although much larger chamber pre-filters, to treat water taken directly from the Thames. Approximately 1,500 tons of Polarite were used for this contract. This was followed by a similar works at Christchurch, West Hants, to treat

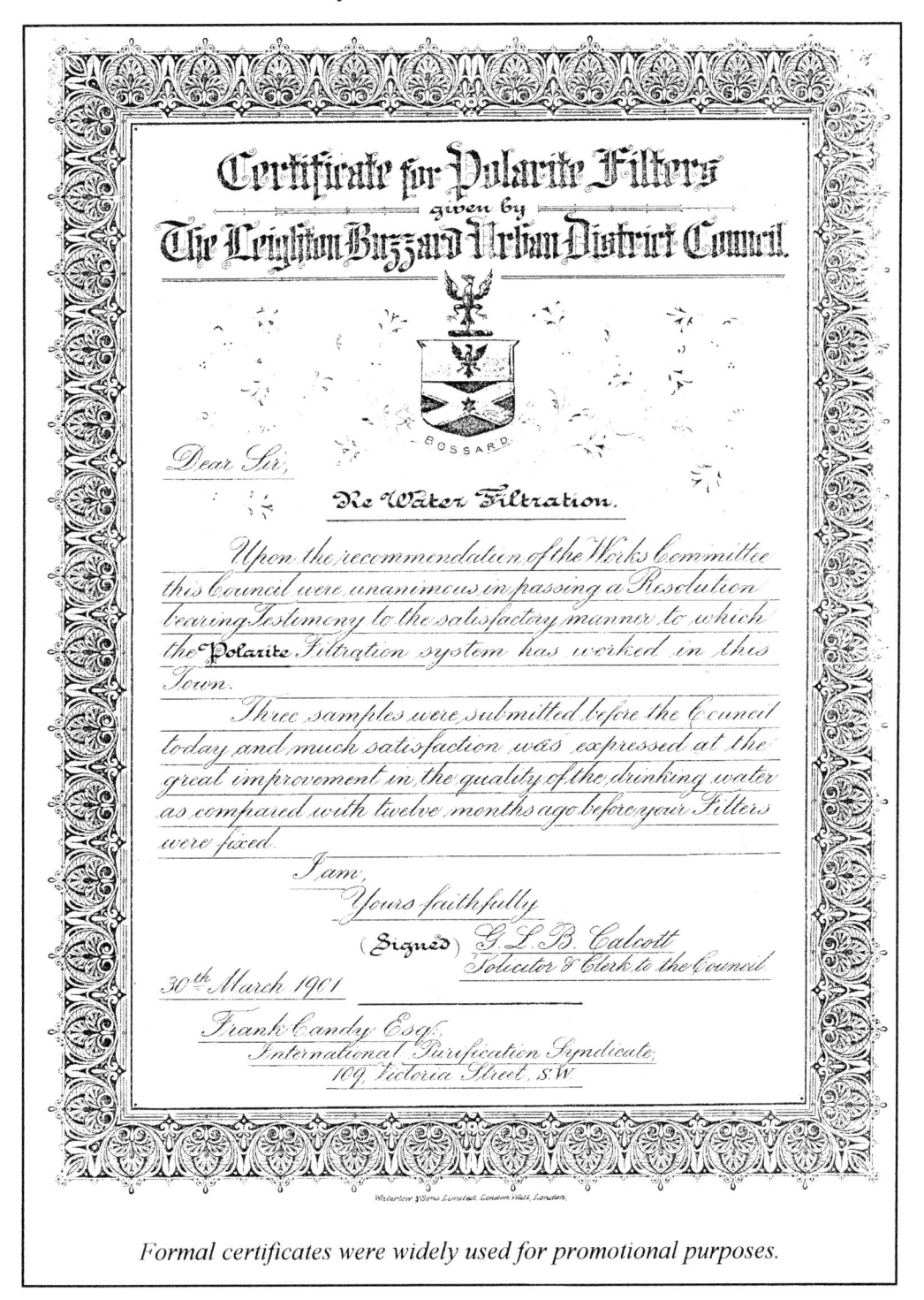

Formal certificates were widely used for promotional purposes.

Chapter 1

River Avon water, and three small plants for Southwold, Teignmouth and Leighton Buzzard.

It is worth recalling that there were then many hundreds of suppliers of water in the UK, ranging from large organisations like the eleven London water companies, later to be combined as the Metropolitan Water Board, to other water boards, large water companies, and towns of all sizes which managed their own water supplies. Apart from the large concerns, few suppliers had facilities for making chemical or bacteriological tests. These services were often provided by public analysts, and suppliers with their own laboratories frequently assisted the smaller concerns in times of difficulty, such as typhoid outbreaks or when there were serious complaints about the quality of the water.

Dr Angell not only helped with the production of Polarite, but he was also medical officer of health for Hampshire County Council. This provided him with facilities for chemical and bacteriological tests which presumably he used to the benefit of the Syndicate. Candy and his son Pullen also developed a close relationship with a Dr John Thresh, who in due course formed the well-respected Counties Public Health Laboratories. These connections enabled Candy to offer services which many of the water supply organisations lacked. Sixty years later Paterson Candy International Ltd offered a similar service through a thinly disguised subsidiary, Water Treatment Advisory Services, until the early 1970s.

The filters for Port Elizabeth leaving the manufacturer in England by train, about 1904

The new century

During this period, Candy developed valuable markets overseas, appointing local agents in a number of areas. The first exports had been mainly Polarite, but they now included batteries of pressure filters. An early example was six 8'3" diameter filters for Port Elizabeth in South Africa, which were in service by 1905. By then, Oxidium was getting considerable publicity as an improved version of Polarite and it was also claimed to be indestructible, with everlasting purifying properties. However, notwithstanding the claimed improvements, the name Polarite is the one which has survived.

Chapter 1

By the turn of the century there was a continuous flow of patents from the Candy stable, and there is the first mention of Alexander Jarvis who was to be Candy's partner in the Candy Filter Company; also of Edgar Ralph Candy, Frank's second son who plays a relatively small part in the story as he died prematurely in 1906.

The business was prospering but the expansion meant that the company needed to be re-structured again and Candy invited his son Pullen to re-join him to cope with the volume of work. It is not certain when Pullen returned but it is known that he had formed his own business by then, and he ran it until 1908, in parallel with his work for the Candy Filter Company.

These photos from about 1904 illustrate the difficulties of transporting heavy equipment at the time.

The filters for the Vaal river plant would have had to be hauled by ox train over the Drakensberg mountains

Candy filters for King William's Town, South Africa, in course of erection at site.

2-THE BELL BROTHERS, WILLIAM BOBY, THE LASSEN-HJORT PARTNERSHIP

The Bell Brothers 1896-1934

Bell Brothers' name has virtually disappeared from the water industry, although many of their installations remain in service and are well regarded, particularly in the north of England. Bell's once occupied an important, perhaps even dominant position in the UK market, and they were Candy's main competitor until about 1920 when Paterson's took over this role.

Andrew and Peter Bell started their business at Ravensthorpe in the West Riding of Yorkshire around the turn of the century. Their names first appear in 1896 on filtration process patents, and their earliest waterworks pressure filter installations date from about 1901.

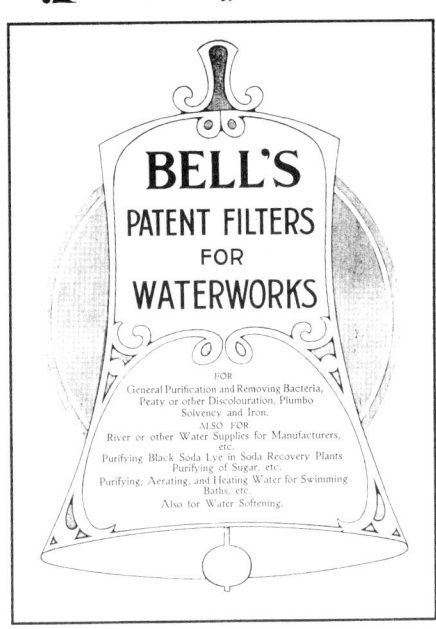

The photo shows a Bell Brothers 16 HP phaeton of about 1908. Bells also made a lorry based on the same chassis and running gear.

Like many entrepreneurs of the period they dabbled in unrelated businesses, and in the early years they produced a number of Bell motor cars and vans based on the same chassis. The car range included 16 to 30 HP touring and saloon models, and they won the Scottish reliability trials in 1906-7-8 and 9. Enthusiastic Bell employees reported that they were very good cars, but with so many manufacturers competing in a limited market, they were clearly not good enough, and the designs were eventually sold to Thorneycroft.

Initially, Bell's main activity was in the industrial market for boiler feed water treatment and filtration of river water for manufacturing. They also advertised plants for purifying sewage and factory effluent, for the purification of sugar, black soda lye and soda recovery, and by 1910 their catalogue listed a great many installations in the same categories as Paterson's. These included eighty plants for paper manufacturing, twenty-two for dyers and bleachers and fifty miscellaneous users.

Bell's were early pioneers in the swimming pool market, and they supplied their first purification plant to the Broughton pool at Salford in 1907. At the time, pools operated on the fill and empty basis, with the water being discarded when it became too dirty to use! Bell's developed swimming pool purifiers with continuous circulation systems and heating and treatment plants, and their record of swimming pool contracts up to the 1930s exceeded the total of their competitors.

Bell's public supply record was also impressive, with some forty-four plants for local authorities in the United Kingdom, mostly in the north of England and Scotland. These plants were used as pre-filters to slow sand filters as well as for direct filtration.

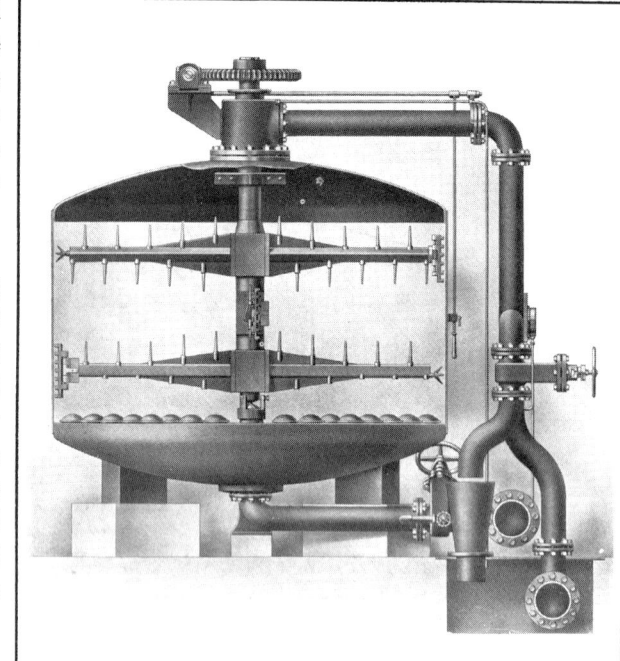

Bells specialised in heavy stirrer gear to clean the sand. Later designs used line-shafting driven by oil or steam engines to drive the rakes of up to eight filters together.

The Bell filter design used heavy mechanical rakes for cleaning the filter sand during backwash, and the earliest models had massive hand-turned capstan wheels and gear drives. Later, steam engines, oil engines or electric motors were used to turn the rakes through external reduction gears linked with shafting, pulleys and belts from the drive engine. Bell's always claimed that only mechanical rakes would clean filter sand efficiently and keep it clean, and it was many years before they introduced air scour cleaning as an alternative. By then their rake systems were no longer competitive, and it is surprising that Bell's made so little effort to get into the growing gravity filters business.

Shortly after the 1914-18 war Bell's acquired the Reeves Filters business from Mather & Platt of Manchester. Reeves was a well established company with an impressive reference

Chapter 2

Two Reeves patent "single contact" gravity filters at Morley in 1898. The capacity was 1 mgd.

list, including gravity filters and a variety of compound filters (a combined pre-filter and fine filter), and other designs which Candy and others would later copy. Mather and Platt offered two models of the rake filter, the earlier with an internal mechanism that was less heavy than Bell's. The second, more interesting design had a rotating impeller fitted in the top of the filter which circulated sand through an induction pipe, and discharged it in a clean condition back to the surface of the filter bed. This concept pre-dates by many years the designs introduced in the 60s which re-circulate the sand outside the filter for cleaning. Several of the Mather and Platt plants were installed in Yorkshire and Lancashire and in due course some were converted to airscour cleaning by Candy.

During the 1920s Bell's competed very effectively with Paterson and Candy and they established strong customer loyalty which brought them much repeat business. Many of their plants were designed to be extended only with their filters, and they had a substantial following from water engineers who were convinced that rake mechanisms from Bell's were essential for efficient sand cleaning, and would not change to airscour.

Bell's owned large workshops at Denton which they used to the full. They carried out heavy work usually done by specialists, including machining and drilling cast iron pipes and fittings bought from a local foundry. They also made items such as calorifiers, aerating vessels, compressors and small turbines, in contrast to Candy's and Paterson's, who by and large used their workshops to provide their own specially developed apparatus, and bought the rest from a very competitive market. The photos of the works at Denton show it to be well-equipped and spacious, and the sketches reproduced from a Bell catalogue of the period give the impression of a prosperous company.

The 1920s brought in several important contracts involving large numbers of filters, generally arranged in batteries, such as those at Derwent Valley which had forty-eight 8 ft. diameter filters in groups of eight that could be cleaned individually, or all eight together. Each battery had its own chemical plant with water turbine driven chemical pumps for aluminium sulphate and lime. Those proportioning turbines are a good example of the ingenious hydraulic devices invented by the industry, and they were widely used by Bell's. The Derwent Valley and Leicester installations are also good examples of the way provision was made for extension, effectively locking in future orders.

In 1924/25 the company decided to go public. Their shares were probably considered a good investment, especially by engineers working in the industry, but apparently the capital and prospects were pitched too high and Pullen Candy remarked, *"If Bell's obtained all the work available within the UK they still would not make a reasonable return on the capital employed."* He was right, and soon afterwards, the company was re-structured as Bell Brothers (1927) Limited.

Bell's were generally more successful in Britain than they were overseas, though one of their important references was an order booked in 1929 for a 1 mgd gravity filter plant for the Straits Settlement Government at Bukit Panchor in Malaya (Malaysia). This was one of few such orders and by 1933 they listed only fourteen overseas gravity filter contracts, of which the largest was for Kinta, also in Malaya, with a capacity of 6 mgd, a modest record when compared with Paterson's and Candy's. (Thirty years later PCI built a 21 mgd works at Kinta).

Bell filters at Birkenhead, Alwen works. Fifty-five filters arranged in batteries of five, with a capacity of 9 mgd. Note the lay shaft (top left) and belts driving the rake mechanisms. These filters were fitted with Bell's high turbine type chemical dosers. Bell's sold many plants of this type.

Chapter 2

Bell's low turbine type chemical doser. Turbines driven by the main water flow, operated reciprocating dosing pumps for alum. soda and chlorine etc. Note the stroke length adjustment for dose control.

By then the founders were nearing the end of their careers, although one of the Bell brothers was still a member of the board. In 1934 William Paterson bought the company with part of the proceeds of a 75,000 £1 share issue, his first of several acquisitions in the industry. When they were taken over, Bell's had a fair volume of their traditional work, and had also set up a domestic water softener organisation known as Bell Brothers Domestic Ltd.

Paterson left Bell's to trade independently, with little interference, and they continued to get orders for extending existing plants, as well as some new contracts. This pattern continued until the late 1960s by which time the company was fading. It ended its life mainly as a specialist swimming pool plant supplier, before being absorbed into Paterson Candy International in the early 1970s and then disappearing entirely in 1975.

In retrospect, Bell's failed to see how the market was changing, and did not adapt with it. They also made the mistake of entering the domestic swimming pool market, despite not having suitable products or a consumer-oriented staff. Their once impressive workshops at Denton dominated and distorted their activities, and eventually became a millstone around the company's neck, which undoubtedly contributed to its demise.

Chapter 2

View of Bells workshops at Denton, showing bays 1, 2 and 3

William Boby Ltd 1897-1972

William Boby was another late Victorian pioneer and first appears when he was running a well-established business making steam engines. The ever present problem of scale in boilers prompted his entry to the water treatment field in 1897 when he formed William Boby and Company, to promote a device called a "de-tartriser" which consisted of a series of cast iron plates heated by steam, to precipitate alkalinity from the feed water.

Following his early de-aerators, he went on to concentrate on lime-soda softeners and filters, and the company developed as a supplier of industrial water treatment plant, offering ion-exchange softeners, demineralisers, de-aerators and degassers etc., as the technology became available. By the early 1920s Boby was also selling American greensand for the early

William Boby 1852- 1938. 1931 photo

Chapter 2

base-exchange softeners. He was also active in the municipal market as evidenced by the photographs of the treatment plant at Gwalior in India, but few details of this activity remain.

William Boby retired in the late 30s and handed the company to his son Vincent who ran it until his death in 1957, when the reins passed to his son Michael.

During the late 1950s Boby's were very successful with their thermal de-aerators. Although the technology was well established, Boby's added a number of improvements and this business was their main source of income.

Gwalior treatment plant. 4 mgd. The triumphal arch for receiving the Viceroy. 1929. This plant was equipped with an electro-chlorine plant which must have been one of the earliest of its kind.

Then in the early 1960s, they entered the ion-exchange market with their first mixed-bed unit, though they had previously done little other than softening plants. For the rest of the 1960s the UK power programme provided them with many contracts for boiler feed-water plants, and Boby's were very successful with de-alkalisation and base-exchange systems. Their entry to the state-owned Central Electricity Generating Board was with the feed-water plant for the Bankside power station, (now soon to become part of the Tate Gallery of Modern Art). This was one of the first automatic mixed bed units, and it was followed by plants for Ferrybridge, Eggborough, Ratcliffe and other power stations.

Boby's also got involved with continuous ion-exchange, licensing the Asahi process to build a pilot plant at Kearsley power station, followed by three 175 t/hr feedwater treatment streams for Shell's Stanlow refinery. But whilst the process worked, the wear and tear on the resins was unacceptable and the market lost interest in these "resin crunchers".

Boby feedwater heater/de-aerator, installed at Reavells, Ipswich in 1898 and still in use in 1951. This may have included his "De-tartriser".

William Vincent Boby 1888-1957

Chapter 2

In the mid-1960s, Michael Boby, in failing health and having no family members interested in the business, sold it to Weir's. The sale brought few benefits and Weir's managed the company from arms length.

During the late 1960s Boby's entered the municipal market, where they quickly became a serious competitor by under-cutting the established suppliers, then PCI, Permutit and United Filters. But, Boby's expanded too fast and much of their work was under-priced, making the company an easy target for take-over when they ran into financial difficulties. There was also friction between the Boby's and Weir board members, and in 1971 a number of Boby's senior managers and board members left to form Dewplan.

A year later Boby's was sold to the Permutit Company and the activities and some of their staff were divided between Permutit and PCI. However, the acquisition produced few benefits for either company, other than the removal of a difficult competitor who might well have gone under anyway, and was promptly replaced by new ones. Though there was some short term work-in-progress, much of it proved to be unprofitable, perhaps partly due to the way in which the work was absorbed into the two companies. The Boby site at Rickmansworth was very valuable. It was soon sold, and this may have justified the purchase.

At the time of the acquisition, Boby's had an agreement with the Graver Company of Illinois, providing access to their Powdex and pre-treatment technology. Although this agreement was ended at the time of the sale, some items such as the Reactivator softener/clarifier continued to be used by both PCI and Permutit-Boby, with the designs supplied from Boby's Australian subsidiary.

Boby's also had licences for the Immedium upflow filter, similar to Candy's original design but fitted with a grid in the top of the sand to stabilise it. The Immedium filter was introduced at just the right time

Michael Boby, 1918-1990. Photo late 60s

This delightful but posed photo shows a Boby type-K dry powder lime softener "on test" at the works. About 1910.

to secure the bulk of the sewage "tertiary" filtration market in the UK. This was a substantial marketing achievement against PCI who had originally introduced the concept of filtering sewage effluent but failed to make the early plants work properly. Boby's then extended the design to the industrial and potable markets and built some plants, but the design was very susceptible to air in the underdrains and this showed up the inherent weaknesses of this type of filter. Excepting for a very few sites, the design was not used afterwards.

Boby upflow filters at Blackbirds sewage works. These filters treated the final effluent before discharge, to produce a "10-10" effluent. Late 1960s.

With hindsight, the demise of William Boby's company began with the purchase by Weir's and the decision to grow the business rapidly by very competitive pricing. They introduced a policy of cutting resin prices, so triggering price-cutting by the industry. Nobody gained from this except the end-users, and from being a profitable side-line, resin sales became a loss-leader. The price cutting was extended to Boby's contracting business to buy market share, and it was only a matter of time before this short-sighted policy overwhelmed them.

Although Boby's were not active in filing patents, they did introduce some new technology. In particular, they pioneered air hold-down during counter-current regeneration at a time when others were using the less satisfactory water hold-down method.

Coulsden, lime softener, capacity 5,000 gph, 1910-11.

Chapter 2

The Electrodialysis (ED) disaster

This story would be incomplete without some mention of the ventures into ED by both Boby and Permutit. At the start of the 1950s both companies took licences from the Dutch TNO organisation for a process that was originally intended for desalting cheese whey. Permutit planned to use it for desalting mine water in South Africa, and because Polystyrene strong base anion exchange resins were very new, they attempted to make ED membranes by polymerising resin monomer in-situ on Kraft paper. Unfortunately, the membranes were not sufficiently robust, leading Permutit to abandon ED until the 1980s when they had another attempt at making the process work, this time aimed at the non-water treatment applications with Asahi membranes. But the venture was again unsuccessful as the potential market was too small and fragmented to justify continuing.

Bankside Power Station, cation, anion, mixed bed.

Boby's persisted with the TNO design for a further twenty years and sold a number of plants to inhospitable markets, but they were unable to solve some of the inherent problems, and the venture did not succeed commercially. The sale of the 4.2 mgd Benghazi plant was a substantial coup at the time, and for a brief while it was the largest desalination plant in the world, though it was beset with problems, a

The Benghazi Electro-dialysis plant, capacity 4.2 mgd, 1970

common feature of many early desalination plants: whilst the science may have been sound the development was incomplete.

In the late 1960s Boby's signed an agreement with the UKAEA to collaborate on electrodialysis technology, and received an injection of funds and engineering input. However, the design remained fundamentally flawed, the materials inadequate for the environment, and neither of these problems was ever properly resolved. The technical director for Boby's at the time offers these thoughts.

- *Don't pioneer - let someone else do it.*
- *If you must pioneer, don't do it in the desert.*
- *Don't get ahead of your supporting technology.*
- *Don't aim for high efficiencies while you're struggling to get the wretched thing to work at all.*

Although the company struggled with the technology for a few years after the merger with Permutit, no further sales of importance were made.

The Lassen-Hjort Partnership 1900-1913

Lassen and Hjort formed their partnership in 1900, based at Blackfriars in central London. Hjort had arrived from Denmark the year before but

BP Baglan Bay Immedium filters treating the feed to the process water plant, all supplied by Boby's. Capacity 275,000 gph, early 1970s.

Lorry mounted purification plant supplied by Lassen-Hjort during WW1.

Lassen, who was his cousin and brother-in-law, was already established as a consulting engineer in refrigeration. The new partnership concentrated on lime-soda softeners and steam separators, initially importing most of the equipment from Europe.

The business prospered, and by 1903 they listed sales to five power stations, two gasworks and a number of other companies, including a first export order for the Buenos Aires and Pacific Railway. The lime-soda softener was their main product, undergoing continuous improvement up to the start of World War 1. They also introduced a hot lime softener. The photograph shows a typical plant with the measuring device mounted on top of the reaction vessel.

In 1906, Lassen-Hjort formed a company called Sofnol to supply lime-soda mixtures, which has since grown into a well known retail chemical business. However, the most significant change in the interests of the partnership came in 1911 when the first base-exchange softener in the UK was installed at Burrill's Wharf in London's dockland by their competitor, Water Softeners Ltd. This plant used the German Gans natural zeolite, regenerated with salt, which the company called the "Permutit" process. The advent of this base-exchange process brought hitherto undreamed of water quality, and in due course led to the development of ion-exchange demineralisers.

The introduction of base-exchange softeners set the stage for major advances in water treatment, permitting the use of much higher temperatures and pressures in boilers, as well as improvements in the design of turbines, condensers,

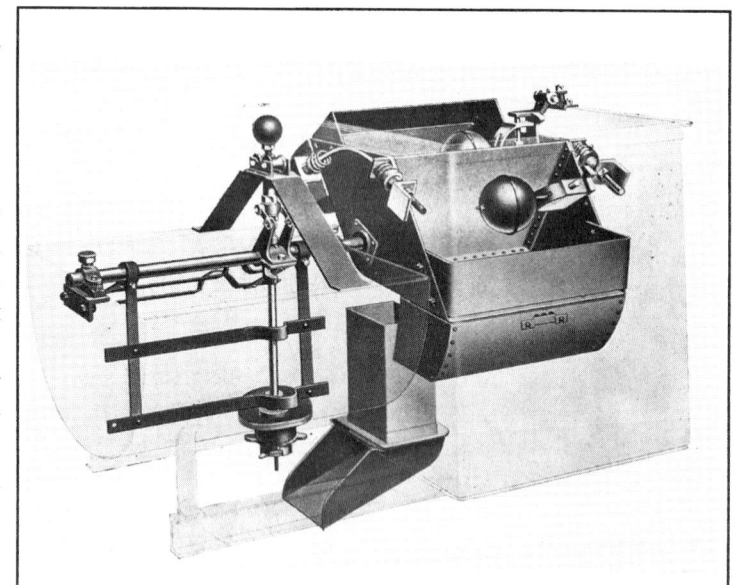

Lassen-Hjort patent continuous automatic measuring and mixing apparatus. It consisted of a twin-chambered oscillating water measuring device side-by-side with a reservoir for the chemicals. Water to be softened filled each chamber alternately until the heavier discharged its contents into a tank. An adjustable double beat valve in the reservoir lifted at intervals due to the rotation of a flow measuring device and caused the addition of a pre-measured quantity of chemicals to the tank. The apparatus was continuously improved up to 1915 and was claimed to be accurate to plus or minus two percent.

heating systems and a wide variety of equipment using water or steam. By 1917, United Water Softeners, as the company had become, had supplied thousands of base-exchange softeners throughout the world, and they claimed to have supplied more than eight times the number of all other water softening apparatus.

United Water Softeners Ltd, 1913-1918

Water Softeners Ltd had been formed by a group of financiers using consultants to design the equipment, and sales were slow against the established lime-soda process. By contrast, Lassen-Hjort were prospering, and in 1913 they merged with Water Softeners Ltd to form United Water Softeners. They also formed a separate company to export lime-soda softeners, with offices at Kingsway in central London.

1912 saw the sale of the first base-exchange plant to the municipal sector, for the West Cheshire Water Board at Hooton, with a capacity of 0.75 mgd. A similar plant was sold to United Alkali at Fleetwood to provide all the boiler feed and works process water.

The outbreak of WW1 stopped imports of the German Gans material so the company was forced to develop a replacement which it called No. 31. This material had a much shorter regeneration time than the eight hours needed for the Gans material, and gave it significant operational advantages.

Lassen-Hjort lime softening plant, c.1905. Note the lime measuring pot mounted on top.

The war years saw full employment and many army contracts, including new mobile treatment units to replace the British army water purifying equipment which dated from the Boer War. The new process was based on super-chlorination, contact, and filtration, followed by de-chlorination with sulphur dioxide. This appears to have been a very early use of the gas, as routine de-chlorination with it was not adopted for public supplies until the 1970s.

United Water Softeners horse-drawn water treatment unit from the first war.

Chapter 2

J.J.Lassen left the company around 1920. He was highly gifted technically but lived beyond his means, and he committed suicide in 1922. Water Softeners Ltd continued to trade until 1937 when it became The Permutit Company Ltd.

UWS base exchange plant at Prenton for West Cheshire WB. Capacity 3 mgd. 1920s

3-THE CANDY FILTER COMPANY 1906-1918

Pullen Candy

In retrospect, Pullen Candy's contribution to the water business was perhaps more important than his father's. He modernised much of what Frank Candy had introduced, and was responsible for the fundamental filter engineering for which Candy's became known, including nozzle filter floors, airscour, and combined air-water backwashing, developments that remain at the core of the technology to the present day. With Caink and Whittaker, he introduced trickling filters which made a major contribution to the treatment of sewage.

Pullen joined his father at the International Water and Sewage Purification Company in about 1889 and spent six years there before deciding to branch out on his own to concentrate on sewage treatment, partly because the company could not afford to employ him. Whilst there he worked on a wide range of ideas before concentrating on water and sewage treatment, and of passing interest are his inventions for improving road hot tar spraying machines and watering carts - so necessary in those days of horse-drawn traffic - and he started a business named the Tar Roads Syndicate, probably with his father.

One of his patents should certainly have changed his career and fortune, and was lodged on the 19th of March 1892, "for improvements to velocipedes, bicycles, tricycles and other wheeled vehicles." At the time, inflated tubes were used without an outer cover or tyre and they lasted for a very short time. Pullen's patent provided for an outer tyre with an inner tube, both held in position in a grooved wheel when the tube was inflated. But he was pipped at the post: a similar specification was accepted just twenty-one days earlier, from John Boyd Dunlop.

Pullen Candy aged about 70, c.1941

Pneumatic tyres continued to occupy him for several years and he took out a number of patents related to them. Perhaps sensing that he had missed that particular boat, he also put his energy into sewage treatment, and by 1895 had lodged eight patents for improving sewage filters. He tackled a whole range of equipment improvements, including the mixing of coagulants and removal of sludge from settling tanks, as well as new designs for vertical and horizontal flow settling tanks. These included cylindrical tanks, vertical flow designs with tangential inlets and surface collecting troughs, as well as inverted pyramid and multi-pyramid designs.

> N° 6126   A.D. 1891
>
> Date of Application, 9th Apr., 1891
> Complete Specification Left, 21st Dec., 1891—Accepted, 13th Feb., 1892
> PROVISIONAL SPECIFICATION.
> Improvements relating to Velocipede and other Wheels, and to Tyres therefor.
> I, JOHN BOYD DUNLOP of 50 Gloucester Street Belfast Ireland, Veterinary Surgeon, do hereby declare the nature of this invention to be as follows :—
> My invention relates to velocipede and other wheels, and to pneumatic or hollow inflatable or air tyres, and is designed to provide improved means whereby the said tyres can be more easily fixed or secured upon the rims of the wheels.
> The said rims moreover are strengthened, and improved facilities are afforded for the repair of the said tyres.
> In carrying my said invention into practice I form the centre of the rim of the wheel more deeply grooved than those in ordinary use. Between the said groove and the edges of the rim there are flat or nearly flat portions, and the said edges are turned up at right angles or approximately at right angles thereto.

> N° 6088   A.D. 1891
>
> Date of Application, 9th Apr., 1891
> Complete Specification Left, 11th Jan., 1892—Accepted, 19th Mar., 1892
> PROVISIONAL SPECIFICATION.
> Improvements in Velocipedes and other Wheeled Vehicles.
> I FRANK PULLEN CANDY of 56 Nightingale Lane Balham in the County of Surrey Sanitary Engineer do hereby declare the nature of this invention to be as follows :—
> My said invention relates to the application of different forms of pneumatic appliances to and in connection with the wheels, saddles, bearings and other parts of velocipedes such as bicycles, tricycles and the like and to other wheeled vehicles. In applying my invention to the rim of a wheel I adopt a simple and efficacious mode of securing and at the same time protecting the inflated pneumatic tyre now commonly used in bicycles and tricycles. As is well known such pneumatic tyres

Trickling filters

The most significant of these improvements was the development of the circular biological filter which used coarse filtering materials such as stones, coke, etc., to give plenty of air space. The effluent was sprinkled over the surface of the filter by small jets or sprays and Pullen had obtained a patent for a revolving distributor powered by the force of the jets discharging onto the filter surface. The drawings showed that if necessary, wind vanes could be fitted to assist rotation, and the top twelve inches of the filter contained a layer of Polarite. These designs, developed from the project at the Acton Sewage Works, were to change the course of sewage treatment by providing a simple and robust system that would be used widely for the next seventy years, and ranked alongside activated sludge in importance.

At about this time, Mr Whittaker and Mr Caink were working on similar lines to Pullen Candy. They decided to pool their ideas, and in 1902 they formed a company called Patent Automatic Sewage Distributors Limited. The company produced an excellent range of sprinkler distributors with special features which were to give them a commercial lead. It is worth describing some of these features as they dominated the design of sprinklers for many years.

Typically, a 100 ft. diameter sprinkler in operation weighed more than two tons. The Candy-Whittaker buoyant sprinkler carried the weight on a float which greatly reduced the friction so the distributor revolved easily from the force of the inlet jets and could be operated without an additional drive.

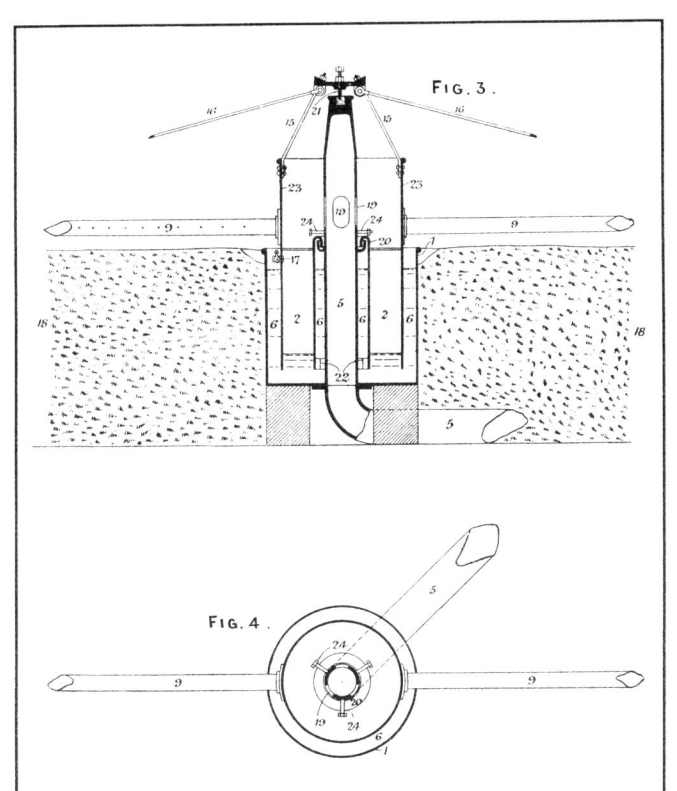

The compensating system of sprinkler arms enabled the sprinkler to work continuously with a large variation in flow, avoiding the need to provide large storage tanks for storm water conditions. The variation was accommodated by discharging from two arms at low flows, and under high flow conditions, the settled effluent rose up the central inlet column to feed two additional arms, set at a slightly higher level. Pullen used an ingenious system of siphons to feed the sprinklers, with master controls for shutting down or bringing on-stream additional sprinklers.

Pullen Candy also developed a frictionless mercury-sealed joint between the revolving parts of the sprinkler distributor and the fixed inlet supply pipe. Although it would be unacceptable nowadays, it was then far in advance of other systems. Bottom bearings and glands had been tried by the company and discarded as being *"not completely satisfactory."*

Extract from patent No.9179, 1902, one of many lodged by Candy. The patent covers a floating sprinkler with self-propelled compensating arms and mercury seal, also travelling versions etc.

An essential feature for satisfactory operation of biological filters is a free passage of air through the medium, and Candy developed and patented an inverted V-shaped tile collector system that interlocked at the apex. The tiles were made of very hard, impervious Staffordshire clayware and they were probably the best system produced for this purpose. By 1905 the company publications stated that *"thousands of yards had been produced."* Some fifty years later the Candy Filter Company occasionally received orders for them and they were still regarded by many as the best drainage and ventilation system for biological filters.

Based on comparative tests at the Reigate sewage works, Candy demonstrated that Polarite gave better oxygen demand figures than stones, although examination of the filter materials showed no putrefaction in either of the trial filters. He used Polarite as the filter medium for many installations, and by 1905, his reference list numbered over three hundred filters including fifty-two at Croydon and thirty-four at Kingston-on-Thames. An extract from the Sanitary Record of the time states, *"One of the most striking facts in the history of the sewage question is the success that has attended the sprinkler system of sewage purification through a comparatively coarse bed, the sewage being sprinkled over its surface by means of either a rotary or travelling distributor and this was originated by and is the invention of Messrs. Candy, Whittaker and Caink."*

Candy's supplied many thousands of these drainage tiles over a period of about fifty years. In theory the inside passages could be rodded if needed.

Coventry c. 1910. Note the dress distinction of the three different classes of people in the photo!

Chapter 3

At the time the pattern for placing contracts was to order odd bits of sewage equipment from a bill of quantities drawn up by an architect or consultant, with poor payment conditions (what has changed!). This did not suit Candy and he generally declined to get involved with these jobs, or projects which included civil works. Nonetheless, as the list of his contracts from the period shows, over several years he had almost a monopoly for his sprinklers, and they became a standard feature of many works.

However, he had rivals, and 1908 his advertisements were referring to *"makers of sewage valves and such like, making a cheap imitation of the Candy distributor, and because it revolves, it does not follow that a good effluent will result,"* which suggests that he was encountering serious competition. Pullen lost his direct interest in the market and handed over manufacturing to Ham Baker in 1926, as the patterns were very worn by then. However, for some time Candy's continued to specify the spacing and orifice size of the jets in the arms using *"Mr Candy's magic recipe."*

The formation of The Candy Filter Company

Newport. One of twelve pressure filters being floated across the Ynis-y-fro reservoir. c.1907. There were two other sites each with six filters

From the Monmouthshire Evening Post, 5 July 1910... "The day was ideal and one hardly knows which was most enjoyable, the drive to the reservoirs and the fine views, or the excellent lunch and tea which His Worship provided. Pant-yr-eos was first visited, the party starting at noon, some in four horse brakes, others in carriages and gigs and motor cars. The prettily situated reservoir, exceptionally full for the time of the year, was visited and admired and then the party turned their attention to lunch... Afterwards the chairman said that Newport now had the largest mechanical filter installation of any in England, and he gave the health of Mr Pullen Candy..."

It is not clear when or why Frank Candy parted company from Dr Angell, but in 1906 he formed the Candy Filter Company Limited with a capital of ten thousand one pound shares and seven shareholders, all members of his family except Alec Jarvis. The new company started with a full order book for home contracts and a growing export business, with orders from South Africa and a large one for Manaos in Brazil.

By then Frank Candy was well established, but there was growing competition from other companies, including Bell Brothers, Mather & Platt (later better known for their pumps), and an English branch of the American Jewell Filters company. The French supplier Peuch Chabal was also active but failed to make much impact in the UK.

Chapter 3

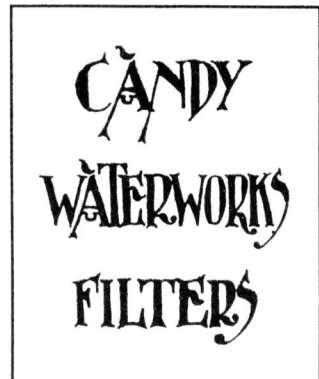

CANDY WATERWORKS FILTERS

Candy's logo changed several times during the early years

The Jewell filter was being used extensively in the USA and Egypt, and there were Jewell plants in the UK at York and Wolverhampton. Their filters were circular, open topped, steel gravity filters, with a rake system for cleaning the sand, whereas Bell Brothers made pressure filters with mechanical rakes that changed very little up to the company's demise in the 1970s. Mather and Platt's filters were similar in structure to Bell's but with a lighter rake system. By contrast, the Peuch Chabal filters consisted of a series of open roughing filters of increasing area set at descending levels, followed by a pre-filter and a finishing filter. They were similar in principle to the chamber system installed by Candy some years earlier at Reading, and they were widely used in France. Candy's filter combined an aerating chamber, followed by a coarse pre-filter, an Oxidium purifying filter, and a final sand filter, all within a single pressure vessel. The resultant water was *"clean, bright and sparkling and of good bacteriological purity"* and it was produced at a filtering rate of 120 gallons per square foot per hour without a coagulant.

New ideas

Pullen Candy continued to look after the Patent Automatic Distributors Company as well as the Bacterial Water Treatment Company (ex-Howard Filtration), and it was not until 1908 that he re-joined his father as a full-time director of the Candy Filter Company. At the time, Candy's were much involved in supplying additional Oxidium chamber filters for Staines which had the last of the old chamber pre-filters. They also designed an alumina dosing apparatus to improve the operational efficiency

Hastings 1903. 2 mgd filters at Brede.

of slow sand filters. This was known as an "alumina filming device" and came into operation for a short period when the slow sand filter was first put into operation after sand cleaning. Although Frank Candy had claimed that alumina dosing was not necessary with his pressure filters, he clearly knew that its use would spread in due course to all filters.

Chapter 3

At a meeting in 1909 Candy announced two significant advances. The first was *"an economical method of sterilising water, at the same time rendering it chemically pure, palatable and refreshing"* and the second *"a simple and inexpensive system for neutralising the peaty acids in upland waters in order to prevent lead poisoning."* These were the first announcements of his Declor and Magnesite filters and although the Declor process was to disappear fairly quickly, the Magnesite filters continued to be used into the 1960s.

As more treatment plants were completed, it was noted in the UK and the USA that this coincided with a reduction in typhoid and other water-borne diseases, as well as lower infant mortality rates. In particular, Hastings and Reading, where Candy had installed his Polarite filters, had the lowest figures in the UK, according to records published at the time.

Harrogate

The Harrogate works was a nice example of Candy's oxidising filters. Two circular, open filters were supplied in about 1905 to treat drainage water from moor and rough pasture, and their performance was compared with slow sand filters. The oxidising filters comprised layers of sand, Oxidium and Polarite, held in position by perforated and slotted grids and backwashed with filtered water. Candy's design was very competitive, and in his report to the Harrogate Water Board in 1908, the waterworks engineer, Mr F.J.Dixon, reported that additional Candy filters to provide 500,000 gpd would cost £2860, against £5203 for slow sand filters, with annual charges of £195 against £420 for the slow sand filters. On his recommendation, the corporation ordered four more of the new filters. Sixty-five years later, Paterson Candy International supplied a very different plant for the same Harlow Hill site.

55

Chapter 3

Magnesite filters

Candy's solution for dealing with "plumbism" was made public by the opening in May 1909 of a new filter installation at Holne, the Dartmoor source of the water supply for Paignton. Like most moorland waters, the supply had a solvent action on lead and it also carried some suspended matter. The treatment was accomplished within the filter by extending the height to house a neutralising medium, magnesium oxide, which Candy called Magnesite. It appears that the raw material came from two sources, India and Greece, with the grading done in the UK.

Four 8' 3" diameter filters, with a height of 10' 6", said to be the tallest made by the company, were installed at a cost of £2,000. The filters were of the compound type, with the pre-filter in the top, followed by a central Magnesite layer supported on silica sand.

After the annual inspection of the works in June 1911, the press reported that the filters were very successful in keeping the water non-plumbo solvent, and that six more were to be installed eventually. The neutralising filter, due to its inherent simplicity, became widely used throughout much of Europe, although large suppliers with lead problems preferred to dose chemicals rather than have to re-charge filters at intervals.

Candy's variable stroke dosing pump, early 1920s. The advanced feature was the indirect hydraulic drive of the diaphragm head, so that the solution did not come in contact with the working parts.

The Declor filter

Nowadays we are used to worrying about minute and probably harmless traces of various chemicals because we have the capability to measure them, and it is hard for us to imagine the public supply in the UK spreading typhoid. However, the following extract from the technical journals of about 1910 shows how different the concerns were at the time. *"During the past summer we understand there have been sixty-six cases of typhoid fever at Strood with unfortunately, several deaths, the outbreak being attributed to pollution of the water supply from wells in the fissured chalk. Although treated with Chloros, the taste and odour of the chlorinated water have been so unpleasant that consumers, rather than drink it, have resorted to old and probably polluted supplies. It has been decided by Rochester Corporation, who supply the*

Chapter 3

Strood water, that the Declor system should be at once put into operation at the Strood Waterworks."

This was the background to Candy's development of his Declor filter, and when he made his forecast of important developments in 1909, work was already in the development stages, once again at Reading. During discussions at the Fobney works in 1907, Candy had suggested providing a trial "bacteria destroying pressure filter" for a period of six months, free of charge. If the trial was successful the filter would be paid for, and additional filters would be added to bring the total quantity from 0.7 to 1 mgd.

Declor filters at Windsor. 1 mgd. 1915.

Candy's experiments and co-operation with Dr Thresh (of the Counties Public Health Laboratories) made him decide that the best approach for sterilising water would be to add one part per million of chlorine to the filtered water, and after thirty minutes contact to enable the chlorine to complete the sterilisation, to then de-chlorinate by filtering through a bed of activated carbon. The complete process would be accomplished by combining the contact space and carbon filter within a single vessel. This scheme was agreed and an experimental filter was ordered in 1909, to be subjected to a six month working test.

From the start of the test, the results were so good and consistent that the Engineer and his council accepted the filter and ordered an additional four units without completing the full six months' test period. Reading claimed to be the first town in the UK to chlorinate the water supply. (However, this claim is disputed in favour of Lincoln where continuous chlorination apparently commenced in 1904). Following the successful test on the "Bacteria Destroying Filter" and before the results became public, Candy re-named it "The Candy Patent Declor Filter System" and registered the name.

The Declor filter gained instant acclaim after the Engineer, Mr Leslie Walker, gave a paper on it to

Chapter 3

> From "The Times" January 5th 1911
>
> "WATER PURIFICATION"
>
> In his monthly report to the Reading Town Council Mr L.Walker the manager of the Reading Waterworks, states that Dr J.C.Thresh and Dr J.F.Beale, both of the London hospital Medical College, recently visited the works, and having thoroughly examined the new system of filtration, expressed themselves entirely satisfied with the working and with the results obtained.
>
> Dr Thresh wrote that, being the first in this country to realise the possibilities of chlorine as a purification agent and to demonstrate the destructive effect of very minute quantities on the bacilli of typhoid fever and cholera, he was greatly interested in the results obtained by Mr Walker with the Declor process.
>
> Mr Walker had not only solved the water purification problem for Reading, but had set an example, which, sooner or later, would be followed throughout the civilised world. Why should any water authority continue to supply water liable to the least suspicion when by so simple a process absolute safety could be ensured?
>
> He congratulated Mr Walker and messrs Candy on a success which he had verified by bacteriological investigations. Dr Beale also offered congratulations on the excellent results of the process.....

the Association of Water Engineers in London. Headlines in the London newspapers varied from the Daily News' *"Pure Water, Reading's example to the whole civilised world,"* to the more sedate Times' *"Water Purification."* The Declor system was probably the first practical method of super-chlorination, contact and de-chlorination, a treatment process that became standard in much of the UK and Europe, and is still the basis of many modern water treatment plants.

The Reading filters were fitted with hydraulically scoured pre-filters in the top and the de-chlorinating filter in the bottom. The pre-filter enabled the original slow sand filters to be scrapped, and by eliminating a break in pressure, the pumping could be carried out by a water wheel in place of the steam driven pumping plant, so saving on coal and labour.

Similar work by other companies, relating to different methods of sterilising water, was in progress in America and Europe, with ozone and chlorine in the form of calcium hypochlorite (bleaching powder) as the most favoured means. However, the success of the Reading installation attracted widespread interest from, among other places, South Africa, China, and Japan. Orders were soon received from the UK as well as overseas water authorities, and to meet different site needs, Candy developed several designs including single bed de-chlorinating filters to be used in conjunction with an existing clear water storage tank. He also offered a range of open, gravity Declor filters, and having taken the precaution of patenting the Declor process as well as the filters, he was able to charge a royalty from suppliers who converted their existing gravity filters.

Between 1909 and 1915 Candy was granted patents for the use of lignite, coconut fibre and sponge for de-chlorinating purposes. It was found that the lignite remained active for about twelve months continual use and it could be re-activated by soaking it in a fifty per

> From "The Daily News" January 6th 1911
>
> "PURE WATER"
>
> READING'S EXAMPLE TO THE WHOLE CIVILISED WORLD
>
> We published yesterday morning brief particulars of the Declor system of filtration of water which was experimentally put into operation at the Southcote works of the Reading Corporation by the Candy Filter Company, under the supervision of Mr Leslie C.Walker, Engineer and Manager of the Reading Corporation Waterworks.
>
> The supply of pure water for domestic purposes is a matter of the utmost importance to public health, and the action of the Reading Town council is an example which might be followed with advantage by other municipalities.
>
> In conversation yesterday with Professor W.R.Smith, the Principal of the Royal Institute of Public Health, our representative learned that the results at Reading were perfectly satisfactory. A full description of the method and results, from the pen of Mr Walker, will be published today, in the monthly journal of the institute, from which we are permitted to make a few extracts.
>
> The use of chlorine is not new, says Mr Walker, but the system offered for adoption by the Corporation was in all respects a complete process, embodying the automatic addition of the chlorine, the provision of a contact period between the water and the chlorine, and the total elimination from the water of the residual chlorine after it has performed its function of destroying the bacteria..
>
> Dr J.C.Thresh.......

cent hydrochloric acid solution for 12 - 24 hours, which would have posed some handling problems!

Copenhagen

A new factor during this period was a significant growth in business from Copenhagen, where Candy's agent Peel Harvey secured work in Denmark, Sweden, Norway, Finland and Russia. Candy also appointed agents in a number of other countries, including China and Japan. A 1916 publicity booklet refers to over 400 plants having been installed for private and public supplies in these countries, and in correspondence Candy also mentions sales to France, Germany, America and Canada. However, the only reference to an actual plant for these last four places is one for Lethbridge Jail in Canada!

Hydraulic scour, Bi-flow, horizontal and upflow filters

The first twenty years of the century produced a variety of designs from Candy's which were adopted by the industry and continued to be made for at least the next fifty years. In 1912 Candy installed hydraulic scour consisting of a rotating distributor just above the filter sand at Torquay, and this became the standard cleaning arrangement for the next decade. The engineer to the corporation reported, *"The system of cleansing and scouring the filtering material marks a great advance on the methods usually employed...the power of the water is concentrated, in turn, on every part of the bed."*

At West Hants (near Bournemouth), in 1913 Candy supplied the first upflow filters as roughing units ahead of slow sand filters. These gave good service for about forty years until they were dismantled, and used as storage tanks after a major reconstruction of the works when the original upflow plant was re-built in the 1950s.

In the early 60s, William Boby Ltd introduced their Immedium filter which was an upward flow, gravity type with the same coarse grade of

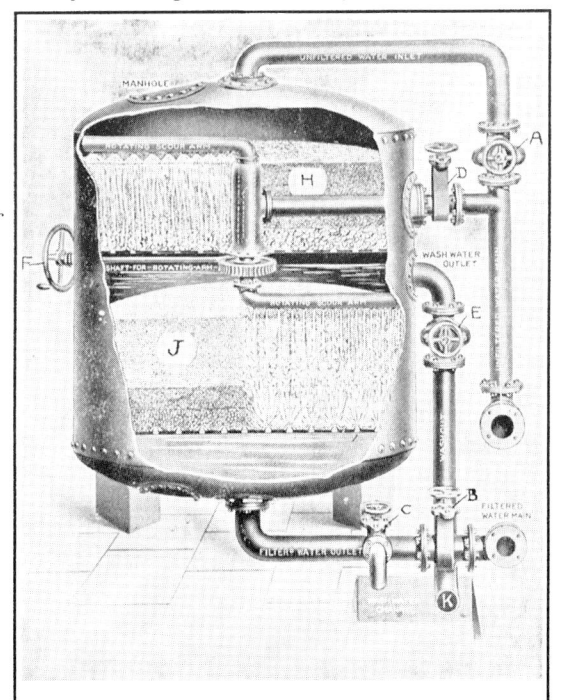

Candy's compound filter with externally operated scour jets working with the back-wash. The degree of agitation achieved looks distinctly optimistic!

Chapter 3

Truro. 1912. Capacity 1 mgd

sand and the same rating as Candy's original design. The first of these plants was used to improve the quality of sewage effluent discharging from the sewage works into the River Lee at Luton. In due course, Boby's became part of the Permutit organisation, which later transferred the Immedium filter business to PCI, which was a roundabout way of acquiring something the company had developed about 60 years earlier!

Although the upflow filter was an elegant concept, it had fundamental weaknesses. Suspended material tended to block the underdrains, and dirt retained in the coarse layers was not removed by backwash. These problems made the design sensitive to air in the feed, so when it was fully loaded it tended to discharge unpredictably into the filtrate and Boby's version worked little better than Candy's.

The Bi-Flow was a more successful design that combined two filters fed through top and bottom distributors with a central outlet, built in a single, tall vessel to provide double the filter area. The design was supplied to China and elsewhere and variants included a roughing pre-filter. This design was widely used by other plant suppliers but died out due to its cost.

The final and most enduring design in this prolific period was the horizontal pressure filter, with Truro in Cornwall having the distinction of being the first town to use them. They were 8' 3" diameter by 21' long, and equipped with hydraulic scour wash operated by a

Christchurch 1913.

Sir, We notice in an article headed "New filtering plant at Clydebank," in your issue of the 10th inst., a statement that the mechanical open gravity filters, each having an effective filtering area of 252 square feet... "are claimed to be the largest mechanical filtration units in the United Kingdom." We would, however, like to point out that such claim is incorrect, as we laid down last year at Christchurch, Hants, for the West Hampshire Water Company, an important installation comprising mechanical open gravity filters, each unit of which has an effective filtering area of rather over 314 square feet....

As the Christchurch filters possess unique features and have been visited by engineers from all over the world, we enclose a photograph in case you may like to illustrate them... and give publicity to this correction.

(For The Candy Filter Company Limited),
FRANK CANDY, Managing Director.
London, July 21st. 1914

gear through the front dome of the filters. Their installation enabled the Truro Water Company to scrap their slow sand filter beds and to use the tanks for storage and settlement of the raw water. The new filters were sited alongside the existing Declor filters and commissioned in 1912.

The First War years

By 1914 Frank Candy, aged 72, was living in Torquay and thinking about retiring. There was a good train service to London, and although Pullen had taken over much of the running of the company, his father was well aware of what was happening in the water supply and treatment world, and maintained a lively interest in the business as well as his correspondence with Dr Thresh.

The company was extremely busy in the UK and overseas, and the outbreak of war opened up new markets. Four months after the war started their advertisements proclaimed *"Five Declor Filter Plants Ordered For Kitchener's Army"*.

For years there had been a debate about the loss of life during the Boer War and other campaigns, when the troops drank untreated water in preference to the heavily chlorinated water supplied to them. Apparently the problem arose from the over zealous use of calcium hypochlorite (more soldiers died from disease than from enemy fire) and the War Office was very conscious of the need to supply the troops with water that was safe, bacteriologically pure, and palatable. In 1914 they established camps to train some 200,000 men on Salisbury Plain, and a large camp at Catterick in Yorkshire, for which Candy's supplied Declor pressure filters and calcium hypochlorite dosing equipment, with capacities of 20-30,000 gpd.

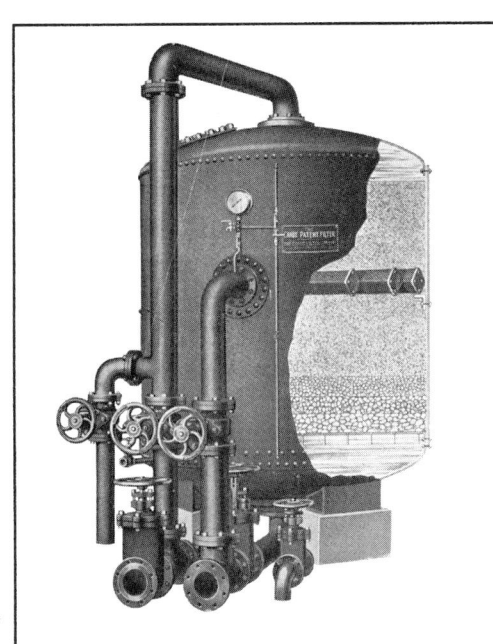

Cross-section of the Bi-flow filter. The raw water entered at the top and bottom, leaving through the centre distributor. The filter was airscoured and backwashed as a conventional filter.

Once the needs of the camps had been satisfied, orders came from the Ministry of Munitions for a factory at Avonmouth and an explosives factory at Stowmarket. As the war progressed, treatment plants were put in at Longmore Camp in Hampshire and for the Royal Flying Corps aerodromes at Manston and Eastchurch.

The war also had some effect on the supplies of bleaching powder, and in correspondence Frank Candy mentions that the company had supplied an electrolytic plant to produce chlorine from salt. The machine was probably obtained from Mather & Platt. However, despite the urgent work for the war effort, the commercial orders for water treatment plant for the home and overseas markets proceeded with little delay.

In 1915 Candy received a letter from Dr Thresh describing a visit from a high ranking officer who had recently returned from the front line in France. He reported that the British Army was expected to move forward shortly and the War Office was worried about the possibility of the Germans poisoning water sources as they retreated. Dr Thresh suggested that Mr Candy immediately start designs for an assembly of Candy Declor filters mounted on a steam wagon (then widely used by industry). The steam engine would be used for driving the wagon and for pumping water and sterilising the filter sand and carbon when the vehicle was static. Unfortunately, the British Army was bogged down for a very long time until tanks were invented and there is no record of any mobile Declor filters being supplied!

As the war progressed Alec Jarvis joined the armed forces as did Burville Candy (Frank Candy's grandson) which left Pullen very overworked. At the end of the war it was decided that he should find a partner in preparation for his father's retirement. Larger offices were also required, together with bigger workshops and test area, so the company moved to 18 Howick Place in Victoria, near the Army and Navy Stores, with additional workshops and stores in Amberley Mews.

Ministry of Munitions, Avonmouth. Half of the 6.5 mgd plant. Note the steel construction, presumably for speed of building.

When Captain Alec Jarvis returned from the war he decided to deal only with Scandinavian work, so he joined Candy's agent Peel Harvey, in Copenhagen, where he established a substantial market for Candy's designs.

Chapter 3

Early flow-proportioned chemical dosing systems

All the suppliers made some form of flow proportioning system for dosing chemicals, using a variety of ingenious hydraulic devices. The new chemical plant for Pontypridd, supplied in 1915, was one of the first to bear a resemblance to modern practice. A flow proportioning turbine was used to drive shafting with pulleys and chain drives to four variable stroke chemical pumps, and to the chemical solution tank agitating gears. The chemicals used were aluminium sulphate and lime, and the doses could be varied easily by the stroke change mechanism fitted to the pumps. The Centrifugal Balancer, described in chapter 9, was one of the last of the hydraulic devices, and was superseded by DC motors and other electrical systems once electronic transmitters appeared, leading to today's static inverter/variable speed AC motors.

Talybont chemical pumps, with flow proportioning control. Although much later than Pontypridd, the layout is similar.

Hastings and the development of the nozzle floor

During the war period a large contingent of Canadian troops was in training near Hastings. The Hastings Corporation found that the supply from the Filsham Pumping Station was depositing suspended matter in the water main supplying the original pressure filters two miles away at West Hill. Following discussions, Candy's designed a rapid gravity filter plant, to be constructed in concrete, with inlet aerating spray jets to remove dissolved carbon dioxide and hydrogen sulphide. The filters would be cleaned by airscour and an entirely new design of filter floor would be used. Furthermore, it would be a package deal, with Candy's being responsible for the design and provision of the reinforced concrete building.

The plant is of particular interest as it was fitted with the first recorded airscour nozzle filter floor which Candy named the "type-A", and it was to be widely used throughout the world for the next fifty years. The nozzle itself was imitated by most of Candy's major competitors over the next few years. The Hastings filters used separate airscour and backwash, and the company ceased to offer hydraulic scour at about the same time.

Chapter 3

A few years later, Pullen developed a combined-wash version with a separate airscour header which is described in chapter 5.

The rivalry with Paterson's

With hindsight, perhaps the most important event affecting the future of the company occurred in 1913 when Candy's competitors, the Paterson Engineering Company, secured an order for Cheltenham at their Tewkesbury Works. The new plant was the first resembling a modern gravity filter installation, with many design innovations. Until then, Paterson's had concentrated mainly on industrial work, but the Tewkesbury order took them into direct rivalry with Candy's.

The war delayed Candy's start of the building of the new filters at Hastings, and in the meantime, Paterson's had won a contract for a similar but larger plant to the Tewkesbury works, for the Irvine District Water Supply. This meant that not only had Paterson's installed the first of what was to become the modern pattern of gravity filter installations, but had quickly followed this with an important order required urgently for the war effort. So pressure was on Pullen to make the new Candy gravity filter competitive and technically superior, and with lower operating costs. Predictably, he rose to the challenge and produced what became the defining gravity filter technology for the next fifty years.

This was the start of fierce competition between the two companies, from which Paterson emerged as the dominant supplier in the UK until the early 1960s.

Chapter 3

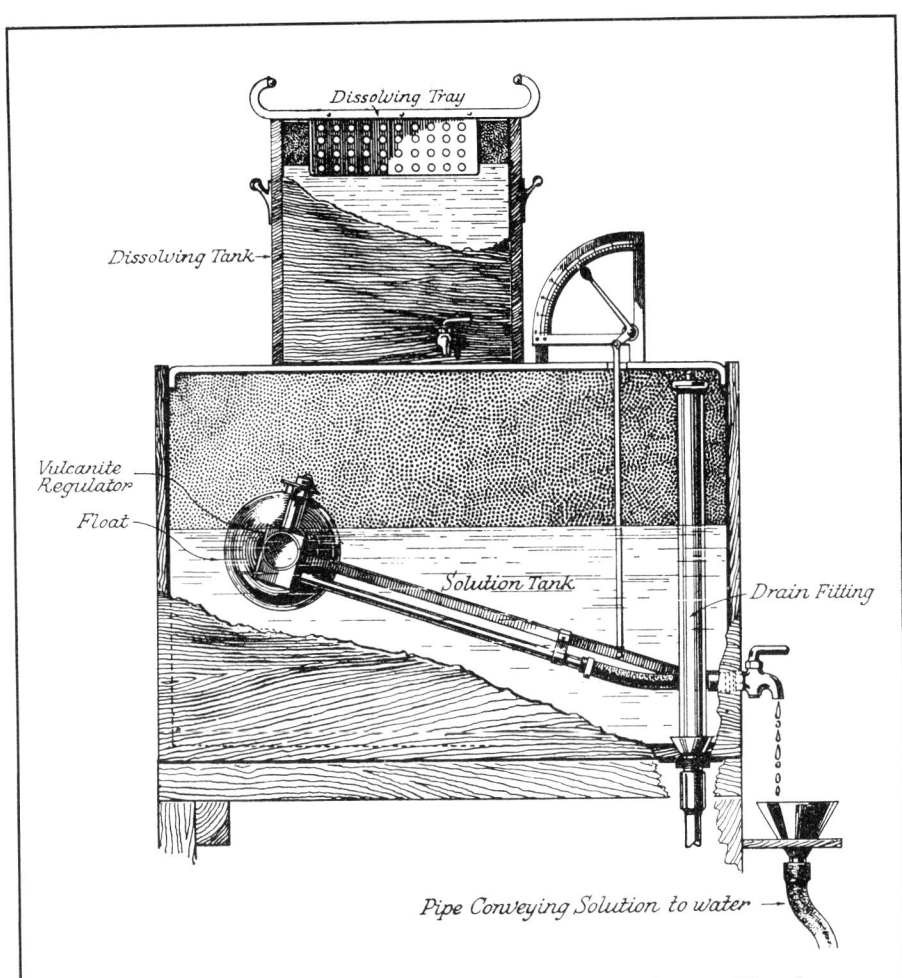

A simple floating draw-off gravity doser for alum solution. The dose was adjusted at the Vulcanite regulator. The quadrant mechanism provided level indication. From a 1926 catalogue

4 - WILLIAM PATERSON, 1902-1955

The early years

William Paterson was born at Lasswade near Roslin in Scotland in 1874 and educated in Edinburgh. After a technical training at Heriot Watt College, he served a five year apprenticeship as an engineer in the workshops and drawing office of James Bertram and Sons, a firm of paper mill engineers. From these early days, his interest in water treatment developed as he became aware of its importance to industry, and in particular, of the large quantities of treated water required for processing and steam generation.

At the time, boiler explosions were a frequent occurrence, especially in the new power stations using tubular boilers and high speed reciprocating steam engines. Paterson became convinced that the trouble was caused by the presence of oil in the boiler feed water, and in 1902, sure that he had the solution to these problems, he decided to start his own business. He was then twenty-eight, and registered his company in Edinburgh as the Paterson Engineering Company Limited with a capital of £700.

William Paterson, aged about 80.

Orders proved hard to win and it appears that the breakthrough came when Paterson attended a meeting of senior engineers and listened to the various suggestions for reducing the hazards of boiler explosions. After some hesitation, he offered his own thoughts regarding the real causes and possible cures for the problems. Apparently his

Chapter 4

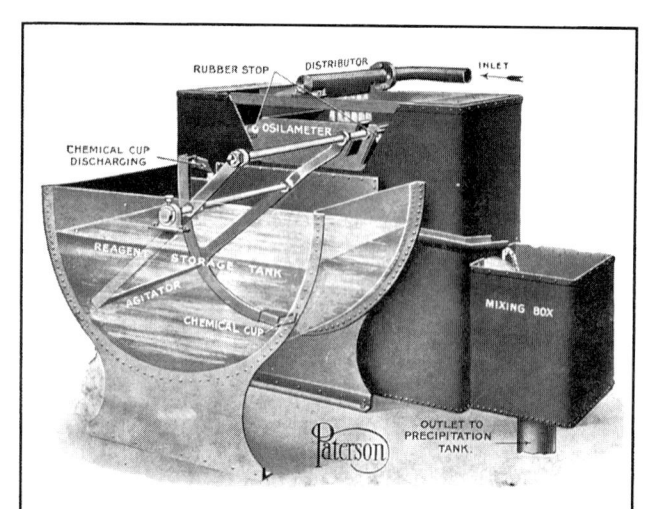

This curious device was the Paterson Osilameter. A tipping bucket mechanism caused a cup to add chemical solution each time the bucket tipped. The chemical was then mixed with the discharge from the buckets. Pre-1912.

ideas were well received, because a few days later, he received six enquiries and to his delighted surprise, four orders followed shortly afterwards. From this small beginning the business grew rapidly, and in 1904 he decided to transfer his office from Glasgow to London. There he shared lodgings with John Anderson (later Lord Waverley) and Alexander (later Sir Alexander) Gray, leaving a representative in the Glasgow area to keep in touch with his many customers.

The Red Book

Paterson's energy was evident from the beginning, and in the year he started his company he published his first technical book, which became known as "The Paterson Red Book". This had illustrations of a limited range of Paterson's well-designed equipment plus much useful information for the steam raising engineer. The 1911 edition shows the outstanding growth of the business as well as the range of equipment he produced. This covered pressure and gravity filters, industrial water supply, exhaust steam heaters and purifiers, as well as oil eliminators and chemical plant. The illustrations show that the equipment was well-designed and solidly built, and the number of repeat orders testifies to his customers' satisfaction. Under the section entitled *"Some representative users of Paterson purifiers for power plants"* are listed two hundred and seventy names, including approximately eighty generating and electricity authorities and eighty-seven contractors for steam-powered generators. There are also sixty-five paper and other mills listed, as well as the Admiralty dockyards, army installations, railway companies and laundries.

Gravity filters for the Royal Arsenal College, Tokyo. 1911, at the fabricators at Millwall. Note the hydraulic scour arms and gear drive mechanism.

Initially, Paterson concentrated on the industrial market, with the bulk of his activity in the UK, though he had already started to export to India, Malaya (Malaysia), South Africa, China, Argentina, Australia and Greece. Apart from three very small installations, he left the public water supply industry alone, having stated in 1902: *"It is our aim to meet the demands for industrial water purifiers by a thoroughly British product."* However, the introduction to the 1911 Red Book covers a wider market and reads, *"Gentlemen, we are the only British firm rigidly specialising in water purifying apparatus for municipal, domestic and industrial supply."* We might find his language pompous but his longer established competitors were soon to learn of Paterson's intention to enter the municipal market.

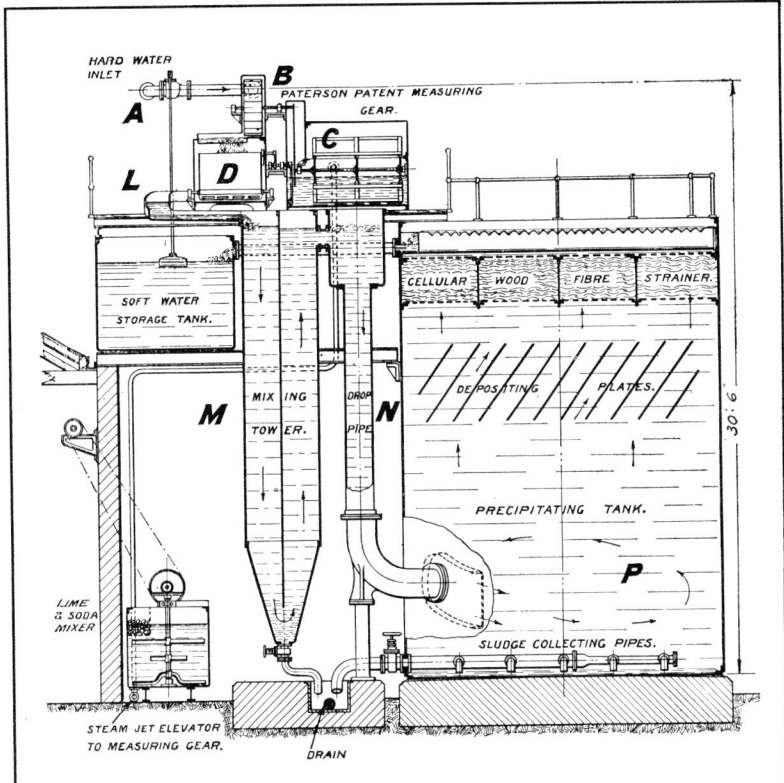

Paterson lime softening plant, capacity 10,000 gph, at Rowntree's cocoa works, pre-1912. Item C is an Osilameter.

Tewkesbury - the first modern gravity filters

[The term gravity filters was used rather loosely and at the time covered both slow sand and rapid gravity filters, the difference being an approximately fifty-fold increase in the rating].

The first, very basic water supply rapid gravity filter plant consisting of concrete tanks made to Paterson's design was installed for the Weardale and Consett Water Company in about 1911 and he supplied all the equipment. This plant had a major impact on the industry, but the Tewkesbury plant built for the Cheltenham Water Company in 1913, with its more sophisticated controls and attractively finished filter house, was a huge leap forward. It is generally regarded as the first "modern" gravity filter installation in the UK. With it, Paterson had developed a straightforward and practical design which he repeated in numerous installations. He was rightly very proud of the Tewkesbury plant which he visited annually for many years.

Then, during 1914, he again shocked his competitors with the opening of a 5.5 mgd plant for the Clydebank and District Water Trust, to supply the Irvine District. This was a very big plant for its time and it was opened ceremonially by King George V.

World War 1 - the first gas chlorinators

The Irvine plant which was mainly for the supply to Nobel's explosives plant, was followed by another with a capacity of 10 mgd for the Ministry of Munitions at Gretna (near Carlisle), perhaps more famous for its weddings.

Clydebank, c 1916. This plant illustrates the layout Paterson adopted for many years. The plant at Tewkesbury was very similar. Clydebank had 10 filters each 24 x 12 ft, with automatic outlet flow controllers, the filtrate being run to waste for up to 15 minutes after washing, "to afford an opportunity for filming".

Paterson's pressure gas chlorinators, designed in the war years, were a major advance in water treatment, and the first installation was for the Metropolitan Water Board in 1917. Another landmark was an export order to the Indian Army Headquarters at Poona. There Paterson demonstrated that the polluted supplies that were the main cause of dysentery and other diseases, could be treated satisfactorily and made safe. This led to many orders for the Indian state capitals and other large towns and so, in 1919 Paterson formed The Paterson Engineering Company (India) Limited, based in Calcutta.

Clydebank 1916. The chemical plant. Note the main flow channel in the centre of the photo.

The development of the Chloronome chlorinator, which was based on a licensed patent, illustrates a basic difference in approach between Candy and Paterson which was to continue until

Chapter 4

Paterson Chloronome chlorinators at Kempton Park filter plant. Each unit treated 48 mgd.

the amalgamation. Paterson was always happy to licence others' technology when he did not have his own design. By contrast, Frank and Pullen Candy developed most of their products themselves, and this difference in approach persisted long after the founders left the industry.

The Chloronome and later derivatives sold in hundreds as chlorine treatment became more widely used for water supplies, and a separate chlorine department was soon busy designing variants of it, with a wide range of capacities and accessories. Amongst these, the BCM chlorinator was the ideal size for small water supplies for which chlorination was usually the only form of treatment. The chlorinators were manufactured by Kingsway Engineering with whom Paterson had a very good, long-lasting relationship.

Paterson was one of the first to apply chlorine treatment to sewage works to prevent offensive odours and deal with "ponding" of sprinkler filters. He also developed the use of chlorine treatment for power station condensers to limit algal growths, a process that was subsequently adopted world-wide. In turn, these applications required the design of new, large capacity machines.

By 1920 the Paterson Engineering Company had replaced Bell Brothers as Candy's chief competitor. William Paterson had built up his company in a very short time and he was to go on to dominate the British market, at home and overseas.

The Infilco licence

During the 1920s Paterson reached an agreement with the International Filter Company of Tucson, Arizona, later known as Infilco. He was particularly interested in using their filter outlet venturi controllers for maintaining constant

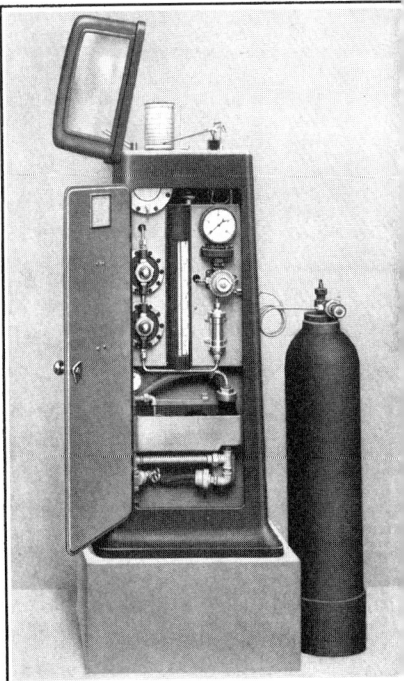

Paterson Chlorograph pressure chlorinator with continuous flow recorder.

71

Chapter 4

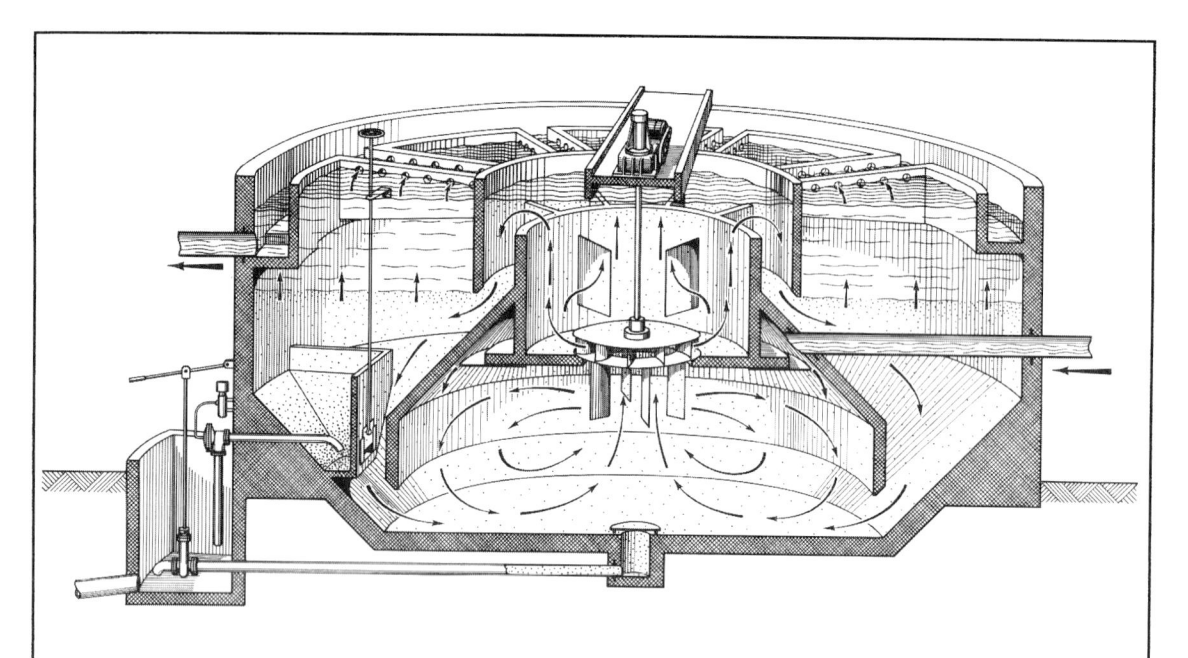

The Paterson Accentrifloc. A very rugged high-rate clarifier/softener used in hundreds of plants.

output from each filter. The control system also embodied means for slow-starting the filters after washing, together with a master control for closing down or varying the flow. This licence agreement lasted for several decades and much of Paterson's future technology was based on Infilco designs, including their filter control tables, used to operate the valves and wash machinery. The tables (illustrated in the photograph) were made of synthetic materials or natural marble, and were generally fitted in spacious control galleries above the tops of two rows of filters. The valves were operated hydraulically using high pressure water, and actuated from small levers mounted on the control table. Loss of head and flow gauges and a flow diagram were also mounted on the table, alongside switches for starting compressors, upwash pumps etc.

In the early 30's Infilco designed their fixed bridge circular clarifier, the Accelator, which Paterson

Filter control table of marble, from the 1930s. The levers operated pilot valves for the water operated slave cylinders actuating the filter valves and penstocks.

renamed the Accentrifloc and used to compete with the Dorr Oliver designs. (Dorr Oliver were very strong in the mineral industry and offered a range of very rugged clarifiers and classifiers). Prior to these developments, British practice was to use horizontal settling tanks or basins that were often specified by the customer to be of sufficient size to give a number of hours contact and settling time, following the addition and mixing of the coagulant, usually aluminium sulphate. Times of four to six hours were commonly specified but sometimes twelve or even twenty-four hours were required. The introduction in the 1920s of the more advanced American settling tanks led to the present-day practice of water treatment contractors offering their own individual designs, rather than working to their clients' designs, except ironically, in the USA where consultants often provide the plant design.

Kempton Park

Paterson flourished in the 1920s, supplying many impressive plants and establishing a number of relationships that brought him preference and repeat orders, including those for the South Staffordshire Waterworks Company, the Bournemouth Gas & Water Company and several gravity plants for the Metropolitan Water Board (MWB) in London.

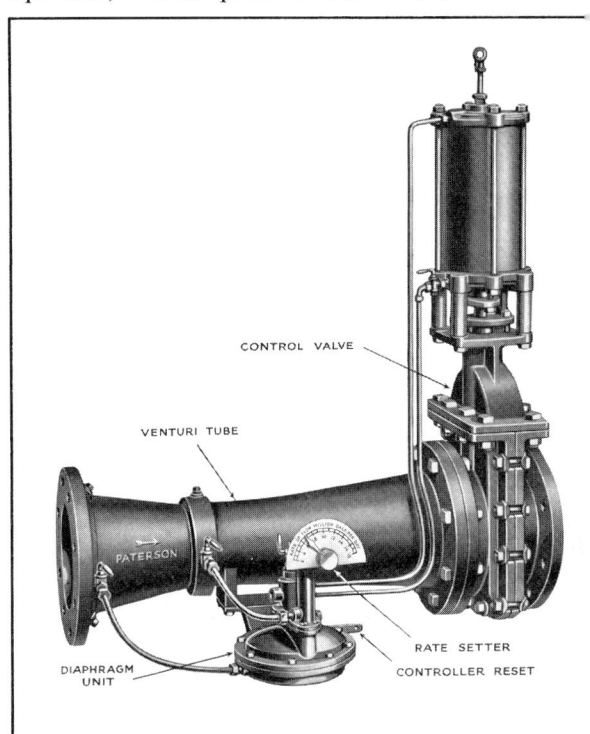

Paterson type-G filter controller. The diaphragm control unit operated at constant differential with a shunt flow through the diaphragm, the difference being provided by the rate setter. The device was water operated.

The large 40 mgd MWB plant at Kempton Park is of special interest because the system used for filter washing infringed a patent owned by Pullen Candy. Candy's system was originally developed for small pressure filter installations in remote areas of the Yorkshire moors which were without electric power but had a high pressure filtered water supply available. An enclosed, horizontal steel cylinder was mounted about thirty feet above the filter floor level and connected to the filtered water main, so that the air in the cylinder was compressed to the mains pressure. When the waste valve was closed the air was used for airscour, and the water in the cylinder was then used to backwash the filter. The outcome of the infringement action by Candy is not known, but the method became commonplace and was much used by Paterson and most of the competition.

Chapter 4

The acquisition years

As the 20s drew to a close, with his business widespread and buoyant, Paterson faced the 1930s with confidence. He began a period of rapid expansion and took over most of his competitors although interestingly, he left them largely free to carry on with their separate businesses. He also floated his own company with a nominal capital of £100,000 which was soon doubled.

In 1934 he took over both Candy's and Bell Brothers, and shortly afterwards he also bought the English and Calcutta companies of the Jewell Filter Company of America. The motive for the Jewell acquisition is not clear, as they had made little impact in the UK. However their Indian subsidiary carried out a fair amount of work in competition with Paterson's in Calcutta, and to a limited extent also competed with Candy's in Bombay.

Paterson pre-filters at Kempton Park, capacity 48 mgd. 1929

The splendid filter house, Rand Water Board. 11 mgd. 1924

So by the middle of the 1930s the three British pioneers and Jewell Filters (UK) were under the same ownership, with the directors aware of the position but the staff knowing little more than rumours. Apart from deed boxes of share certificates and similar material passing from one bank strong room to another, there were few changes, but significantly, details of all sales enquiries were copied to Paterson. The principal result of the acquisitions was that Paterson was often able to pick the jobs he wanted by dictating the price at which his subsidiaries could bid when they were in competition with him. In future years this became a hindrance, but that is a later story.

There was practically no dealing in Paterson shares and there is little in the annual reports to show the true

Filter house, Kobe, Japan. 8 mgd, 1925.

Chapter 4

Adverse conditions. The plant at Tallin Estonia. Capacity 5.6 mgd. 1924. The works was entirely covered to cope with winter conditions of minus 45 degrees F.

worth of the company during the early years, a policy of non-disclosure that continued until the take-over by Portals.

Ozone, big softening plants, paper etc.

The original Langford plant at Southend, built by Paterson in the late 1920s, caused considerable interest and publicity, and the same excess lime treatment process was adopted for subsequent plants at Hanningfield and elsewhere. The process, which was imposed by a government requirement at the time to deal with the water quality, needed the softened water to be stabilised, and various methods were tried including coke gas, underwater burning of propane and later, commercial carbon dioxide.

In the 1934-35 period Paterson's became involved with ozone sterilisation and installed an impressive-looking plant for the Maidstone Water Company at Boxley Pumping Station. They went on to supply a number of other ozone plants, including many for swimming pools, notably for the Helsingsfors Olympic Games. However, the cost of using ozone for potable supply was regarded as too high compared with conventional chlorine gas treatment, and in 1938 Paterson said in his annual report to the company, "We have spent a considerable sum of money on this ozone system

South Staffs Water Co, Sandfields. 4 mgd, 1926. Note how Paterson's design had developed from the Clydebank plant built only 12 years earlier. This was a very modern plant for its time.

Chapter 4

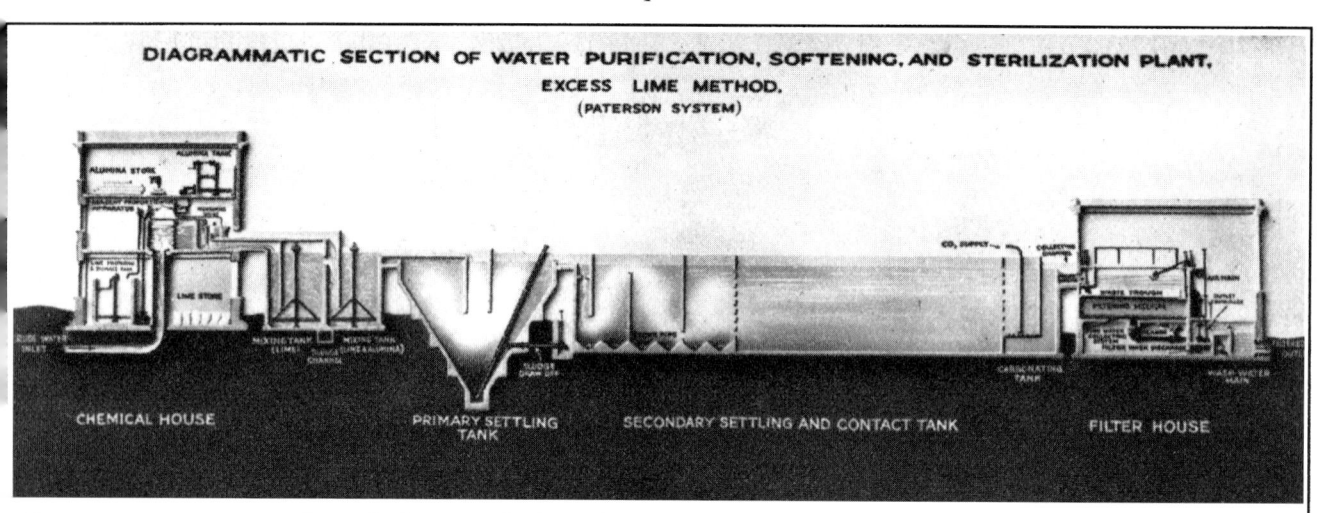

DIAGRAMMATIC SECTION OF WATER PURIFICATION, SOFTENING, AND STERILIZATION PLANT.
EXCESS LIME METHOD.
(PATERSON SYSTEM)

CHEMICAL HOUSE — PRIMARY SETTLING TANK — SECONDARY SETTLING AND CONTACT TANK — FILTER HOUSE

Diagrammatic section through the Langford works. The water was mixed with lime for 20 minutes ahead of the primary settling tank, to produce a very heavy precipitate. The plant treated 7 mgd of impounded river water. Powdered activated carbon treatment was added in 1930 to deal with a taste problem. The excess lime process was a government requirement at the time and imposed on the water company to sterilise the water through the high pH reached in the softening tanks, but the softened water needed treatment to neutralise the excess alkalinity. The plant used filtered coke oven gas to produce carbon dioxide gas for stabilising the softened water, and this, together with processes for re-claiming and re-calcining the softening sludge, were the first of their kind in the UK.

which in my view is the best, but it is clear that it is a losing battle." Notwithstanding this view, the company continued to supply ozone plants for swimming pools until the 50s.

Paterson's had always been very active in the industrial market. In 1930 the order for a 4 mgd clarification and filtration plant for the St Anne's Board Mills at Bristol was a key development which put Paterson's in a commanding position in the paper industry. The value of the original contract exceeded Paterson's annual UK turnover for that period. The plant was extended several times to a total of 29.5 mgd by 1956.

Ozone generators, South Staffs WC, Huntington, 1937. The units appear to be from Trailigaz. The design remained little changed until the 1950s.

Chapter 4

Chellow Heights, Bradford. 1928. 4 settling tanks and 16 gravity filters. Capacity 2 mgd.

Clark and Milton join UWS

During the late 1930s, United Water Softeners (UWS - later the Permutit Company Ltd) unexpectedly decided to enter the municipal water treatment market. To achieve this, they recruited J.G.Milton, an engineer, and R.Clark, a project engineer, plus some draughtsmen, from Paterson's, to set up a new department for UWS. It appears that before breaking away, Milton and Clark had demanded seats on Paterson's board. Paterson and Burrells (the company secretary) were in India at the time and reacted predictably and in very few words! Soon afterwards C.G.Boyton, a project engineer, together with a draughtsman from Candy's, also joined UWS. These moves enabled UWS to take an important share of the municipal market and become a serious competitor to Candy and Paterson.

Overseas expansion

In South Africa, Paterson supplied the Rand Water Board in 1921 with an installation of gravity pre-filters of 15-20 mgd capacity, as well as treatment plants to a few other towns, which was of considerable concern to Candy who regarded the territory as his. However, these orders were just part of Paterson's substantial overseas expansion, and the 1932 edition of "Modern Water Treatment Plant" illustrates some of his extensive world-wide

MWB Green Lanes, 1936. One of the pre-filters arranged to show the construction of the under-drains, packing layers and siphons.

Chapter 4

Rio de Cobre, Brazil. 1.76 mgd. 1933.

references. These include a 23 mgd primary filter plant for Rotterdam. The twenty-two filters, each 40 m² area, used Paterson's high level wash system with washout siphons and valves that were hydraulically operated by water pressure. Of interest is the construction of the filter house which was built on a concrete raft supported on timber piles. Another reference describes a 1 mgd plant for Karkh to supply Baghdad. For this plant, Paterson supplied a heavy duty scraped pre-settling tank to deal with the very high level of solids present at times in the River Tigris.

Egypt had come to be regarded as Paterson's territory, and he had a number of medium-sized plants in service and some large ones expected in the near future. Amongst these was the very large contract for the Fayoum Water Grid Scheme, which Paterson won in 1937 against strong international competition.

Some figures

Some of the financial statements from the period are of interest. In his review of 1937, Paterson said that the profit of £25,000 net on an issued capital of £175,000 was a *"fair and equitable return"* (14.3%) and that the yearly turnover was approaching three-quarters of a million pounds, *"a figure which shows our profit is a modest one"* (3.3%). The turnover figure must have included the overseas subsidiaries to whom Paterson supplied materials at cost plus 20%. Better comparisons are to be found in 1939 when the profit from Paterson's trading was £19,695, with dividends received from subsidiaries amounting to £13,695. The Candy contribution

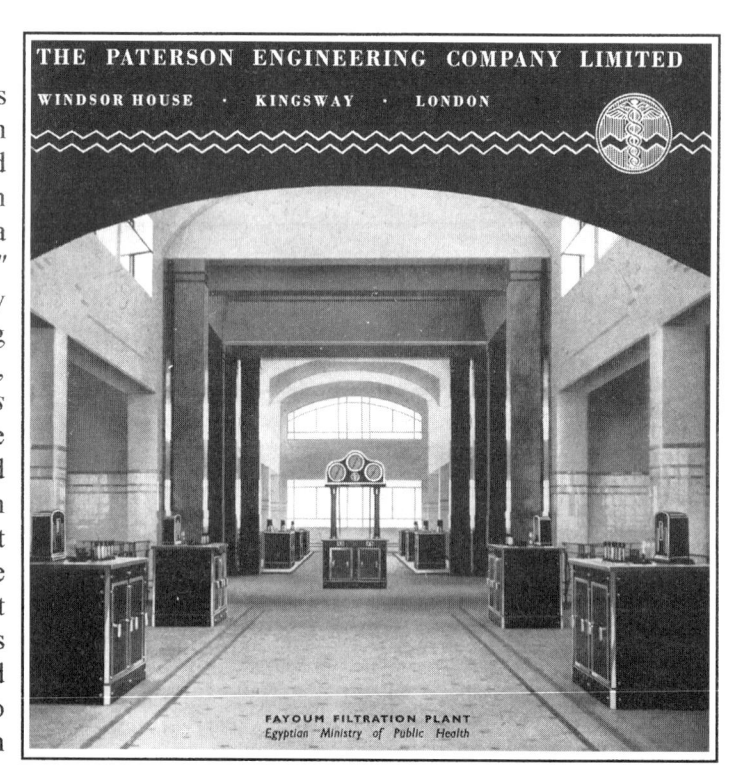

THE PATERSON ENGINEERING COMPANY LIMITED
WINDSOR HOUSE · KINGSWAY · LONDON

FAYOUM FILTRATION PLANT
Egyptian Ministry of Public Health

to these was £5,375 and their profit of £8,183 came from a turnover of £107,638. Included in Candy's turnover figure was £18,000 for materials supplied to the Indian and New Zealand companies, again with a 20% margin, indicating a profit of around 9% on turnover. It's probable that the UK activities of the three companies were producing about the same return, so they were financing their operations from their own resources.

Wavy lines have been used by several companies in the water industry. Candy used an image like this for his logo and more recently, Thames Water adopted a very similar emblem.

His legacy

William Paterson was undoubtedly one of the major figures in the history of water treatment, and for most of his working life he was more successful commercially than his rival, Frank Candy. Like Candy, he supplied treatment plants to most of the world and he was responsible for introducing a number of important developments in water treatment, including the use of ozone as a sterilising agent. In this, he was ahead of his time and the process did not find widespread acceptance for treating public supplies in the UK until the late 1980s. By then, it had been standard practice in much of mainland Europe for many years so the equipment sources are now outside the UK. Paterson's process for treating cooling water with chlorine gas, originally applied in 1923, resulted in substantial gains in power station efficiency.

In the course of his career he filed over seventy British patents, many of them fore-shadowing improvements which were not developed on an industrial scale until years later. He had an ability to choose good men who worked for him for many years, including such well-known names as Oscar Kerrison, Horace Coulson, and Walter Smalley who was the chief engineer for nearly fifty years.

Birmingham Water Dept., Whitacre filter house, 3 mgd, late 1920s.

Chapter 4

During the Second World War Paterson was increasingly involved with his subsidiaries in contributing to the war effort, and these activities are described in another chapter. He retired in 1955 and died only a year later, aged 82, having presided over his company for over fifty years. By then, his companies had become perhaps the foremost water treatment organisation in the world, due in part to his policy of keeping Paterson's, Candy's and Bell Brothers as separate concerns, an approach that enabled him to control much of the market.

In the mid-60s, under the new ownership of Portals, the company was amalgamated with Candy's to form PCI. By then, as has happened so often, William Paterson's company had started to lose its way, and with ageing technology and management, was declining in the world market.

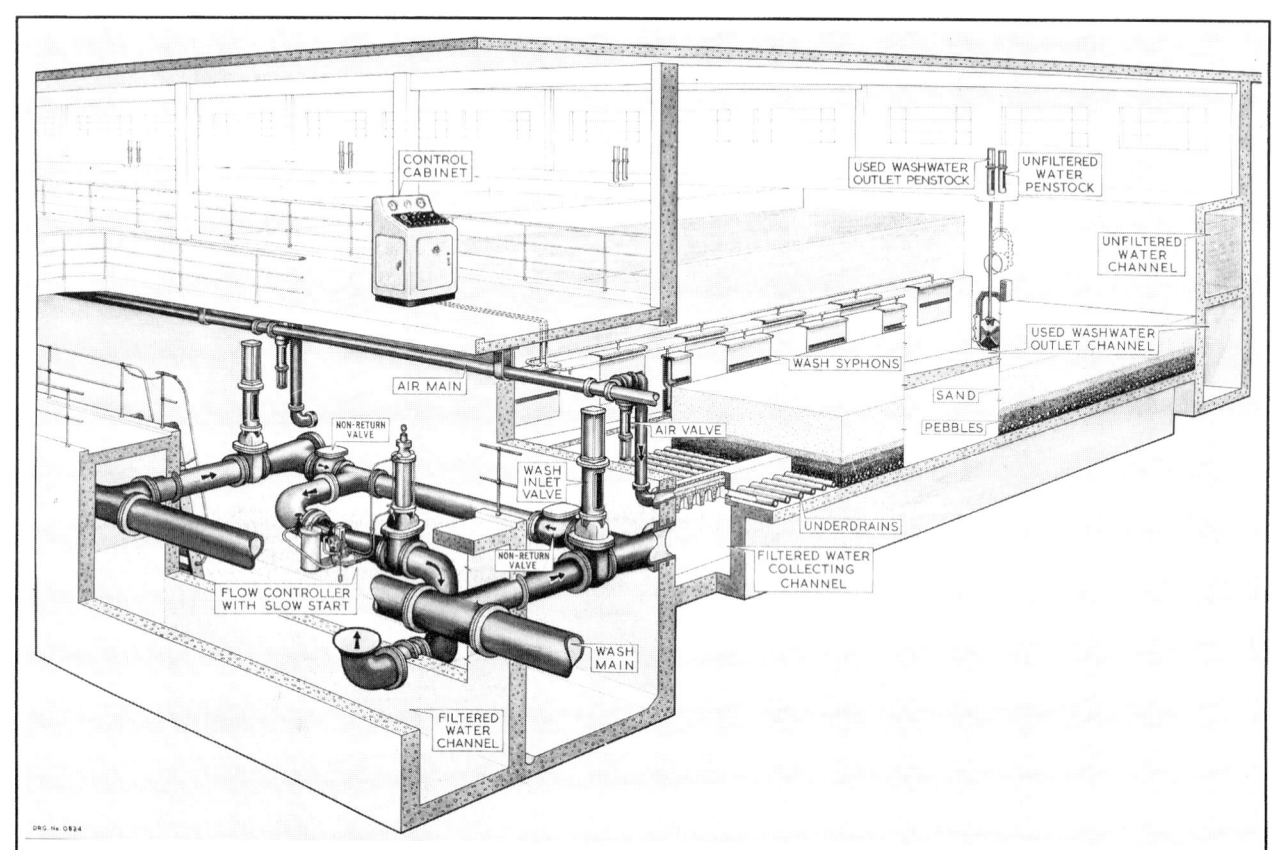

A publicity diagram of Paterson's double filter from the 1960s. The filter is arranged in two halves with a central washout bay and siphons. The divided wash arrangement meant that the upwash and airscour machinery could be reduced in size as the two halves were washed separately. The filter floor is Paterson's perforated lateral airscoured type. Early versions used the then popular asbestos-cement pipes for the laterals.

Chapter 4

Surviving employees remember Paterson as a strict disciplinarian, although the many stories of help and concern he felt for employees who were suffering illness or bereavement showed a human and caring man behind the brusque facade. His autocratic style led him to issue peremptory dismissals, such as that to a member of staff who was caught smoking at a time when it was not permitted, but Paterson was usually persuaded to re-instate the hapless individual. Presumably there

Centrifloc clarifier, St Anne's Board Mill, 1956

were no labour tribunals to bother him at the time! However, senior contemporaries remembered him in his later years as humourless, arrogant and dictatorial towards his customers, and staff at Candy's recall "P-department", as Paterson's were known internally, interfering continually in Candy's chlorinator business. This was hardly surprising given that this was the cause of the original dispute between the two companies.

What is not in doubt are Paterson's extraordinary achievements over the bulk of his working life. He was survived by his wife Dorothy, a very fashionable lady, who he married in 1911, and their daughter, Mrs Norah Gordon.

Steenbras treatment plant, overlooking False Bay, Cape Town. Late 1930s

Chapter 4

HM King George V opening the filters at Clydebank, 1914. The heavily re-touched pillar was actually wrapped with cloth in the original photo!

5-THE CANDY FILTER COMPANY, TECHNICAL EXPANSION 1918-1940

The Type-A floor

Pullen Candy is credited with inventing the airscour filter nozzle which was the basis of his type-A floor. It had the unique feature of a separate air distribution hole drilled in the stem below the nozzle head, and is now the most common method of collecting the filtrate as well as distributing the backwash water and airscour. The design remained in service with the company, almost unchanged, until the early 1980s when PCI introduced the K (for Karkh) floor which was a combined wash floor. The nozzle concept was copied by much of the competition, particularly in the UK and Europe, although Paterson's continued with perforated lateral floors until the formation of PCI. Candy's floor achieved a very even wash, and because he practised threshold fluidisation of the media as opposed to the more common expansion approach, he was able to claim a very low consumption of washwater.

The type-A was a separate wash floor, an approach Candy's were to use until the advent of the K-floor, although there were many exceptions, and some very large combined wash plants were built using a separate air distribution header buried in the media (known as type-B). Presumably the problems of keeping sand out of the underdrains, resulting from the mixing of the support layers, caused Candy's to stick with the separate airscour method. Combined wash also needs a much greater instantaneous wash flow rate, larger pumps etc., and Candy's were very conscious of the need to design economical plants. Whatever the reasons, despite having originated combined wash, Candy's retained the separate wash system long after most European specialists had adopted combined wash.

Chiquinquira, Colombia, 1.5 mgd, 1920s. Note the brick construction of the filters.

Chapter 5

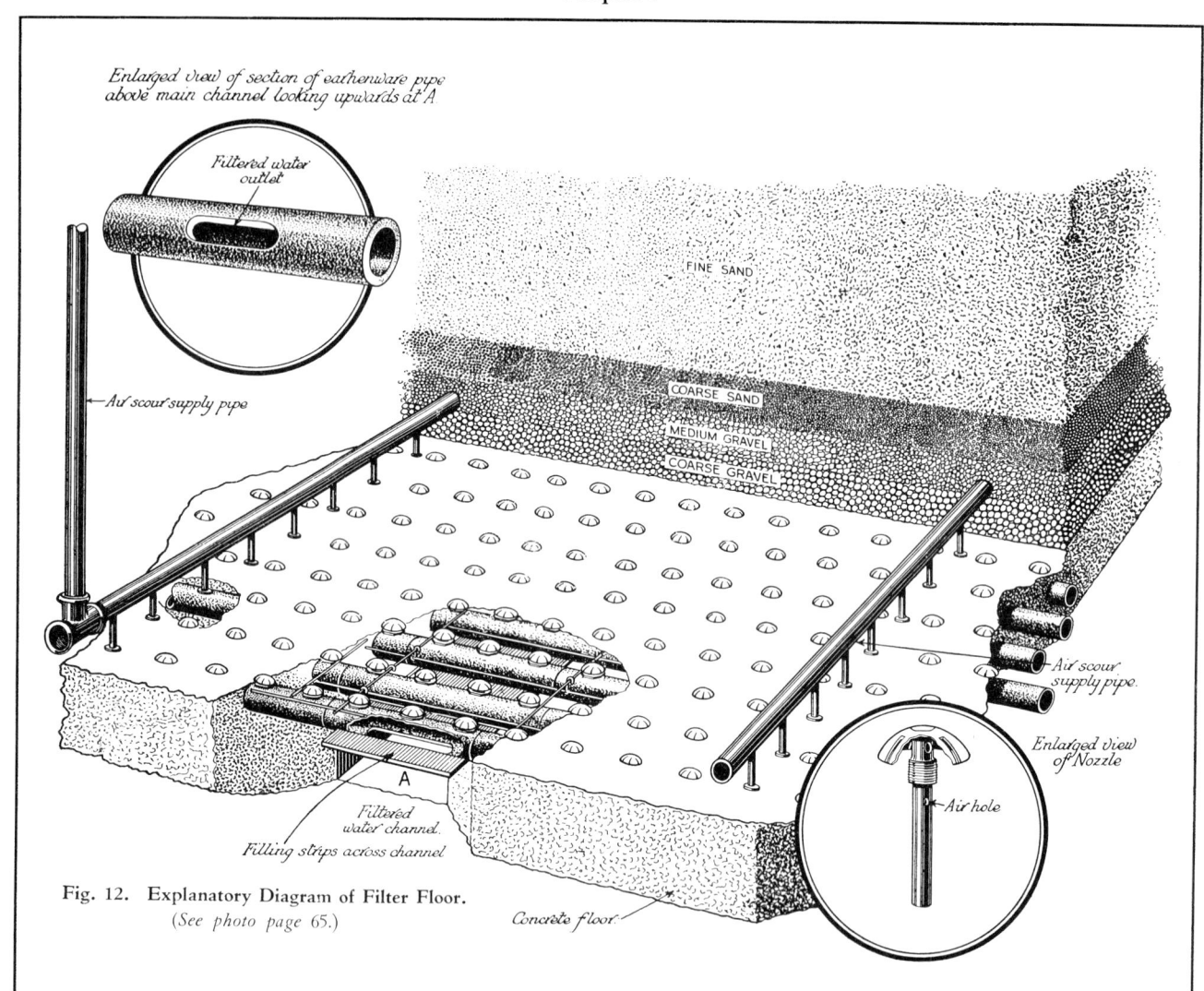

Fig. 12. Explanatory Diagram of Filter Floor.
(See photo page 65.)

Candy's type-A filter floor.

The airscour pressure depressed the level of the water in the collecting pipes, so uncovering the air metering holes. This simple concept enabled the nozzles to distribute the backwash water and the air separately and evenly over the base of the filter. The design provided for some tolerance for levelling the nozzles. Varying the size of the metering holes enabled the floor to be adapted easily to different backwash rates. The invention was an elegant solution to these distribution needs and when correctly installed, it formed a robust and maintenance-free filter bottom integral with the concrete structure.

The original nozzles were fabricated from copper or brass and these remained in production up to the advent of mouldable plastics. The air-headers were made of cast iron and were gradually replaced by uPVC when it became available. The floor required accurate installation to ensure levelling of the clay pipes and the placing of the concrete infill was also critical. The floor's major weakness was that it could stand limited back pressure but this was not a problem where the plant was correctly designed, and floor failures were generally associated with poor laying.

Chapter 5

Over the 60 years of its commercial life, the type-A was regarded as one of the best filter bottoms available, and thousands of filters have been equipped with it. In 1948 at the Public Works Exhibition at Olympia, Paterson (by then Sir William) paid a visit to the Candy stand. He looked for what seemed to be a long time at the exhibit of the type-A floor and then said to Warwick Dufour (Candy's MD): *"That well-designed filter floor has held me back for twenty years,"* which seems an extraordinary remark given that he had owned both companies for the previous fourteen years.

The floor was available in two sizes, with the smaller three inch collector version used for horizontal pressure filters and very small gravity filters. The type-A was designed for use with graded packing layers under the filter sand, but the availability of modern engineering plastics in the 70s allowed the nozzle slots to be progressively narrowed until at 0.25 mm they were able to retain fine filter sand without blocking. This approach was adopted for the type-K floor, now Paterson Candy's standard.

Frank Candy retires

The discussions which led to the recruitment of F.D.C.(Freddie) Allen as a partner and joint MD with Pullen were part of the preparations for Frank Candy's retirement in March 1920 at the advanced age of 78. The Company

Laying filter floors at Kobe, Japan. 16 mgd, late 1920s.

would have two managing directors until 1934, each having an equal shareholding which he could sell only to the other, and there would be a royalty arrangement to provide an income for Frank Candy during his retirement. The royalty was based on a payment of 6d (2.5p) per square foot of gravity filter floor sold and 4d per square foot of pressure filter area, on orders above the first £10,000 per year.

During his last year with the company, Candy had the great satisfaction of knowing that the first of the newly-designed concrete gravity filter plants was being built and would soon be operating at Hastings, the scene of his first 0.5 mgd pressure iron removal plant, designed some twenty-five years earlier. During that period the so-called "Hastings Filter", regarded initially with some scepticism by the industry, and later called the mechanical filter, had gradually replaced many of the slow-sand filters used over the previous century.

Chapter 5

Frank Candy died in 1934, aged 92, still mentally and physically fit. We do not know whether he lived to see his company taken over by his principal competitor William Paterson but his inventive genius is still apparent in modern water treatment practice.

The war ends

The ending of the Great War in 1918 enabled the backlog of work held up by the war effort to be released, and new premises in Howick Place in Victoria provided the company with extra office space. Nearby mews buildings were readily converted to stores and a small development and test bay. A larger mews at Amberley, near Paddington Station, housed a small fitting and machine shop, and from this small works the first open Module flow controllers were shipped to China. Pullen also designed an enclosed Module for pressure filters, and Candy's early gas chlorinators made their appearance. The company employed 15 to 18 people with Pullen looking after new design work, tendering and seeing customers, whilst his new partner, F.D.C.Allen concentrated on improving the finances and opening up new markets, as well as doing some tendering work.

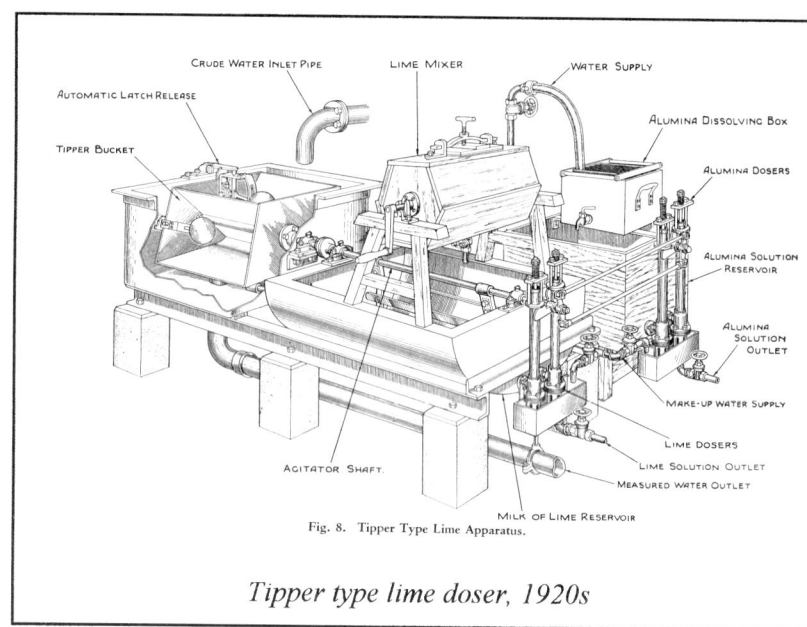

Tipper type lime doser, 1920s

By the end of the 1920s, the sewage business had largely dried up although for many more years the company received a small but continuous flow of profitable orders for Candy sprinklers and biological filter tiles. They were active and successful in the swimming pool treatment market, providing concrete gravity filters for the large open air sea-water pools at Blackpool, Hoylake, Wallasey, Rhyl and Colwyn Bay. Candy's also supplied Bi-flow pressure installations for pools at Nottingham, Southall and Richmond.

Pullen adapted the type-A floor to pressure filters, abandoning the hydraulic scour systems and compound designs pioneered by his father. He also produced a range of chlorinators and accessories, variable output chemical dosing pumps and chemical handling plant. Polarite disappeared except as an iron removal catalyst, although

Chapter 5

Candy's continued to supply most of the iron removal plants in the UK for the next sixty years.

It was a period of low inflation when increased costs were rare, there were few strikes and the public authorities normally made payments promptly, a situation unfamiliar in more recent years. The company entered 1930 with a sound base. The competition from Bell's and Paterson's had developed over predictable lines and it was reasonably easy to forecast which of the three concerns would get a particular contract from a particular water supply authority.

New gravity filters

The earliest gravity filters supplied by Candy were installed from about 1913. These were generally pre-filters to slow-sand filters and were cleaned by backwashing, combined with hydraulic scour by a rotating arm fitted with jets, and this approach continued until it was overtaken by Paterson's new designs.

Waitakere, Auckland, New Zealand. 5 mgd. 1920s

Paterson's successes at Tewkesbury and Irvine shook Candy, and his most urgent task became the design of a new gravity filter using reinforced concrete structures. For this he developed a revolutionary air scour system for filter cleaning, based on his newly patented filter nozzle. His requirements were that a filter floor must be non-corrodible, and should perform three functions:

- The even collection of filtered water,
- The even distribution of air for scouring the filter medium,
- The even distribution of backwash water.

Additionally, the design would have to tolerate some margin of error in levels when the floor was constructed, without affecting its essential functions.

The result was the type-A floor which he patented and first used for the Hastings Filsham supply. He could hardly have imagined how his design would influence the concept of gravity filters over the next sixty years, and his general specification remains the fundamental basis of design for filter bottoms to this day.

These new features were successfully installed at Filsham, and the design was modified to replace the washwater collecting channels which were about eighteen inches above

Chapter 5

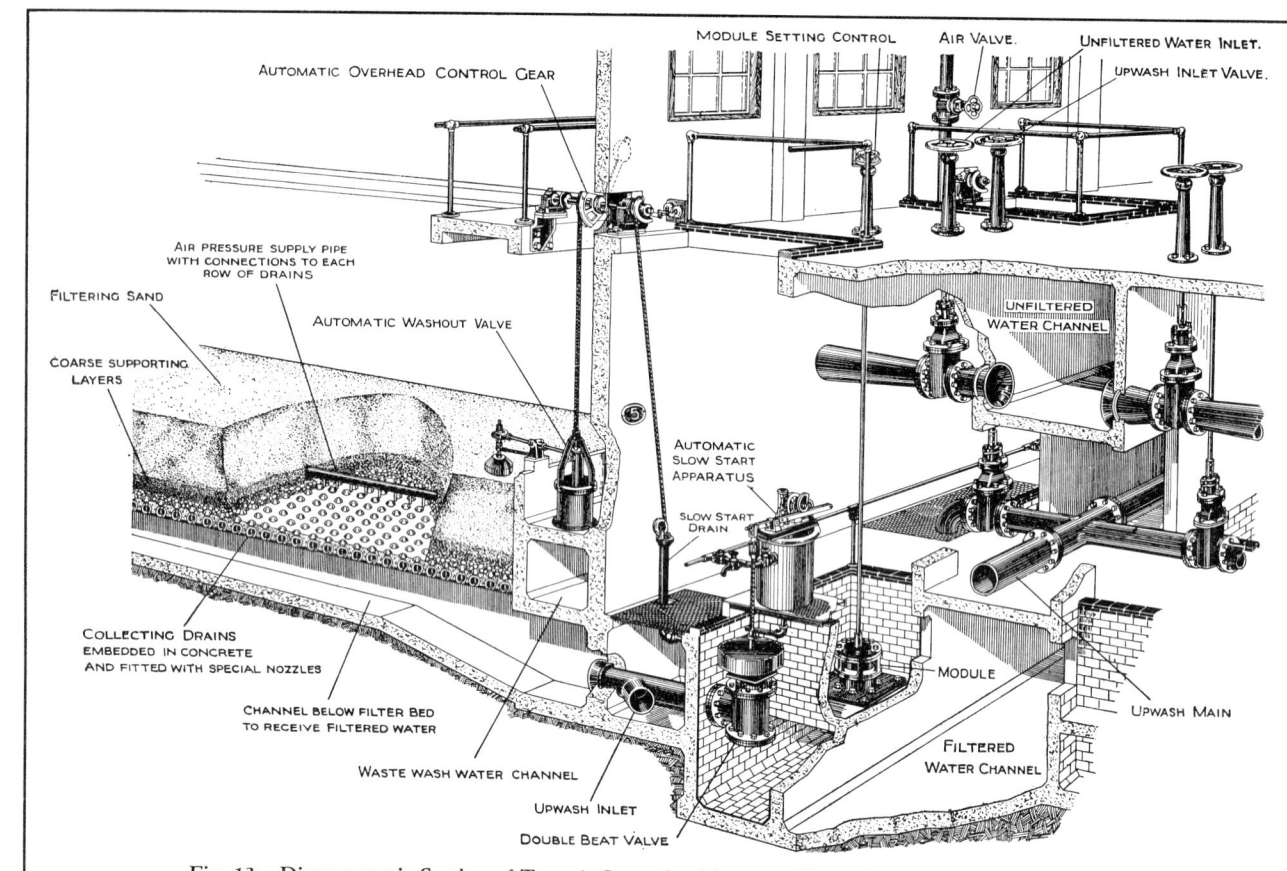

Fig. 13. Diagrammatic Section of Type A Control, with controlling valves on upper gangway.

Diagram from a 1930s catalogue showing Candy's Type A control system for gravity filters. The double beat valve on the outlet acted as an isolating valve for the filtered water with the Module providing flow control. Later versions of the Module acted as isolating valves as well, eliminating the need for the double beat valve.

the sand with a low draw-off weir. This low washwater draw-off system, with the cill four inches above the sand bed, eliminated the retention of a considerable volume of dirty washwater and reduced the amount of washwater used. It has been a standard feature ever since.

The 1920s saw substantial development of the design of gravity filters as the controls became more sophisticated, with ingenious hydraulic flow control systems. Some beautiful drawings survive in the catalogues from the period. The illustration is one of several from a 1930s catalogue, and most suppliers used similar drawings to show their equipment.

Chapter 5

The Candy Module

Amongst Pullen's many designs was a balanced double beat valve for controlling filter flow, which he called the Candy Module. The Module was typical of the hydraulic devices invented by the industry to provide control of flow and automation of treatment plants prior to the appearance of electrical, pneumatic and much later, computer controls. Surprisingly, the catalogues from the 1920s and 30s show that the principles of filter plant design were as well understood then as they are today, and the controls were very sophisticated, given that treatment plant designers were limited by the non-availabilty of pneumatic or electronic controllers. All of the principal suppliers made some sort of filter controller based on double beat valves or venturi devices. To these were added a wide variety of overall plant controls using floats, weirs etc. This equipment had to survive for decades in a corrosive environment, with little or no maintenance. Many of these devices were very elegantly designed and most were made from bronze or other copper alloys, although the housings were often made of cast iron.

The main function of a filter controller is to maintain a constant filtrate flow (excepting declining rate filters), irrespective of variations in head or filter head loss. In addition to this, Candy's Module also acted as a filter outlet stop valve and filtrate rate of flow indicator. The Module was essentially an adjustable balanced valve, and the diagram (from a post-war catalogue for clarity) shows the main components.

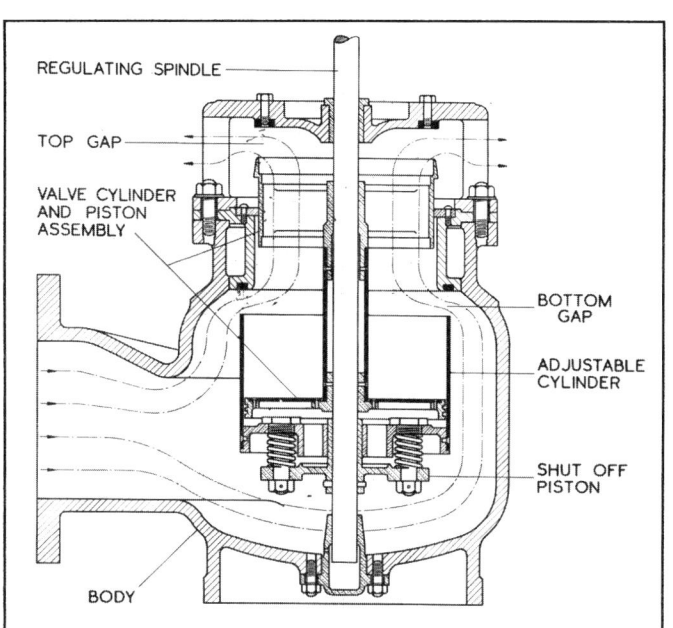

The Candy Module.

The adjustable cylinder was fixed to the regulating spindle (which also provided flow indication) and could be moved up and down by a handwheel to alter the bottom gap. The valve cylinder and piston assembly was free to move on the spindle. Holes in the base of the adjustable cylinder connected the Module inlet pressure with the underside of the piston, applying the pressure difference across the bottom gap to the piston which at a critical flow, balanced the weight of the piston and valve assembly, causing it to float. Because the valve was balanced, the force required to raise it and so throttle the discharge through the top gap, remained constant, irrespective of the Module inlet pressure or the drop in pressure across the top gap. Consequently, the bottom gap maintained accurate control of the flow, as an increase or decrease in the critical flow through it caused the piston-valve assembly to rise or fall, and so alter the top gap to restore equilibrium.

Chapter 5

This essentially simple device was made in a variety of formats and sizes, and it was linked to slow-start mechanisms as well as overall filter plant controls. The basic design patented by Pullen Candy in about 1920 remained much the same until it was discontinued in the 1960s. By then, the largest version (15") was too small for the larger filters being built, and the bronze construction made it uneconomical against the new electronic devices becoming available. The Module was a very reliable and exceedingly robust device that required no maintenance between major overhauls, perhaps every 15 to 20 years.

Slow-start controllers

Pullen also introduced his patented slow-start controller in 1920 for the Filsham plant. Up to this time, the practice was to run the filter to waste for 10 to 20 minutes after washing, until the filtrate turbidity reduced sufficiently. The slow-start controller was designed to increase the filter output gradually to enable the filter to settle after backwashing, without wasting water. The device also shut down the filter automatically for backwashing and a further automatic feature opened a bucket-type washwater drain valve. The diagram (p.91) shows an early version with the slow-start unit acting on the filter outlet double beat valve. Later versions connected the unit to the Module.

In the 1970s, for commercial reasons, the importance of slow-starting a filter was down-played in favour of simpler (and cheaper) controls, but with the advent of much more demanding quality standards from modern waterworks filters, the slow-start has been re-introduced and it is once again recognised as an essential part of filter controls. A case of plus ca change, plus ca va!

Tuborg Brewery Copenhagen, 1909. An early attempt to produce a "clean installation."

Overseas

Candy's agents in Scandinavia, Harvey & Jarvis, were very successful in developing the market and royalty payments appear regularly in the accounts during the 1920s. Captain Alec Jarvis was probably the link as he dealt with Peel Harvey from the UK in the

Chapter 5

pre-war and early war period, when plant was shipped to Scandinavia. After the war when he joined Harvey, only specialised equipment was sent from the UK.

Another market that suddenly became active during these years was China. Valuable contracts were obtained from the Shanghai Inland City Waterworks for a 7 mgd gravity

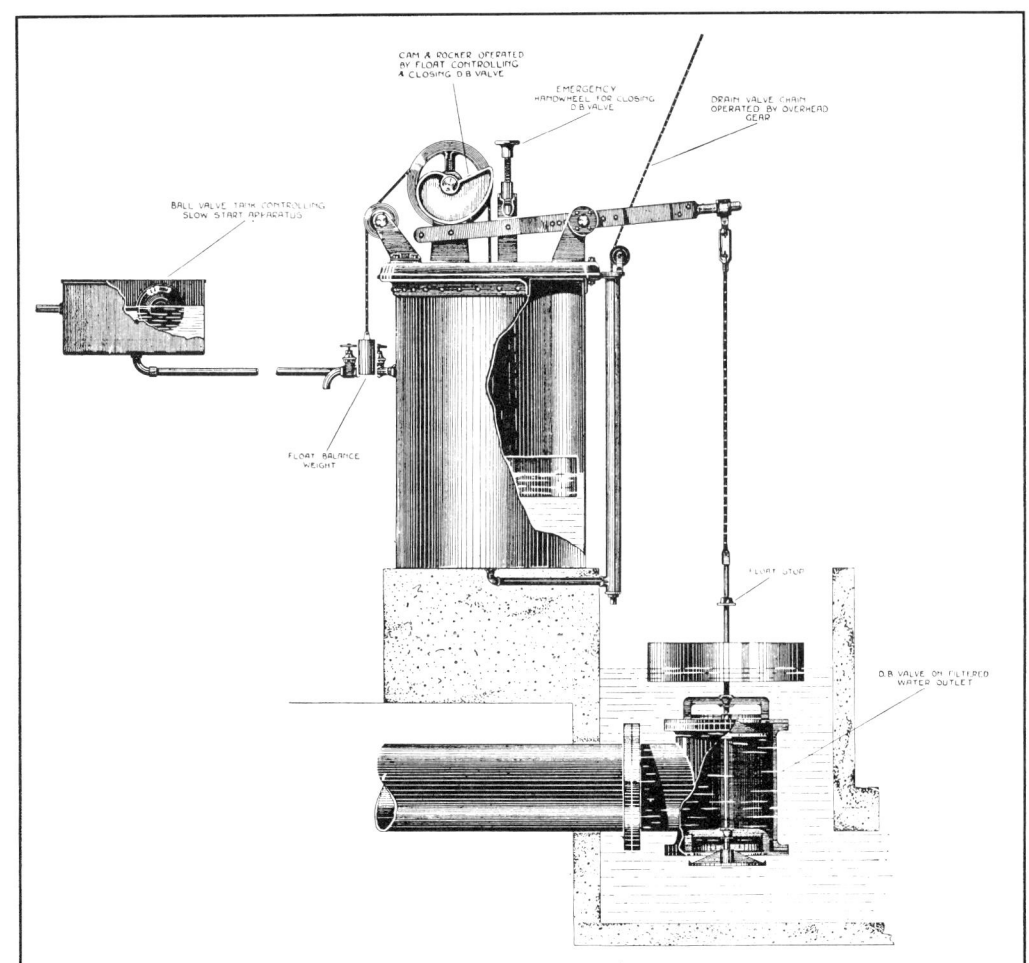

Candy's patented Slow-Start controller. 1930 catalogue.

The mechanism consisted essentially of a float in a tank. The float was connected to and rotated a camshaft which acted on a lever, in turn acting on the Module regulating spindle. With the tank full, the Slow-Start controller did not affect the setting of the Module but when drained by low level in the filter, the float dropped and caused the module to close. As the tank refilled, the rising float gradually allowed the Module to open. The device was adjustable so that the slow start period could be varied from about 20 to 60 minutes by means of the tank re-filling valve setting. The camshaft provided a simple but ingenious means of gradually increasing the rate of increase of the filter flow.

plant, as well as a 1 mgd compound Bi-flow plant for the British Municipal Waterworks at Canton, and a 3 mgd Bi-flow plant for a Canton cotton mill. From Japan, the Kanegafuchi Spinning Mill Company ordered an 8 mgd gravity plant, described as being exceptionally profitable. Japan appears to have been a substantial market for Candy's during this period, and the 1930 issue of "Gravity Filters" lists fourteen references including a 16 mgd works for Kobe and a 12 mgd plant for the Imperial Steelworks.

At home, by the mid-1920s it was apparent that Candy's needed additional capital together with larger premises. A site was chosen in Church Road, Hanwell that was to be the company's base for the next thirty-six years.

Cape Town, Kloof Nek, 1920s

Marginal chlorination - the demise of the Declor filter

The Declor filter served its purpose at a time when the practical sterilisation of drinking water was poorly managed. With the arrival of Wallace and Tiernan's marginal chlorination method, market demands altered, and signalled the end of the Declor filter. There were, of course, difficulties with taste where the water had organic matter present, but the marginal dosing technique persisted for several years. Both Frank and Pullen Candy had always believed that a dose of 1 ppm or more, with 30 minutes contact, followed by de-chlorination, was the best safeguard against pollution and taste problems, and in this and other instances, they were well in advance of their contemporaries.

At about the same time, the introduction of the W&T vacuum chlorinator effectively ended the reign of pressure chlorinators, although both Candy and Paterson supplied many of them until the early 1970s, particularly overseas where the more robust design survived poor maintenance much better.

Cheltenham, Dowdeswell Filter House

In turn, marginal chlorination gave way to the breakpoint approach (also introduced by W&T), which was a major step forward in water treatment. It is now the standard method used throughout most of the world, although some authorities also add ammonia after breakpoint treatment, to take advantage of the greater stability of the chloramines (formed by reaction with chlorine) for protecting the distribution system against re-infection.

F.D.C.Allen

Freddie Allen read maths. at Caius College, Cambridge and graduated with a first. He went straight from university in 1915 into the Army to serve in the Artillery, from which he was de-mobbed with the rank of major in 1918, when he took a job in the Commercial Union Assurance Company's actuarial department. After a year, he looked for a post with more scope and some time in 1921 he saw Pullen Candy's advertisement in "The Times"

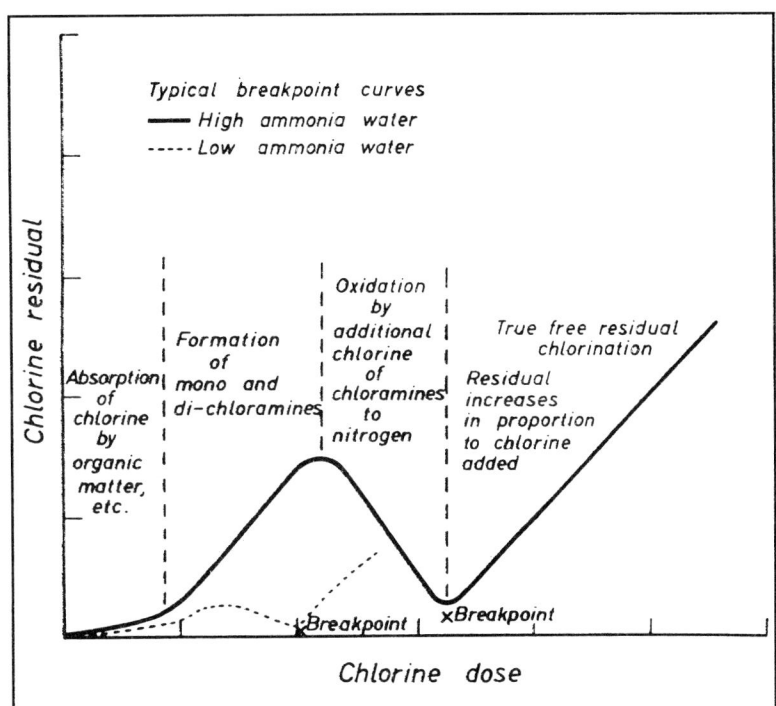

Chlorine demand curves.

Breakpoint chlorination. Where a water already contains ammonia, chlorine will react preferentially with it to produce chloramines (the "combined" or "marginal" chlorine process introduced by W&T early this century). Chloramines are longlasting compared with free chlorine but much less effective as a disinfectant. Once the ammonia demand is satisfied, further chlorine oxidises the chloramines, causing the drop in measured residual chlorine. The addition of more chlorine then takes the curve through "the breakpoint" to establish a free chlorine residual. The chemistry is of course, much more complex than this simplified summary.

offering a partnership on a 50/50 basis in return for a minimum investment of £1,000. He became joint MD in 1922 at the age of 30, and he was soon very active in developing the company.

By 1925, Paterson's were securing most of the gravity filter schemes in the UK as well as sharing many of the pressure filter jobs with Bell's. However, Candy's had secured a number of overseas projects, so Allen went on an extensive, three and a half month tour that included the USA, Japan, Australia, and New Zealand. He returned with several orders which led to many others. Whilst he was away, he left Dufour who had joined about a year earlier, to act for him, with the instruction to *"see that Mr Candy doesn't do anything silly and keep the bank quiet."* Whilst we might regard an absence of this length as extraordinary, getting to those faraway places before air-travel would be very daunting to today's businessmen. This was just one of a number of overseas trips; he also visited the West Indies and South America.

Two years later, Allen decided to open a company in India where Paterson was already established, and made a tour with his wife, of which little is recorded, but Candy Filters (India) was to flourish and prove a good training ground for some remarkable men.

However, by 1934 Allen was giving only part of his time to the company and was working part-time for the John Lewis Partnership as Director of Buildings. The dispute with Paterson (chapter 6) had resulted in a very acrimonious relationship between Allen and Kerrison, then MD of Paterson's, and Allen resigned.

Bob Williams records that Allen was full of energy, a strict but fair administrator with a sharp brain for the commercial side of the business. He worked for the company for fourteen years, re-building its fortunes so that when Paterson took over Candy's, he acquired a flourishing business despite the recession of the 1930s. Allen's departure at a time when Pullen Candy was nearing 65 meant that much of the management load fell to Warwick Dufour, and it proved to be in safe hands.

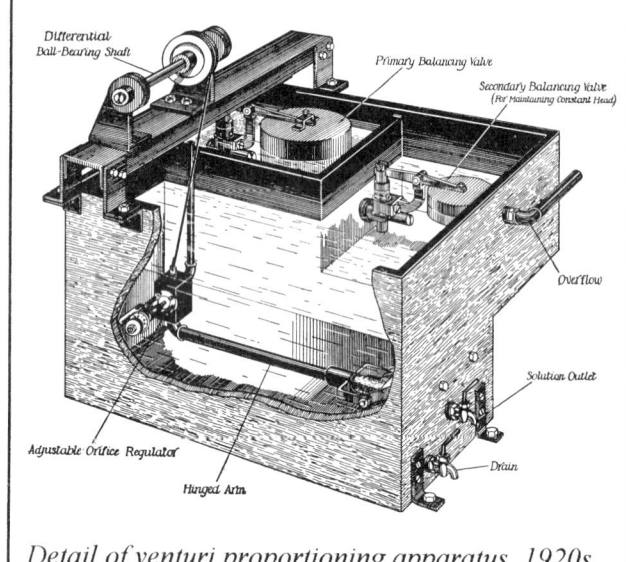

Detail of venturi proportioning apparatus, 1920s

Warwick Dufour

W.F.H.Dufour joined Candy's in 1924 direct from university under terms of engagement unusual by present standards, as Allen took on two engineers from his old college, Caius, on the understanding that after six months one of them would leave. Dufour proved to be the more adept in the test plant and so got the job.

The company was then at 18 Howick Place, in very cramped and dilapidated accommodation. On Dufour's first day he was asked to sort through the correspondence on a possible move out of the centre of London and to recommend suitable premises. *"The one that seemed the most suitable to me - on the scantiest possible briefing - was*

Chapter 5

the property in Church Rd, Hanwell....the proximity to my home in North Avenue, West Ealing, was an advantage."

Dufour's first meeting with Pullen Candy was at Amberley Mews where *"the Old Man was in an overall coat helping to unload galvanised pipes."* For the next four months, Dufour worked in the test plant calibrating the first of the newly-patented slow-start equipment and Modules for Launceston in Tasmania. They needed lots of modification and when they were despatched the drawings were correct only in outside dimensions!

In 1926 Candy's secured the orders for extending the Nihotupu and Waitakere plants for Auckland, and Dufour was detailed to take charge of erection and start-up. Prior to this, he had been involved in a variety of tasks including tender preparation and numerous plant start-ups. He left for New Zealand in February 1927, expecting to be away for about six months, only to return two years later, having established Candy's new business in New Zealand, and having got married in New York on the way back.

Dufour records: *"For the journey to New Zealand, I travelled tourist class on the Atlantic, ordinary rate on the trains and first class on the Pacific. The only expenses chargeable to the firm were meals and hotel bills and tips on board but no drinks or any other expenditure whatsoever. My salary was £4-5s a week plus £1-10s for board and lodging and remained at that for one and a half years until C.F.Co (NZ) was formed and I became manager, when my pay became £6-10s with no boarding allowance. No bonus found its way to me at either of the Christmases abroad and no present from the firm on my marriage, but they were not really expected in those days".*

Warwick Dufour, aged about 65

The return home was enjoyable. *"After the hectic last weeks at work it was like going into a dream world to sail off into the Pacific on the S.S.Tahiti. On this route to San Francisco there was only one call - 24 hours at Papeete, Tahiti. I became friendly with a Spanish - Australian, Mr Zalappa...and the days passed very pleasantly. Zalappa was on his twice yearly tour of the islands around Tahiti where his practice was to hire a large sailing boat and go round the islands buying and bartering for pearls and copra. He was very well in in Papeete...and organised what in those days was almost an orgy for a party of about 20 of the passengers, including myself and the Captain. We docked at dusk and immediately went to the hotel which was on the waterfront with tables on the pavement, French style. In due course we had dinner of truly local food*

Chapter 5

and all delicious, and a flow of French wines. At about 10 pm when nobody cared very much...taxis came and we all went to a villa 2 or 3 miles along the coast. Another taxi brought crates of champagne. At the villa the main room had been cleared and there was a native band with five hula-hula girls, topless, in grass skirts, who danced to the music. Before long the band took to playing Western dance tunes and those who had no wives to restrain them, danced with the girls which was quite an experience for a totally inexperienced young man who had been waiting two years to join his fiancee and get married. This was the extent of the orgy and nothing more wicked happened."

On his return to the UK he was immediately sent to Rumania in pursuit of various projects, none of which materialised for Candy's. This trip illustrates the lengths to which the company went to pursue business, and Dufour's main recollections are of interminable and incomprehensible meetings, awful hotels and cars, and long drinking sessions with officers in corsets! However, he had already demonstrated his sound judgement and administrative ability and in 1929, with Burville Candy and W.W.Pullen (no relation) he was appointed to the Board of Candy's.

Auckland, Ardmore Works, 60.5 mgd, 1960s. Ardmore was the first overseas automatic wash plant supplied by Candy's.

The year after the sale to Paterson, Dufour took over as MD, a position he held for the next thirty years. He also became chairman in 1959 when Pullen Candy retired, aged eighty-eight. Throughout this period and until he retired himself, he prepared tenders (and managed his contracts) for the West Country, Australia, New Zealand, South and West Africa, at the same time as running the company. This personal approach was the normal method of doing things at the time and it was one of the strengths of the company. Dufour's designs were generally simple and robust, if unambitious compared with those of his colleagues, but they resulted in fewer cost over-runs.

96

Chapter 5

Dufour states that in the 1930's the company was *"very light-hearted and experimental,"* although the period perhaps signalled the transition from amateurism to professionalism. The arms-length and elaborate management systems which now consume so much effort, were long in the future, and Dufour's style was paternal and direct. He was held in great respect by the staff and the industry, and he was on very good terms with his colleagues, particularly Simmons and Griffiths, who was a regular visitor to Dufour's home where he performed conjuring tricks for the family.

At the start of 1966, the man who had been sent down from Cambridge *"for an escapade"* (he was one of those intrepid night climbers who put chamber pots on the spires of the college!) formally handed over to Leo Rabeneck and retired after forty-two remarkable years and sound stewardship of Candy's. He died at home in 1976.

Humphrey Griffiths

Candy's has been blessed with clever men and Griffiths was outstanding for his prodigious output and innovation. He made a major contribution to water treatment, particularly in the UK where his legacy includes several landmark and pioneering plants.

At the time of his recruitment to Candy's, Griffiths was working for the Metropolitan Water Board, after reading engineering at Cambridge. His first job on joining the company in 1929 was to gain experience at Wakefield, and to show the plant to a delegation from Skipton. This subsequently resulted in their order against tough competition from Bell's and Paterson's and it was the first demonstration of Griffiths' many such successes over the next forty years.

Humphrey Griffiths at the opening of Pitsford, late 1950s

The man appointed to run the newly established Indian company had proved unsatisfactory, and shortly after joining, Griffiths was sent to take over, initially working alongside the local management. He set solid foundations and secured much of the business, and he is credited with the development of the Candy Tank which he sold widely in India. However adoption by the parent company was somewhat more cautious and the design only became widely used in the UK when Griffiths returned.

Griffiths relished a challenge and his approach to the design of water treatment plants invariably sprang from the question, *"what is the most suitable treatment for this water?"* This lead him to producing designs that were not always economical or competitive, but his unbounded enthusiasm got him orders and he regularly took on seemingly intractable treatment problems. The treatment plant at Church Wilne, which he built for the supply to Nottingham, is a good example of his approach. Considerable doubt had been expressed as to whether the raw water from the very polluted River Derwent could be treated for potable use, but Griffiths arranged to do the necessary laboratory tests and proved to the client and a public enquiry that the water could be treated reliably.

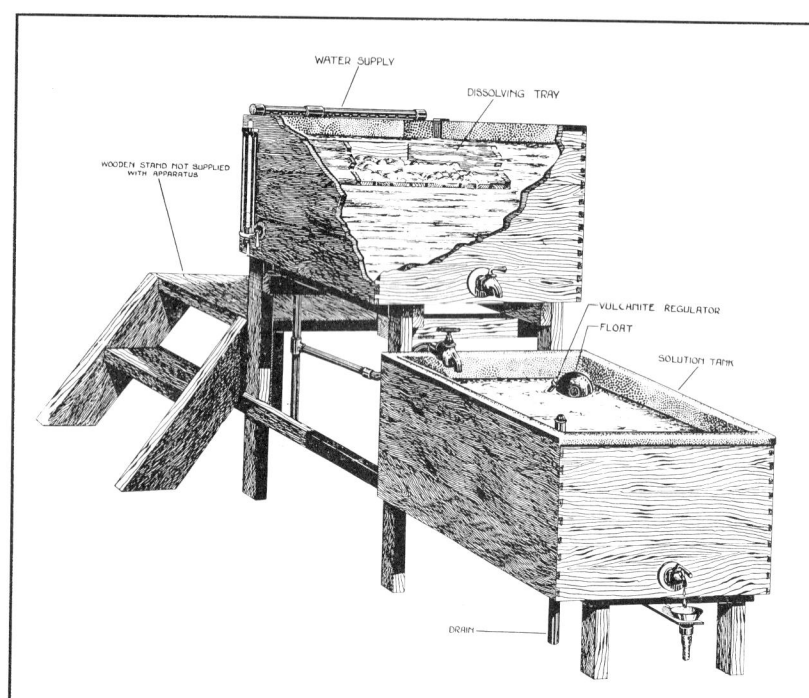

Medium type hand-proportioning Alumina apparatus, 1930 catalogue.

His questioning approach introduced many original ideas, including the systematic use of automation to handle the massive quantities of chemicals needed for the complex treatment plants. The big softening plants he built in the 60's have since been modified as softening has gone out of favour but they were outstanding in their time and worthy of a separate mention elsewhere. (See chapter 9.)

A sometimes difficult and always demanding man to work with, Griffiths was very good company, well educated, with a fine mind, and he lived his life to the full. He was a member of the Inner Magic Circle, and as a young man he enjoyed motor rallying, skiing and other fast sports, and his love of fast cars continued for most of his life.

Towards the end of his career at Candy's, Griffiths fell out with his fellow directors and in 1967 he resigned to join Binnie and Partners, as a well-respected water treatment consultant.

Chapter 5

The Candy vertical flow tank

Whilst Griffiths was in India in the 1930s, he developed a hopper - bottomed clarifier which was to make a major contribution to the clarification of water. The basic tank was already well-known as the Dortmund tank and used for settling sewage. Griffiths extended the inlet pipe to near the base of the tank and increased the inlet velocity of the feed. This converted a simple settlement tank to a sludge blanket clarifier, producing a better quality effluent and operating at a much higher rate. The design became known as the Candy Tank and it was used throughout the world until the late 1960s, when it became uneconomical due to the construction costs. Griffiths' development may not have been the first sludge blanket clarifier (sludge recirculation tanks such as the Infilco Accelator pre-dated it) but it was an elegant, very simple device which was widely copied.

In the 1960s, Candy's supplied a number of hopper tanks adapted for clarification and precipitation softening for several major softening plants, with considerable success, but it was not until the 1970s that the fundamental mechanisms were properly understood. Work by the company at this time, particularly on the mixing of the coagulant and the sludge removal system, enabled many installations to be substantially uprated.

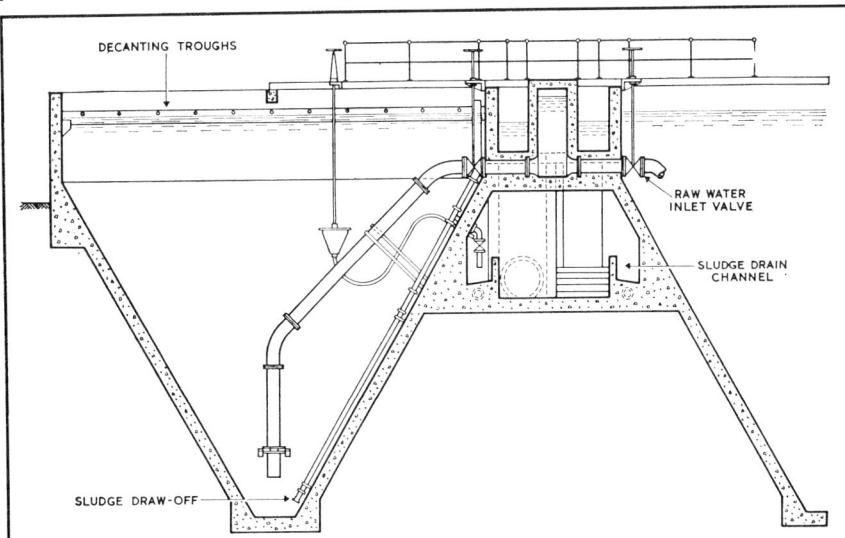

Griffiths' clarifier had no moving parts and the water was flocculated in the tank, hydraulically. The square version of the tank led to efficient use of space, common construction walls etc. Many variants of the sludge blanket concept have since been developed, and almost all modern clarifiers rely on passing the coagulated feed through a suspended "blanket" of sludge to achieve the ratings and quality of clarified water. The first installation in the UK was a small plant at Ryton for the supply to Coventry, installed during WW2.

The hopper tank clarifier took many forms, including batteries of square, inverted pyramid tanks in concrete, conical tanks in steel, and some spectacular conical tanks in concrete for the RTB strip mill in South Wales. These clarifiers were placed on high central support columns to eliminate a pumping stage.

Early versions did not have the sludge concentrator but relied on the main sludge discharge. Later versions were fitted with much larger concentrators, as the behaviour of sludge blanket tanks became better understood.

These developments also led to the design of PCI's flat-bottom clarifier. This much cheaper concept provided the company with a clarifier able to compete with Degremont's Pulsator designs, but it effectively ended the commercial life of the Candy hopper tank.

Combined-wash systems - the type-B floor

It is not clear when Candy's introduced their combined wash floor. A reprint from "Water and Water Engineering" of 1937 describes a combined-wash floor which used perforated laterals for water collection and distribution, with a separate air distribution header installed about twelve inches above. The design was relatively expensive and prone to failure of the copper gauze, but the reprint lists twelve substantial plants around the world equipped with the type-B floor, including a 22 mgd plant for the Rand Water Board in South Africa. The separate air distributor approach was used by many suppliers, including Paterson's, but usually for separate wash. The availability of stainless steel gauze largely overcame the problem and wrapped distributors are now widely used in a variety of process units.

With the advent of modern plastics, a combined wash nozzle (pioneered by Degremont) simplified the construction, although early versions of these suffered from sand ingress to the filtrate collection system. The very fine slots of PCI's K nozzle finally eliminated this problem.

Type-B floors fitted to horizontal filters at Talybont, 1930s

The air headers were of copper with gauze tied over the dimpled perforations to keep out the sand. Candy's claimed a one third reduction in washwater volume and improved cleaning of the sand compared with their type-A system.

The filter had Candy's "low draw-off system" as well as surface flush following the wash, to clear the surface of residual solids. It must have suffered from substantial sand loss. The Candy surface flush was introduced in 1935 and was a major commercial feature for the company for thirty years.

Chapter 5

The Great Depression

The 1930s started well for Candy's as the water treatment market was expanding at home and overseas and they were getting a good share of the available work. The Indian and New Zealand companies were also busy. However, the general trade depression had a firm grip on the UK. At this unpromising time, the directors decided to provide for future growth by extending the Hanwell workshops to provide more office space and to re-model and fully enclose the test plant which was open to the elements on one side. They were able to let most of the additional space, though they had to take it back four years later as the company expanded.

Whilst Candy's were doing well, Paterson's had taken key orders for Alexandria in Egypt with Infilco designed Accelator clarifiers. They also had orders for Halifax in Yorkshire and for the Metropolitan Water Board's plant at Kempton Park. The Halifax plant included a massive battery of eighty-four 8ft diameter pressure filters, and the Kempton Park plant was for 48 mgd gravity pre-filters which are still part of the supply to London. Losing these projects spurred Candy's to become more competitive. The product range designed in the 1920s needed revision and the growing use of settling tanks as pre-treatment to filters required new designs, so C.E.G.Simmons was appointed as chief engineer to take charge of the drawing office, research and development, as well as checking the hydraulic calculations for the new, larger and more complex plants that were being designed.

> MINUTES OF A MEETING OF THE BOARD OF DIRECTORS
> held at 14, Church Road, Hanwell, on
> June 1st. 1932.
>
> Present:- F.P. Candy.   Chairman.
>   F.D.C. Allen   )
>   W.F.H. Dufour   ) Directors.
>   J.A. Pullen   )
>
> The question of a Bonus to the Staff out of the Profits of 1931 was considered and it was decided that, provided the Bloemfontein Plant was finally successful and the money paid, a Bonus would be paid on the same terms as last year, namely:-
>
> All Directors,   1 month's salary.
> Heads of Departments and Engineering Staff,
>   2 weeks' salary.
> Remainder of the Staff, 1 week's salary.
> Works: 1 week's pay.
>
> It was further decided that the Bonus to the Works should be in addition to the fortnight's holiday.
>
> It was further agreed that any of the Staff wishing to have their Bonus before their holidays would be entitled to do so, on the understanding that if the Bloemfontein Contract was not paid for, they would have to refund it by deduction from salary over the following 12 months.

Extract from the Board minutes, 1932

In this climate of confidence Candy's took the then unusual step of introducing a profit sharing scheme for all employees and a letter to the staff stated that, *"The first charge on profits was salaries and wages and the second, a reasonable dividend on the actual capital employed in the company. Thereafter, the remaining profit should be divided approximately equally between extra dividends on the ordinary shares and a profit bonus for all company members including the works."* It was estimated that every four per cent of additional dividend on the ordinary shares would be accompanied by one week's extra pay as a bonus. Furthermore, both staff and works employees would get two weeks annual holiday as well as the bonus. The board hoped that this would make members feel that they had a stake in the

MWB Walton. The Candy filter gallery. 20 mgd

company and would do everything to improve output. Not surprisingly the scheme was well received but it is uncertain how long this forward-looking policy paid any bonuses.

The Bloemfontein contract

The City of Bloemfontein ("flower fountain") is approximately mid-way between Johannesburg and Cape Town in South Africa, and a long way from both. The story of this contract is interesting because it concerns the battle between Bell's rake filters and Candy's airscour system, whose outcome was to determine the buying pattern for the giant plants to be installed on the Vaal River to supply the Witwatersrand area.

In 1931, the City Engineer called for tenders for pressure filters to treat 3 mgd of water from the Modder river, to replace the existing slow sand filters. Offers were received from Bell's, Paterson's and Candy's, with the order to going to Bell's, despite their price being nearly £10,000 more than Candy's. This was too much for F.D.C.Allen of Candy's to take and he protested, informing the client that *"whatever Bell's could accomplish with their plant, Candy could do equally well and probably better."*

Bell's had persuaded the client that only their rake filters could clean the filter sand efficiently, and they had installed a 0.5 mgd plant at the same site three or four years earlier. Bloemfontein's Engineer suggested that Candy's should supply a similar 0.5 mgd plant in a test to compare the two systems, though unless the results were equal or better than Bell's, Candy's would have to remove their plant and make good the building. Allen replied that in his view the right approach would be for Candy to install the complete plant for the total flow, and prove their case.

Chapter 5

His arguments prevailed and the plant was supplied via Candy's South African agents, Dowson and Dobson. It consisted of six 30 ft long horizontal pressure filters that were shipped in pieces for riveting together at site. W.G.Williams was sent by Candy's to supervise the construction and subsequent tests. He recalled that he arrived at site to find a large pile of steel plates, cast iron pipes etc., and a workforce of some sixty African labourers, six local Boers and a Dowson and Dobson fitter. Williams spoke no Afrikaans and they no English, but between them the plant was assembled and set to work.

Alongside Williams, James Massie, the Bell's engineer, was re-furbishing the pilot plant and apparently they shared a bungalow and looked after one another's sites during absences. The tests in 1932 vindicated Allen's claims and so the client confirmed the draft contract entered into with Candy's in 1930. The Bell's pilot plant was re-used elsewhere.

The Bloemfontein test had wide repercussions because it was fully publicised at the South African Water Engineers Congress held shortly afterwards, and the city's Engineer presented a paper about it. During the test period, the Rand Water Board invited tenders for extending the Paterson pre-filters at Vereeniging, the supply for Johannesburg and the Rand mining district. Candy's were successful in getting this contract and

Density Controller at Aitken's Hurleston, Mid-Cheshire plant. 1960s. This device weighed the chemical solution flowing through a tube and continuously adjusted the dilution water flow to maintain the weight of the sample (and by derivation, the solution density) constant.

R.W.Aitken
Bob Aitken was the son of Candy's representative in Jamaica. He graduated from Oxford and came to the firm in 1934 after spending a year at Harvard as a Rhodes Scholar, under the renowned Professor Fair, then Head of Sanitary Engineering.

In 1938 Aitken went to India to take over from Humphrey Griffiths. He returned to the UK after the War, and he became a director of the company in the 1950's. Aitken is credited with introducing a number of new ideas including "tertiary treatment" - the use of coarse sand filters for polishing sewage effluent - at Luton, although the idea may actually have come from the works superintendent. He retired in 1973.

Chapter 5

since then have supplied all the filter plants for the Rand Water Board, totalling a massive 900 mgd by 1990. Most of the larger towns ordered from Candy's until the 1960s, when Degremont became the main supplier to Durban and Paterson to Cape Town. More recently, the market has further fragmented, although PCI (SA) continued to get much of the work.

Godwin Simmons

Not much is recorded of Simmons, although with Pullen Candy he was responsible for much of the company's engineering excellence which was to last long after he had left. Simmons joined Candy's in 1931 as Chief Engineer, but he left soon afterwards to join ICI. By 1934, he had had enough of shift working in ICI's soda ash plant at Billingham and so re-joined Candy's, staying for four years before leaving to work for Tate and Lyle. During his brief time with the firm, he made many badly needed improvements to existing designs, including modernising the somewhat archaic look of much of the equipment, and he designed chemical dry feeders and flow proportioning systems. He introduced the use of high pressure oil hydraulic systems for valve actuation, based on an exclusive licence for Lockheed's aircraft systems. These

Simmons' M pump

were to provide a reliable alternative to the troublesome water actuators used by the industry at the time, and they remained Candy's standard until the mid-1960's when, for economic reasons, they were replaced by a low pressure oil system which was never entirely satisfactory.

One of Simmons' important achievements was the design of the Autominor water meter operated proportioning pumps and the Minor dosing pump, later re-named the M-pump. Whilst the Autominor idea was not original (it was based on a Proportioneers' (USA) design), Simmons substantially improved the design for the pumps. In contrast, the Minor was original in all respects and it incorporated an ingenious stroke change mechanism. The Minors and Autominors were put on the market at just the right time to take advantage of a campaign by the Ministry

Autominor dosing pump

104

Chapter 5

of Health to persuade the water authorities to chlorinate all their supplies. This was in about 1936!

Over the next thirty years, Candy's supplied thousands of chemical metering pumps throughout industry. In the 1960s the chemical pump department was hived off as a separate company, Metering Pumps Ltd, and soon afterwards was sold to Mono Pumps. The last M and G pumps were made in the late 60s, but some remain in service today.

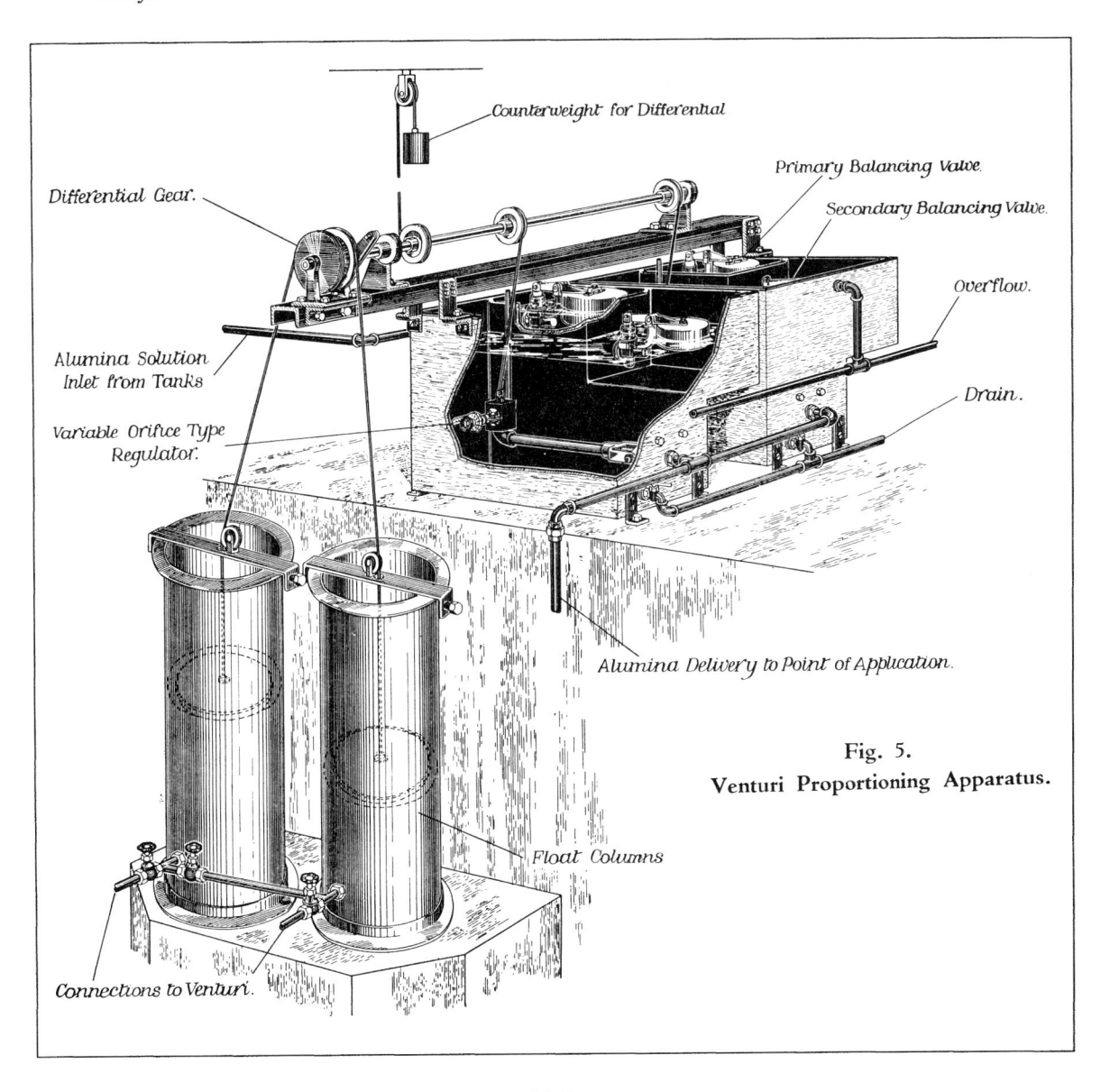

Fig. 5.
Venturi Proportioning Apparatus.

Chapter 5

William Jenkyn-Thomas

Simmons' departure for Tate & Lyle in 1938 caused some dismay, but the man who succeeded him was to prove equally important to the company. W.D.Jenkyn-Thomas came to Candy's with a background in chemical and hydraulic engineering gained at English Electric and ICI. Once again the company had obtained an outstanding engineer who immediately set about new designs, including a range of large capacity chemical pumps called the "G" (originally for giant!). These were fitted with a remarkable stroke change mechanism with a linear response and for their time they were very accurate. This design was characteristic of Thomas' fertile brain, and he was to produce a long list of ingenious hydraulic devices to meet the needs for control in the time when pneumatic controllers were not available and electronic devices were far in the future.

Thomas was a delightful man with the habit of querying everything, and "it won't work," was a stock comment. He was usually right and then he proceeded to tell you how to make it work! He believed and practised the principle "if it ain't broke, don't fix it," and he contented himself with retaining well proven company designs until they ceased to be economical. This same approach was present in his attitude to design - "stop work when the design is adequate to do the job" - a concept that is often difficult for enthusiastic but less focused engineers to grasp.

He was not a process or treatment unit innovator but he could turn others' ideas into reliable equipment, and he provided a stable engineering base for the company until his retirement in the late 1960s. Thomas was a quiet, basically shy man, without the love of fast cars of his more flamboyant colleagues. In his later years his daily routine was to back his car into the wall of the car park, get out to examine the damage and shake his head, to the gentle amusement of those watching. Unable to have a family of his own, Jenkyn-Thomas wrote children's stories which he and his wife read to the young patients in the local hospital.

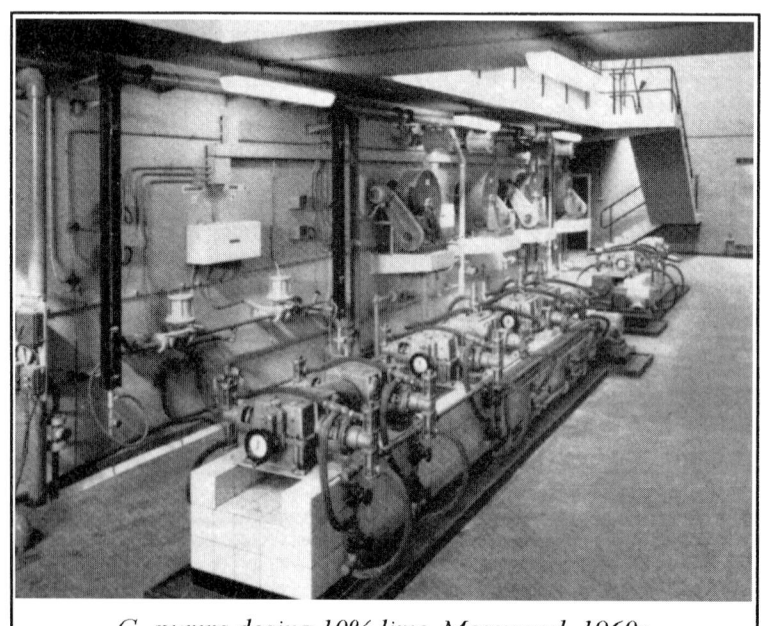

G -pumps dosing 10% lime, Mosswood, 1960s

Chapter 5

Leo Rabeneck

Rabeneck joined Candy's in 1937 and was a member of the group that managed the company's affairs for the next forty years. His most important contribution was perhaps from the mid-60s to the mid-70s and his notes are included in a later chapter.

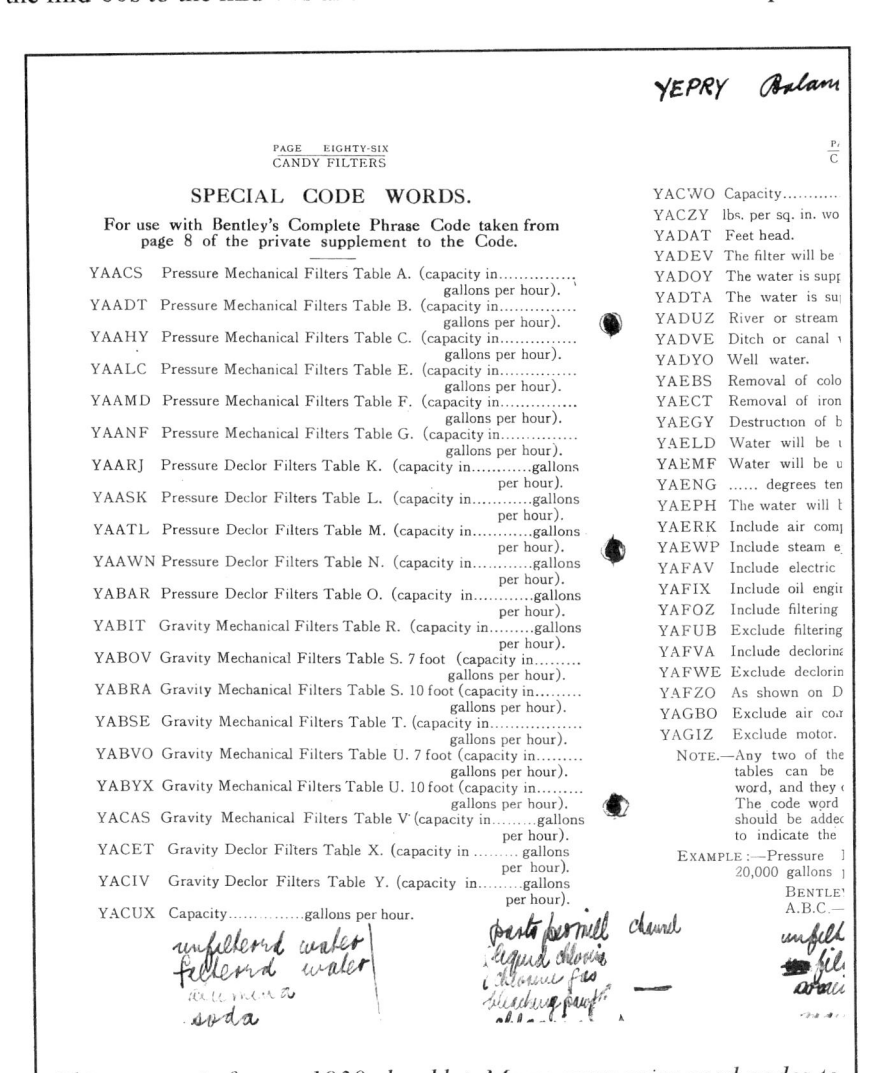

YEPRY *Balam*

PAGE EIGHTY-SIX
CANDY FILTERS

SPECIAL CODE WORDS.

For use with Bentley's Complete Phrase Code taken from page 8 of the private supplement to the Code.

YAACS	Pressure Mechanical Filters Table A. (capacity in............ gallons per hour).
YAADT	Pressure Mechanical Filters Table B. (capacity in............ gallons per hour).
YAAHY	Pressure Mechanical Filters Table C. (capacity in............ gallons per hour).
YAALC	Pressure Mechanical Filters Table E. (capacity in............ gallons per hour).
YAAMD	Pressure Mechanical Filters Table F. (capacity in............ gallons per hour).
YAANF	Pressure Mechanical Filters Table G. (capacity in............ gallons per hour).
YAARJ	Pressure Declor Filters Table K. (capacity in............gallons per hour).
YAASK	Pressure Declor Filters Table L. (capacity in............gallons per hour).
YAATL	Pressure Declor Filters Table M. (capacity in............gallons per hour).
YAAWN	Pressure Declor Filters Table N. (capacity in............gallons per hour).
YABAR	Pressure Declor Filters Table O. (capacity in............gallons per hour).
YABIT	Gravity Mechanical Filters Table R. (capacity in............gallons per hour).
YABOV	Gravity Mechanical Filters Table S. 7 foot (capacity in............ gallons per hour).
YABRA	Gravity Mechanical Filters Table S. 10 foot (capacity in............ gallons per hour).
YABSE	Gravity Mechanical Filters Table T. (capacity in............ gallons per hour).
YABVO	Gravity Mechanical Filters Table U. 7 foot (capacity in............ gallons per hour).
YABYX	Gravity Mechanical Filters Table U. 10 foot (capacity in............ gallons per hour).
YACAS	Gravity Mechanical Filters Table V (capacity in............gallons per hour).
YACET	Gravity Declor Filters Table X. (capacity in ....gallons per hour).
YACIV	Gravity Declor Filters Table Y. (capacity in............gallons per hour).
YACUX	Capacity.............gallons per hour.
YACWO	Capacity............
YACZY	lbs. per sq. in. wo
YADAT	Feet head.
YADEV	The filter will be
YADOY	The water is sup
YADTA	The water is su
YADUZ	River or stream
YADVE	Ditch or canal
YADYO	Well water.
YAEBS	Removal of colo
YAECT	Removal of iron
YAEGY	Destruction of b
YAELD	Water will be
YAEMF	Water will be u
YAENG	...... degrees ten
YAEPH	The water will b
YAERK	Include air com
YAEWP	Include steam e
YAFAV	Include electric
YAFIX	Include oil engin
YAFOZ	Include filtering
YAFUB	Exclude filtering
YAFVA	Include declorin
YAFWE	Exclude declorin
YAFZO	As shown on D
YAGBO	Exclude air co
YAGIZ	Exclude motor.

NOTE.—Any two of the tables can be word, and they The code word should be added to indicate the

EXAMPLE:—Pressure 20,000 gallons BENTLE' A.B.C.—

This extract is from a 1930s booklet. Many companies used codes to reduce the cost of telegrams at a time when the surface mail could take six weeks to reach New Zealand. The notes are probably by Pullen Candy. The references to Bentleys code remained on Candy's notepaper until the early 60s.

Chapter 6

Extract from A New Method of Filtration by Ascent; by James Peacock of Finsbury Square, Architect. Printed for the author, 1793.

The document describes an upflow filter having layers of media of decreasing size, down to dust, held down by larger gravel. Periodically "not more than five or six times a year"! - the filter could be cleaned by reverse flow to remove "all feculencies and obstructions". The "percolator" was also very effective in removing finings from Porter but achieved "no sensible difference in its flavour" when tested on sea water. Clearly, nothing is new!

[5]

Among the various subjects evidently designed by Providence to ask amendment at the hands of men, there is one of immense importance, which has not yet received it in the degree it is capable of, and that is WATER.

This element, necessarily of such universal use, and particularly in food and medicine, is suffered to remain laden with a great diversity of impurities, and is taken into the stomach, by the majority of mankind, without the least hesitation, not only in its fluid state, however turbid it may happen to be; but also in the forms of bread, pastry, soups, tea, medicines, and innumerable other particulars.

Medical gentlemen can readily point out the probable advantages towards the preservation of health, and extending the period of human life, which would result from the use of soft water, cleared from the earthy, and the living, dead, and putrid, animal, and vegetable substances, with which it is always, more or less, defiled and vitiated.

But independent of this consideration respecting health, an intimation of this nature must be not a little alarming to delicacy; and most certainly had better have been entirely suppressed, if adequate means had not, at the same moment, been offered to quiet such alarms. Such means, however, simple in their nature, and easy in their process, are pointed out, in the following pages, with demonstrative evidence; whereby pure soft water may be had at all times, and in any quantity, as clear and brilliant as that from the finest springs.

Many are sensible of the indelicacies of turbid soft water; and are thence driven to the use of hard water, although they are not unapprized of the probable danger to their health, from its petrifying quality, or from the metalic, or other mineral, taints, too frequently suspended and concealed therein.

Others

6-PATERSON TAKES OVER CANDY'S

During the early part of the century Paterson and Candy were keen competitors, and from about 1914 they often bid for the same project and sometimes sharpened their prices to the point where there was little reason to take the work. It appears that following their contest for the original works at Longham (near Bournemouth), the two discussed some form of co-operation or perhaps even amalgamation. With this background, it is perhaps not surprising that the two firms did ultimately combine, but the circumstances which brought this about did not relate to those tentative discussions.

The chlorinator lawsuit

Although in reality it was a relatively minor issue, the chlorinator lawsuit resulted in William Paterson's take-over of Candy's business. Sometime before 1929, Candy's developed a pressure gas chlorinator which, with various devices, produced flow-proportional dosing of chlorine gas. They installed one of these at Cork in Ireland, where it was seen by a Paterson engineer. William Paterson had a licence for chlorine solutionisers (from a Mr Ornstein) and he sued Candy for patent infringement. Pullen Candy had a similar patent of his own which pre-dated Ornstein's, and he protested that there was nothing new to the design and that the basic principle of dissolving gases in a scrubber with a minor flow of water passing through, had been used for many years in the gas industry. There is no doubt that the chlorinators made by the two companies were very similar in appearance and design. There may also have been a dispute over the pressure-reducing valve which was fitted on the outlet of the chlorine gas bottle; but since the pressure reducing valve was essentially a spring loaded diaphragm, this seems unlikely.

The 2 mgd plant at Cork

Due to illness, the judgement was delayed until 1932 when Paterson lost his case. Unexpectedly, he decided to appeal, and to the surprise of the industry, his appeal was successful. However, the Candy Board and their advisors were so sure of their case that they decided to take it to the House of Lords. In December of that year Allen and Candy were invited to meet Paterson and Kerrison, and during the discussion, there was mention of the Kempton Park job which the two companies had recently fought over. Their prices were within a few hundred pounds of one another, both near cost, with the next tender about forty per cent higher. This led to a renewed discussion about creating some form of joint holding company, and was followed by exchanges of information about the possible value of the companies. No real basis for an agreement emerged, and the matter reverted to their advisors.

Some months later, at a meeting with Paterson's secretary, Allen was shocked to receive a demand that he accept Paterson's terms for ending the litigation as a pre-condition to any further discussion on amalgamation. Allen refused in view of the strong probability that Candy's would win in the Lords and said, *"Although Candy's were anxious to complete an arrangement satisfactory to both parties, it must be a treaty between equals and not a dictated treaty as though Paterson was victor and Candy a vanquished foe."*

A week later, Paterson's lawyers announced that the

Candy type-M pressure gas chlorinator, 1920s, showing the main components.

whole matter was off because of Candy's attitude to the litigation and in a letter to his advisors Allen remarked sadly, *"As you know, the same thing happened to United Water Softeners* [presumably a similar discussion] *and we never really knew why they broke off. Some people suggested that Paterson's financial position is not so strong, but I do not think so myself, in fact I hardly know what to think."* His concern must have been soundly based, as three months later Paterson's became a public company.

Chapter 6

An unofficial approach by Candy's lawyers had concluded that the best course would be to come to terms with Paterson, so Pullen Candy and Allen agreed a strategy to offer to drop the appeal to the Lords and pay Paterson £1,000 for half his legal costs. In return, they wanted Paterson to drop his claim for damages and for both sides to continue amalgamation discussions. Negotiations were re-opened but it became clear that Paterson and Kerrison would not settle for less than the acquisition of all the Candy shares, then jointly held by Pullen Candy and Allen.

The discussions were successful and the litigation saga ended, but it took until June 1934 to get the final agreement and a valuation for Candy's business. The price agreed was £47,508 which included £10,000 for the value of the Hanwell works and offices, together with the subsidiaries in New Zealand and India, both by then well-established.

It is not clear why Candy and Allen chose to settle and effectively sell the company to Paterson, although Dufour recorded (many years later) that they were faced with hefty legal costs, the prospect of having to pay substantial damages and possibly have their chlorinator business killed off, except as permitted by Paterson. Furthermore, the affair had dragged on for two to three years and by then, Allen was working only part-time for Candy's and increasingly involved in the John Lewis business, and perhaps he was concerned about the effect the legal struggle was having on the normal business.

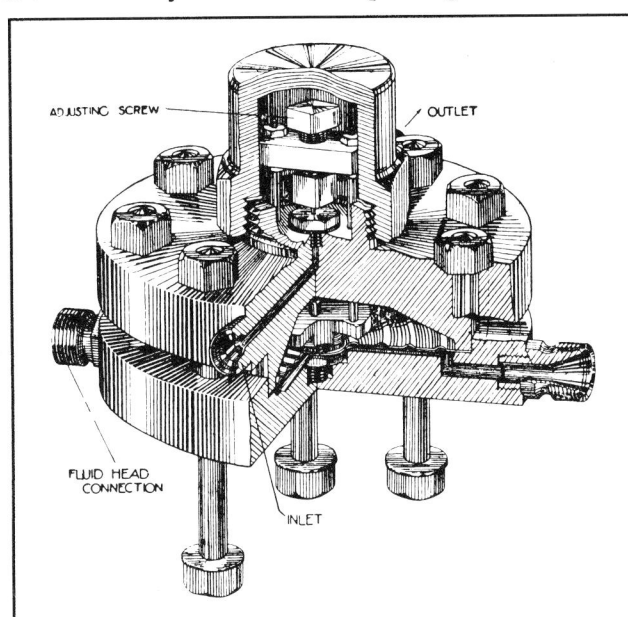

Candy's patented fluid control pressure reducing valve which regulated to the "greatest nicety".

As regards Paterson's interest in settling, Dufour suggests that Kerrison realised that Candy's were ahead technically in many areas, and he was anxious to acquire this strength rather than put them out of business. By the end, it appears that Kerrison and Allen had taken a strong dislike to one another, although Candy himself remained on quite good terms with him. Allen then resigned and left with half the sale price as his share of the business.

The pattern of the relationship between Paterson's and Candy's was soon established. Technically, Candy's were entirely free to do what they wished and there was no formal or informal passing of technical information in either direction. Similarly, there was no interference on management, organisation or wages, other than the directors' salaries. Dufour records that the only queries on performance arose from the annual accounts and these were almost all helpful, although other staff recollect that there was frequent bickering between the companies at lower level. The one control imposed was that Candy's should report all the sales enquiries that were received, and where both companies were quoting, Paterson had to approve Candy's price. This gave Paterson a tremendous commercial advantage but was a powerful spur to Candy's to secure work at higher prices by technical merit, by close personal attention to the customers' ideas and by avoiding *"the dictatorial or patronising approach for which Paterson himself became renowned"* (Dufour). The arms-length ownership continued until the formation of PCI in 1965, and the details were largely unknown to many of the employees or indeed the customers! Paterson himself rarely visited Candy's, leaving Kerrison to manage the relationship. Apparently, during a visit to the Hanwell works in about 1950 Paterson was accidentally sprayed with lime from a hose which came loose from a chemical pump under test and it was his last visit to Candy's.

In the same year that he purchased Candy's business, Paterson also bought Bell Brothers and Jewell Filters (UK), effectively taking over the majority of the UK

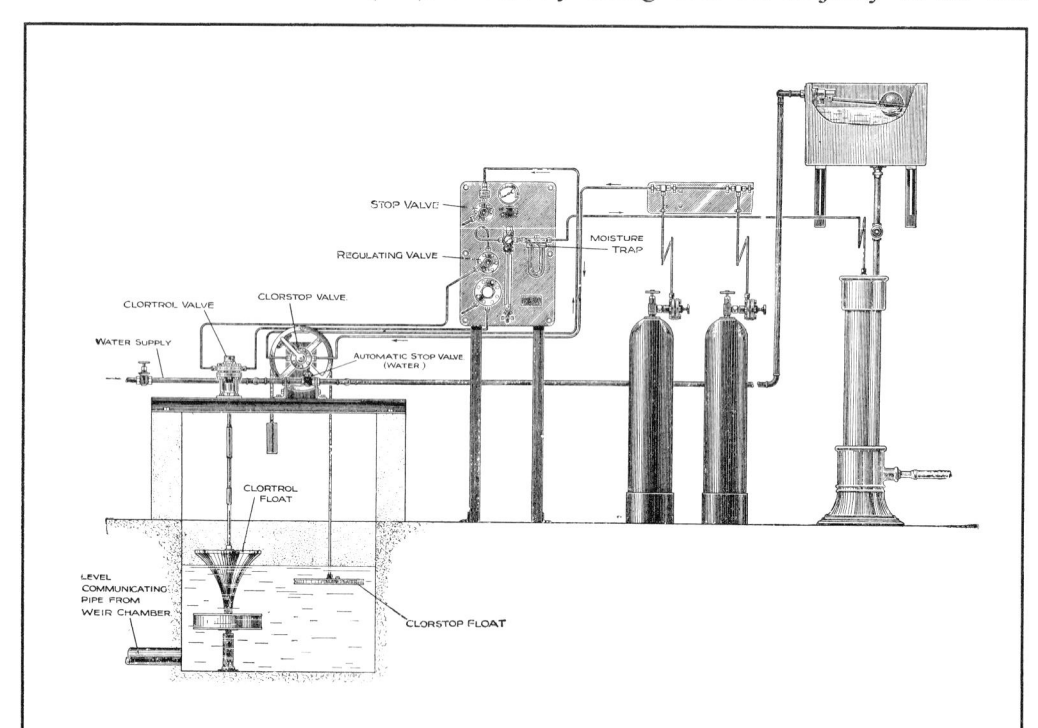

Weir type proportioning system. The Clorstop isolated the gas supply at no flow. Both the Clorstop and the Clortrol valves could be used with either weir or venturi proportioning systems. From a 1930 catalogue.

specialist treatment plant suppliers. Given the strength that the British companies had in the world market at the time, this put Paterson in a commanding position which he maintained until the 1950s.

This remarkable change of fortune was to have far-reaching consequences for the whole industry, and Candy's remained the smaller company for the next thirty years. However, due to their sound technical base they maintained a strong position in the UK market, and enjoyed very wide goodwill overseas, obtaining much of the work in South Africa, the Colonies, Australia and New Zealand as well as a reasonable share of the Indian market. The attention to economy and excellence of design guided the company's activities until the 1970s when it began to lose its way. But by then the roles had been reversed and William Paterson's great company had declined and been absorbed by Candy's.

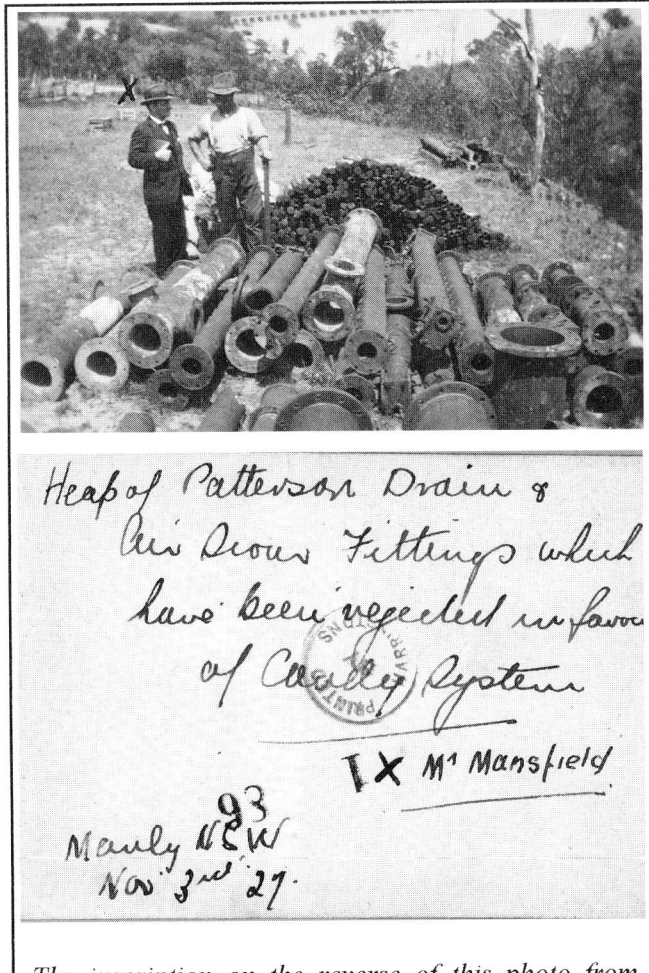

The inscription on the reverse of this photo from 1927 illustrates the rivalry between the two companies!

Chapter 6

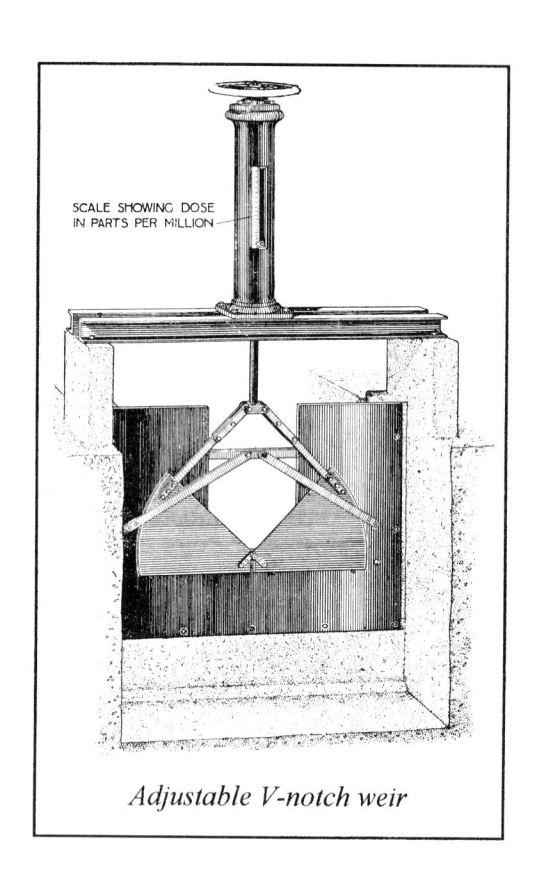

Adjustable V-notch weir

7-PERMUTIT

United Water Softeners in the 1920s

From their beginning as the Lassen-Hjort partnership, United Water Softeners were firmly established in the Aldwych in London, and by the end of 1918 had branched into a number of unrelated interests. In the water treatment field they held an agency from Wallace and Tiernan of the USA covering the UK, Europe and the Empire, for their chemical dosing equipment. This was extended in the 1920s to their gas chlorinators, and it was very lucrative until W&T formed their own UK company and launched the "Agene" process (marginal chlorination). Other agencies included Sharples centrifuges, and UWS had also acquired an interest in a company called KEK Ltd, which had developed a pin mill for pulverising foodstuffs.

Amongst other off-shoots from their main business, UWS had formed a company called British Synthetics for the production of dyestuffs. This development stemmed from a Dr Higgins who had joined UWS in 1919 after a period of internment in Germany during the war, having been responsible for building chemical works in Germany and Russia up to the outbreak of hostilities. The dyestuffs factory at Brentford was later gutted by fire and the company was sold to British Alizarene and ultimately to ICI.

By the end of the 1920s, all these activities had been rationalised and UWS was once more concentrating on water treatment. However, because of their dependence on the industrial market, the great depression that followed WW1 saw them in severe difficulties by about 1930.

During the period between the wars, sales of lime-soda softeners, which had provided the foundations of the company, gradually tailed away, partly due to the general depression. There was a temporary improvement at the beginning of the 30s when the London Midland and Scottish, and the London and North Eastern Railways, opted for the process. The development of ion-exchange techniques also overtook the older treatment method and the arrival of American hot lime-soda softener designs just before the second war was too late to establish an important place in the market.

Chapter 7

Domestic water softeners

UWS were producing base-exchange softeners for the domestic market soon after the end of World War 1, under the trade-mark "Permutit". The early models, which used the German Gans material, gave way to the No. 31 resin versions at the start of the first war, and in 1920 New Jersey greensand was introduced. In parallel, Crosfield's, who had been working on new materials for some time, produced a sodium alumino-silicate which they called "Doucil". They offered this initially to UWS but eventually the commercial rights were given to William Boby, and UWS opted in favour of the greensand. Unfortunately, after much hard work establishing the New Jersey material in the market, it was overtaken by a better performing greensand from Australia for which UWS did not have the rights. The company only regained its leading position in the base-exchange softener market when sulphonated coal was introduced between 1934 and 1936.

Side by side with the development of the ion-exchange materials, the plant was continuously improved. Versions introduced in 1929 were more convenient than the

Lassen-Hjort continuous automatic lime-soda softener on the London, Midland and Scottish Railway, at Castlethorpe, Bucks. c.1930. Note the loco. picking up water at speed from the trough between the rails.

direct salting designs but little more efficient. In 1935 an early design of multi-port valve was introduced. It failed to perform well so it was replaced by valves imported from Permutit New York. Then in 1931 the first volumetrically-measured, saturated brine softeners were introduced, called the DL after the first unit that was installed at Denham Laboratories, and this concept remains the basis of most current softeners. The domestic softener was well marketed and it had become a substantial part of the company's business by the start of WW2. The term "A Permutit" became synonymous with base-exchange softeners, and kept its market cachet until the 70s when the business was passed to Houseman and Thompson, then part of the Portals group, who failed to exploit the value of the name.

Chapter 7

The Permutit trademark

The use of the Permutit name has always been confusing since the originator Riedal sold the rights separately in a number of countries. For some time Roland Pemberton, the UWS MD, had tried to obtain an agreement with the other licensees on territorial rights. By 1930 he had succeeded with Permutit New York and Permutit AG, Berlin. Two years later, he reached agreements with Phillips et Pain, Paris (who were to go out of business in 1957). The co-operation covered territorial rights and interestingly, the pooling of their various research efforts, at no cost. However, the outbreak of the second war disrupted the agreement and it was thereafter maintained only between Permutit New York and London. Then in 1949, US anti-trust laws resulted in the agreement being narrowed and in 1962 it was reduced to the original territorial rights only, and the three remaining licensees ceased any collaboration.

The SD (salt dry) Softener with prototype multi-port valve, c1935.

The trademark issue resulted in UWS adopting the name "The Permutit Company" only for the licensed territories, and for a number of years they continued to trade as UWS elsewhere. The fragmented right to use the name led to some complicated arrangements and the company was later forced to adopt other names, including Zerolit, with inevitable market confusion at times. In this chapter the names UWS and Permutit are synonymous and I have ignored the other trading names used by Permutit.

R.T.Pemberton

Roland Pemberton joined UWS in 1924 after a period in the navy during the first war, followed by a brief spell with his father's company. He was soon appointed sales manager and in 1927 he became joint MD with Dr Higgins who remained with the company until his resignation in the early 30s.

Roland Pemberton was the architect of the company and he remained at the helm for forty years until 1970 when Portals took over. For most of this period he looked after the City's interests, set the business strategy, and with A.J.R.Walter, he established the firm as the foremost industrial water treatment specialist in much of the world.

R.T.Pemberton, late 1960s

Chapter 7

A.J.R.Walter

If Roland Pemberton was the guiding hand behind Permutit's development, A.J.R.Walter was probably the key to their world-wide sales successes (and indeed to their survival during the dark years of the 30s depression). He joined the firm in 1931 as general manager and was also responsible for export sales. Walter had spent several years with Babcock and Wilcox in Spain where he had also started a successful business of his own, until political turmoil caused him to look for opportunities elsewhere. UWS was in difficulties due to the depression, the staff numbers had been reduced and those who remained had taken a pay cut. Having no other firm offer, Walter agreed to try and re-build the company's fortunes and to investigate the prospects for new business in South America.

A.J.R.Walter

Walter and Pemberton, together with Milton and Clark who joined the company from Paterson's, provided Permutit with a strong management team that spanned more than three decades, and built its success until they retired in the late 1960s. They had many "modern" ideas, and introduced training programmes for the staff, R&D, and good staff communication as well as an excellent apprenticeship scheme. Apparently they used to fight between themselves and in common with most companies during this period the firm was very hierarchical, with small privileges at each level in the organisation.

Railways across the seas

Without Walter's success with the Argentine railways, Permutit's future might have been very different. His arrival at the company coincided with an enquiry from the chief chemist of the Buenos Aires and Pacific Railways who had written to a number of water treatment companies to discuss the problems he was having with the difficult waters in his Cuyo district. Without further ado, Walter sent literature and technical details via the very expensive air-mail service then provided by the Graf Zeppelin airship and Dragon Rapide bi-plane. Walter offered to visit and make a survey and his proposal was accepted. This and subsequent visits resulted in an offer to send three

An early UWS fully automatic base-exchange softener, c.1930.

large base-exchange softeners for test. Because the railways were used to lime-soda softeners and little money was available, UWS agreed to supply the units at no cost for a year, to be paid for if the tests were successful. It appears that this was a do or die effort on the part of UWS but the gamble paid off and resulted in orders for a further twenty-five plants.

This was the start of a very successful and profitable sales effort in South America and another two hundred and fifty plants were shipped to railways there during the next two to three years.

Following his successful campaign in Argentina, Walter went to Brazil and sold twenty-three plants. His next target was Rhodesia where he obtained orders for all the main railway lines; from there he moved to South Africa, again repeating his success. However, these orders were held up by the chemist of the South African Railways who preferred lime-soda softeners, and because the Rhodesian Railways used his laboratories, he also affected their orders. Walter responded by offering some of the plants for test as he had done in Argentina, and by 1941 Permutit had become the main supplier to South African Railways, displacing Paterson's, who had until then supplied most of the railway water plants in southern Africa. From there, Walter went on to supply treatment plant to power stations, the mines and many other industries in southern Africa.

W.A.Low

Bill Low joined UWS in 1929 after serving an apprenticeship with Flavell and Churchill, who were general machinery manufacturers. His early career typifies the ups and downs of the 1930s and the uncertain life of an erector. During his first two years with UWS he was shunted around the UK installing and commissioning plant - a rather lonely existence on poor wages. He became a victim of the redundancies of 1931 and rejoined Flavell and Churchill, but a year later he accepted an offer from UWS to supervise the installation of the first plants for the Argentine Railways.

W.A.Low.

Upon arrival in Buenos Aires, Low was given a Spanish dictionary and packed off to the site by train where he was to live in a caboose for the next six months, with a gang of Spanish speaking peons as his only companions. He returned to England in 1934 after a type of wild-west existence which would make a good story in its own right. He had met and resolved many technical problems and he established double regeneration as a means of dealing with very hard waters.

Low then married and went to Argentina, this time with his wife, and their son was born there. The outbreak of the second war prevented him from returning to the UK and so he took his family to South Africa, where he was involved with the plants for the Rhodesian and South African Railways. He remained there for the rest of his life, building Permutit's dominant position in the industrial market.

The difficulty of obtaining supplies of plant from the UK during the war resulted in their local manufacture and the "one man band" grew into an efficient and profitable company, which Low managed until he retired in the 1970s after about forty years of successful service. He played a crucial part in the uranium recovery plant orders of the early 1950s and he secured most of the power plant market in Southern Africa. He was "Permutit (South Africa)" and his retirement, coupled with the amalgamation with PCI (South Africa), signalled the decline of this once dominant supplier, although by then the main industrial investment programme had slowed substantially and several local competitors were well established.

The move to Chiswick

The Aldwych offices had become much too small for the expanding company following Walter's initial success in Argentina, and so the business was moved to purpose-built premises at Chiswick. They remained in use until the early 70s when the site was re-developed.

Type-C dosing pump, 1937

Clark and Milton - again

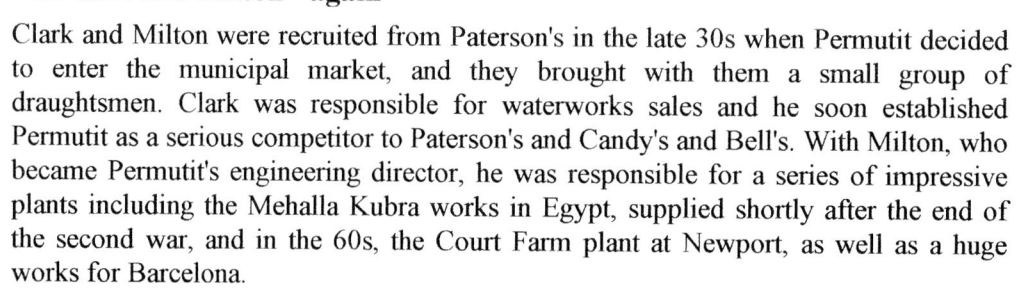

Clark and Milton were recruited from Paterson's in the late 30s when Permutit decided to enter the municipal market, and they brought with them a small group of draughtsmen. Clark was responsible for waterworks sales and he soon established Permutit as a serious competitor to Paterson's and Candy's and Bell's. With Milton, who became Permutit's engineering director, he was responsible for a series of impressive plants including the Mehalla Kubra works in Egypt, supplied shortly after the end of the second war, and in the 60s, the Court Farm plant at Newport, as well as a huge works for Barcelona.

Clark was an easy-going and very approachable man, in contrast to his colleague Milton who was outspoken and irascible but a very good engineer. Apparently the two men

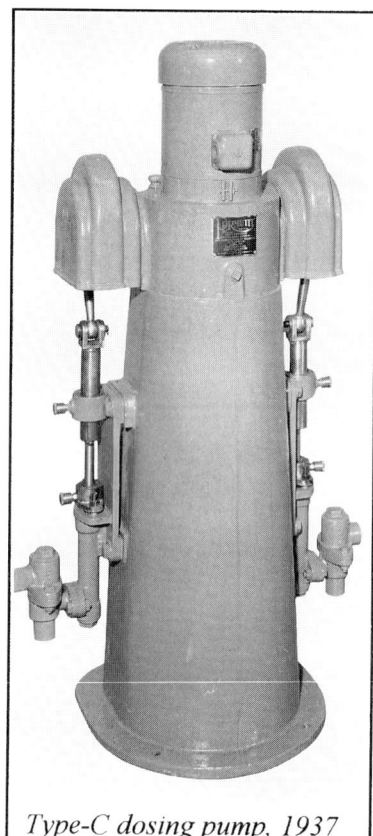

Chapter 7

disliked each other intensely but they made a major contribution to Permutit's success. Milton was later awarded an OBE for his part in the design of the nuclear reactor cooling and waste treatment plants.

Demineralisation

Although Permutit took a substantial part of the waterworks business and established the domestic softener, the company's real claim to fame is its outstanding contribution to ion-exchange demineralisation. Many researchers were active in the field so it is difficult to say who did what first, but Permutit can certainly claim the first two-bed demineraliser, the first mixed-bed plant and the invention of the de-alkalisation process, which they called "starvation". The company is also credited with the development of condensate polishing and resin transfer. The first commercial plant which had both processes was built in the early 60s at the Drakelow power station.

The main filter control gallery at Mehalla Kubra, Egypt, c.1954. The plant supplied 10.5 mgd of water to the textile mill and the potable supply for 24,000 workers. Orders for Aswan, Sherbin, Beni Suef and others resulted from this plant.

There were many other important contributions to the technology, built on the back of Permutit's combination of in-house resin manufacture coupled with its design and contracting activities. This close link between development and application gave the company great strength and depth that would lead to the domination of the market in the 50s and 60s.

In 1934-36 a landmark development occurred with the invention of the revolutionary sulphonated coal ion-exchange material, almost simultaneously in Germany and Holland. All previous exchange materials could be used only for sodium exchange but the new material opened the field to the removal of alkalinity by

Permutit (Candy type!) settling tanks and gravity filters at Barcelona, capacity 96 mgd. c. 1952.

Chapter 7

The world's first two bed demineraliser, 1937.

hydrogen ion-exchange and so, direct competition with lime-soda softening, and the promise of demineralisation.

The next major development came with the invention at the National Physical Laboratory at Teddington of an anion exchange resin by Adams and Holmes in 1935. UWS obtained the exclusive rights to manufacture the material and recruited Holmes to work on its development. This was probably the most important invention in the history of industrial water treatment, as it enabled cation and anion exchangers in sequence, to demineralise water, previously only possible by distillation. The first commercial application was for the Friary, Holroyd and Healy's wine distillery at Guildford in 1937, and was followed in 1939 by the first demineralising plant for a power station at Ferrybridge. By the outbreak of the war, three more power station plants had been installed and a revolution in water treatment had started, bringing immense advantages to the power industry.

The company went on to supply thousands of demineralisers throughout the world for hospitals, power stations, chemical plants, refineries etc.

The Second World War

The advent of war brought lots of work for Permutit. Walter sold eleven hot lime-soda softeners in 1938 as part of the re-armament activities; these were followed by many large contracts for munitions factories during the war years. The scale of the involvement is hinted at in this extract from Pemberton's letter of December 1945, to his agents around the world.

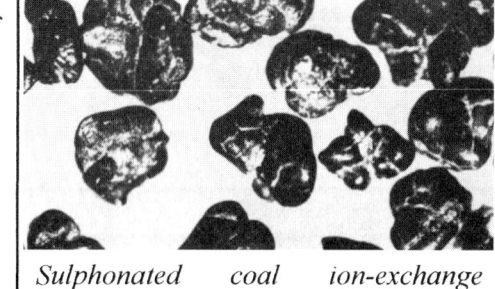

Sulphonated coal ion-exchange material

"During the war years we have often thought that our agents and representatives in all parts of the world must frequently have felt cut-off from Head Office...The development of our sea water desalting kit occupied a great deal of our time, but we are extremely proud that we have been able to add to the products of war one which saves lives. We feel the time was well spent...

Chapter 7

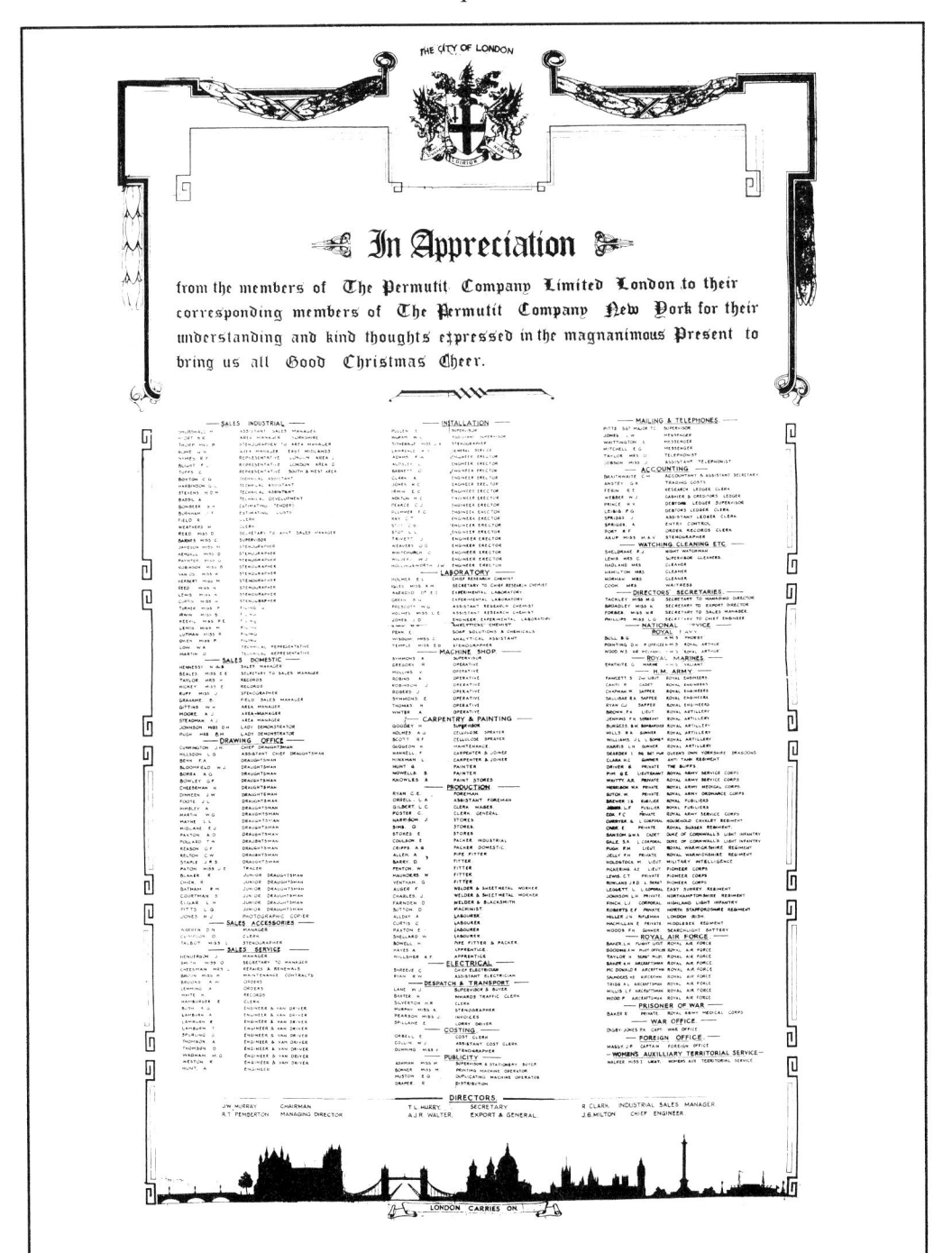

Extract from a "Roll of Honour" from Permutit London to Permutit NY in appreciation of food parcels at Christmas

Chapter 7

"As we have mentioned above, 'Drinking water from sea water' was just one of our contributions towards winning the war. You will probably be somewhat surprised to know that we actually began production in 1937 of the first 500 pound gas bombs which, for secrecy reasons at that time, were disguised as water softening containers and were known up till 1940 as 'Permo No.3'. This began a continuous series of government contracts, without a break, from 1938 to 1944 for equipment for Royal Ordnance Factories alone...This does not take into account numerous smaller types of equipment for British and American camps and hospitals...

"And Russia: This could be a story to itself of plants vital for her power stations, involving among other things, lettering on drawings and valves in Russian characters, special working instructions and endless lists of parts. Some of our first consignments unfortunately went to the bottom of the sea, so we began all over again...

"Then do you remember reading that the trans-Iranian Railway had to be re-constructed in order that supplies to Russia could be sent by an overland route? Permutit was on the job again - six sets of equipment etc....

"Before D-day there were 'hush-hush' visits to the South Coast for the overhaul of the softening plants on passenger and cargo boats...

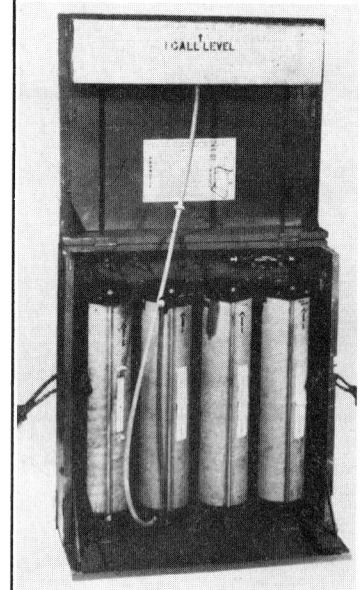

Mixed bed demineraliser used by the RAF during the war for topping up aircraft batteries and diluting glycol.

"After D-Day, portable 'Deminrolit' units were carried by the 2nd Tactical Airforce and used on the beaches and at advanced enemy aerodromes in Europe for topping up batteries and splitting glycol mixtures...There is much more that we could tell you......"

The Mixed Bed

Perhaps the most important of all the ion-exchange processes was invented to meet the needs of the services. The mixed-bed, literally an intimate mixture of anion and cation resins, came about as the result of a requirement from the Royal Air Force for a small water demineraliser for filling aircraft batteries, although these early units had to be discarded when they were exhausted, as the mixed resins could not be separated. In 1941 the concept was adapted to produce the aircrew survival kits, based on silver-barium-zeolites, and many thousands were produced and issued to the Allied air

Chapter 7

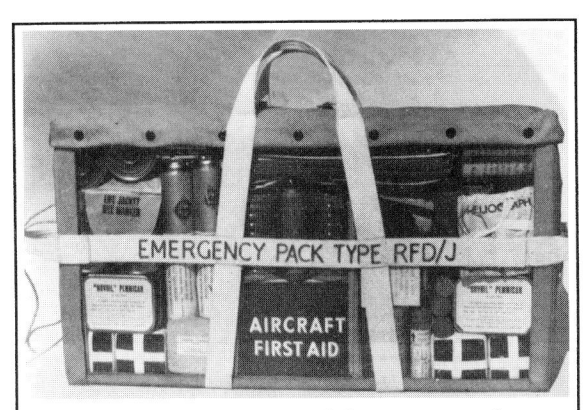

Emergency pack carried by aircrew during the second war. The Permutit sea water kit is at the bottom right hand corner of the pack. The kit consisted of silver-barium-zeolite briquettes which were added to sea water in a bag and kneaded by hand, to produce about three pints of drinking water, enough to survive for a few days in the dinghy.

forces. This extract from the BBC Home News bulletin of 10 November 1945 is worth reproducing:

"One of the most useful of our wartime discoveries was the invention of an apparatus for turning sea water into drinking water without using cumbersome equipment. The idea originated with Admiralty research scientists, but its final development and manufacture was carried out by a famous British firm who produced an apparatus that could be carried by our airmen as well as being used in boats and rubber dinghies. The 'pack' our airmen used was no bigger than a pocket camera but it could produce three pints of drinking water- enough to save many a ditched pilot from dying of thirst..."

Whilst these early mixed-bed units demonstrated the concept, the process was of limited industrial use until the resins could be separated and regenerated, and its future was not for desalting sea water but for producing super-pure water for industrial use and power generation. The breakthrough came about in 1944 at the General Electric Company in the USA, with the development of synthetic cross-linked polystyrene resins. The anion version was much lighter than the cation resin, so permitting hydraulic separation, and this opened the way to processes capable of producing water of undreamed of quality and so, the construction of very high pressure boilers.

Permutit's first industrial mixed-bed plant was built in the 50s, and the first automatically regenerated units were supplied to the Shell Haven refinery in Essex. The device is now a standard feature of many ion-exchange plants.

Post-war development, and the service department

The immediate post-war years were a period of transition for industry in the UK. Most manufacturing concerns took some time to divest themselves of government-sponsored

The first automatic mixed-bed demineraliser at Shell Haven refinery, Essex.c. mid-60s.

work and resume their pre-war business. Markets which had lapsed had to be revived and new markets had to be investigated and developed. The Permutit Company was fortunate to obtain government work during the war that was similar to their business in peacetime, so almost immediately after the war they were able to prepare for an expansion of trade, and planned new offices and works near Heathrow Airport. These plans were frustrated by the government development agency which directed them to build their new chemical factory near Cardiff in South Wales.

Other priorities meant that the domestic softener business had been curtailed during the war period, and so the company leased a showroom in Regent Street to promote its activities. This remained in use until the 60s.

The service department started life in the late 30s as an initiative from Walter. In the post-war period the workload increased to such an extent that a separate building was leased for its staff in Commerce Road, Brentford. Under George Sansom, the business flourished and became a substantial and very profitable part of the company. Later in the 70s, as the market needs changed and Group [Portals] re-arrangements moved the standard plant business away from Permutit, the residual service department declined because the service requirements for the large plant market could no longer support the business.

George Sansom, a wartime photo

Resins production

The production of ion-exchange resins, which had started before the war at the Chiswick works, had to be moved to the nearby Power Road site and then to Pontyclun, South Wales. There, in 1946 the new works began production of cross-linked polystyrene resins, after the company found a way around the American patents. These materials were marketed under the names Zeo-Karb and De-Acidite which became well known in the industry. The products were generally well-regarded and some of them were outstanding.

The development of the cross-linked polystyrenes opened up many new markets in the 60s. The new materials were chemically very stable and they had much improved exchange characteristics that enabled ion-exchange processes to be used for a number of non-water applications, ranging from the purification of glycerine, gelatine and sugars, to the stabilisation of wines. Permutit also achieved considerable success in the industrial waste and re-cycling markets, with plants to treat plating swill waters for companies such as Pye, Bepi Electronics, Flight Refuelling, Ericsson etc., and car body wash waters for British Leyland and Ford. (Paterson's also supplied several plants to this market).

Following the acquisition by Portals in 1970, the resin business was set-up as a separate company that traded under the name Zerolit, and exported over sixty percent of the production. However, there were problems. Much of the product line was beginning to age, as were the production facilities in South Wales, and with the split from the main company much of the technical support faded away. In 1976 Portals sold the resin business to the Diamond Shamrock Corporation. The integration of resins development and manufacture with the design and contracting business had given Permutit a huge advantage which they had exploited very successfully for many years. By the late 60s, resins were already an industrial commodity and the separation of the businesses had some commercial logic, as well as enabling the main business to shop for the best resins, rather than be tied to sometimes second rate in-house products. On the negative side, the separation inevitably meant that the application support work declined, and this weakened the resin company's technical strength.

Automatic uranium recovery ion-exchange plant in South Africa, early 1950s.

The uranium plants

This chapter would be incomplete without a mention of the uranium plants built during the "cold war" in the 50s. The urgent need for uranium rapidly outgrew the traditional sources which had, until then, provided the very small quantities needed. The new sources were mostly in the form of low grade ore from which the traces of uranium could be extracted by acid leaching in the presence of an oxidising agent, but the uranium then had to be separated from the other metals in the leach liquor. The discovery that this could be done by anion-exchange was made in America, partly by accident as so many good discoveries are, and in 1950 the first pilot plant was set up in total secrecy at Western Reefs in South Africa. This resulted in an order for Permutit New York to supply the production plant, but because of the American anti-trust laws, the co-operation with Permutit London had ceased and there was no communication

Chapter 7

Sugar decolourising plant, Suomen Sokeri Osakeyhtio, Finland. Late 1960s.

about it. Bill Low only learned of the development in 1952.

After some difficulty with persuading the UK government that a British company was competent to build such plant (!) the first order was obtained and Permutit went on to secure some two hundred sets of ion-exchange equipment, which was about half the total of plants built. Of necessity, these installations were fully automatic, and in addition to the plants in South Africa, Permutit supplied ion-exchange units for uranium recovery in Australia at Port Pirie, Rum Jungle, Mary Kathleen and other sites. In Canada, twelve very large plants were supplied via their Canadian subsidiary, and installations were also supplied to France, Sweden and Spain.

Towards the end of the 50s the demand for new plant declined but the company was able to apply the technology to the treatment of nuclear reactor cooling and waste waters and they supplied plants to the Aldermaston, Harwell and Winfrith laboratories and later, to many of the nuclear power stations.

Overseas expansion

In addition to the uranium plants, Permutit were very busy with sales to South Africa for the synthetic fuel company and for power generation, and to India, Australia, Canada, Iran, Norway and the Eastern Bloc states, including Russia and many others, for a variety of applications. All of these were dwarfed by the huge plants supplied to Anic Pisticci in Italy and Anic Gela in Sicily. Completed in the early 60s, the Sicily plant was the largest ion-exchange demineralising plant in the world, with a capacity of 2.64 mgd.

The post war years were also good for Permutit's overseas subsidiaries. The Australian company, established as an agency by Walter in 1939, was flourishing and it went on to dominate the industrial market until the late 70s, when a series of poor management decisions in the UK

2.64 mgd demineralising plant at Anic Gela refinery, Sicily. c. 1963. A similar plant was supplied for the Anic Pisticci refinery in Italy.

derailed the business and eventually led to the closure of the Sydney office in the early 90s. In its heyday, Permutit (Australia) built many fine and sometimes ground-breaking plants, including in the 80s, a massive precipitation softening and reverse osmosis pre-treatment plant for the zero-discharge Bayswater power station.

Permutit's Indian company was formed as a joint venture after the war and it developed rapidly with the help of technology from the UK, including the setting-up of a local ion-exchange resin factory at Ambernath, to make Permutit resins. Ion-Exchange (India) sold many thousands of water treatment plants but ultimately, the Indian government's restrictions on repatriating profits meant that there was little commercial reason for continued UK involvement, so the business was disposed of to local interests. Thereafter, as with PCI's Indian activities, the only work of real interest was that funded from outside the country, but even these projects were fraught with the endemic commercial problems

Automatic demineralising plant for high pressure boilers, Norsk Hydro-Electrisk, Oslo. Early 1960s.

Ion-Exchange Canada was set up to supply the Canadian uranium plants, and it did not survive many years after the programme ended. By the 70s Permutit's interests were transferred to an agency and they had declined entirely by the time of the merger with PCI.

Changes in the UK

The rapid development of Permutit's business meant that by the mid-50s the premises at Chiswick were too small, and in 1956 the company opened a new works at Ealing. The new factory provided a wide range of services, from vessel manufacture to constructing electrical power and control panels, as well as making standard plant items such as softeners and small de-ionisers. The works was well equipped, modern and fully occupied with the company's supply needs; however, by the early 70s it no longer made sense for a

Automatic filters and demineralising plant at Inverkip power station, Scotland. 1977

Chapter 7

Swill water recovery plant at Fescol, Staffs. This plant reclaimed over 90% of the swill water used in metal finishing. Late 1960s.

company like Permutit to manufacture vessels and pipework and the volume had declined sharply. The works was closed and sold in 1974 and the standard plant assembly activities moved to the South Wales factory.

Moving the works from Chiswick to Ealing provided a short term increase in office space although this was in the converted workshops and not ideal. By the early 60s, space was again a problem and offices were rented in Kew to house some departments, including the excellent apprentices' training school, from which many of Permutit's competent staff originated. In 1966 the company moved to new "modern" premises at Isleworth where its successors remain. Built in the 60s with too much glass, it is cold in the winter and hot in the summer and the location near the flight-path to Heathrow precludes opening the windows.

The power station business reached its peak in the middle 60s with Permutit dominating the market in much of the world. In the UK, they supplied many manual and automatic demineralisers for the new power stations, most notably the automatic plants supplied to Drakelow in 1966, Tilbury 1968, Fiddlers Ferry and Longannet 1973 and Inverkip in 1977. These installations also brought in the need for additional plant such as filters, de-gassers or de-aerators and as at Drakelow, condensate recovery units.

As the 60s progressed and the large plant sector declined, the company concentrated on developing markets for packaged plant. They had considerable success, for example, in securing most of the new launderette business, although the volume never replaced the big plant activity.

Permak

The period also saw a major push into the effluent treatment market with a range of well-designed packaged sewage plants, sold under the name Permak and a later version called Permex. These units met the needs of small communities, holiday camps, remote hotels etc., in the UK and overseas. The Permak combined a settling tank and extended aeration unit in

Spiractor pellet lime softener, Kingston Power Station, 1966

a site-assembled circular tank, usually of steel, although concrete versions were also built. The Permak needed little attention and was simple to operate, and it remained competitive until the early 80s, when it was overtaken by other packaged treatment units. By then, PCI were responsible for the municipal parts of these plants, and although they sold a number of the units, there was little corporate interest in them.

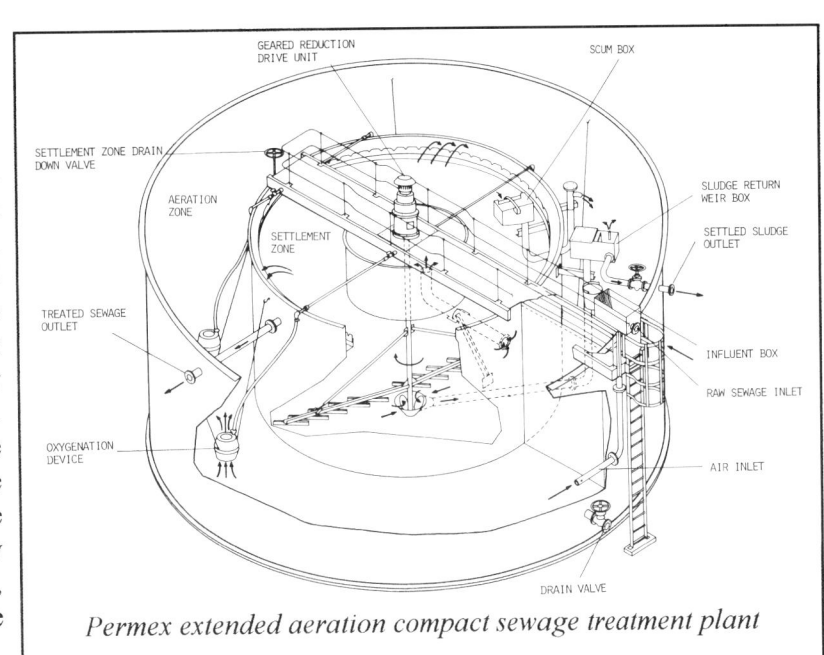

Permex extended aeration compact sewage treatment plant

Stella-Meta Filters (SMF)

The Stellar filter story is really part of Paterson's history (see chapter 8) but Permutit's contribution was also important. Following the amalgamation of Paterson's and Candy's, the pre-coat filter business moved to Laverstoke in Hampshire, and in the general re-organisation resulting from the Permutit acquisition, it was attached to Permutit, since its activities were principally in the industrial field. Although SMF still had a position in general filtration, with sales to breweries and the gold mines in South Africa, it was increasingly dependent on military orders which were very profitable but inevitably intermittent. SMF were able to adapt and modernise their products to meet the expected needs of nuclear, bacteriological and chemical warfare, and this extended the life of the by then ageing Stellar filter, which had changed very little since its conception during the war.

Permutit took the Stellar filters into the power stations as part of condensate recovery and polishing systems and they were also used in the mobile reverse osmosis units.

Metafilters for beer liquor treatment at Scottish and Newcastle Breweries, Edinburgh

In the 90s, by then a separate company, SMF was merged with PCI Membranes which is no longer linked to Paterson Candy Ltd.

Chapter 7

The Portals era

When Portals bought the company in 1970 they already owned PCI, together with another very old British firm, Houseman and Thompson. This was the start of a period of continual change and ultimately, the end of the Permutit Company. By then, Permutit had rather lost its way and the strong managers of the 50s and 60s had retired. The huge power plant market had come and gone and the company (which was quoted on the London Stock Exchange) was struggling to find enough profitable work to occupy the staff, so it was an easy target for acquisition. There was a brief competition between Slater Walker and Portals, with the company management preferring the latter.

Portals' hand was generally very light and they mostly left the companies to run their own affairs, but the break-up of Permutit's activities, so logical from a conventional business viewpoint, was to result in the original large plant business being unable to sustain itself. Perhaps the moves simply highlighted the fact that the business needed to adapt as the market had changed, and the profitable service and specialist filter businesses masked the true position. The standard plant activities were transferred to Houseman's, and Stella-Meta Filters became a division and then a separate company. The loss of the standard plant business resulted in both Permutit and Houseman's neglecting the middle ground which represented much of the market at the time. Houseman's did not have the skills needed for the contracting activities associated with the standard plant or the technical ability to develop the engineering; Permutit didn't have the small plant needed to be competitive in this market. None of this should have been beyond the management of the two companies but there was inevitably much petty rivalry and protection of interests, to the detriment of the business.

Stellar filters treating boiler feed water and condensate prior to ion-exchange demineralisation. Drakelow power station.

In the late 80s, with the sale to Thames Water of all but the very profitable Houseman chemicals business, the standard plant activity became a stand-alone company trading under the Permutit name. It struggled unsuccessfully to make a living and it was soon sold, together with the Permutit name, to US Filters. On the way, the domestic softener business had been sold to Sketchley Textiles who did little with it.

Chapter 7

The Hegro fiasco

With the transfer of the standard plant business to Houseman's in 1974, Permutit's technical input to the product line declined, and against their advice, Houseman's management made an ill-judged acquisition of Hegro, a small Swiss company that made its own softener valves. Hegro knew quite a lot about plastic moulding but very little about water softeners, and their products were based on obsolete technology. The sale was marked by a splendid party. Houseman's flew dozens of perplexed staff from across the Group to Italy to visit the factory, together with a number of journalists. The visitors were greeted by a band at the airport and treated to a marvellous lunch on a lake steamer, the band still in attendance, and returned to the UK even more mystified, after a most enjoyable day! Oh yes, they did visit the factory but the exercise didn't result in any profitable sales and the name and products were quietly dropped soon afterwards.

Stellar military nuclear, biological and chemical treatment unit, 1980s

Later developments

The 1970s saw some very interesting technical developments by Permutit (by then trading as Permutit-Boby Ltd). The electro-dialysis (ED) plants built using faulty Boby technology were exciting at the time and the company sold several substantial units which were to divert its technical resources. Ironically, Permutit's own ED technology had been licensed to Ionics in the USA who very successfully exploited the market with the patented tortuous path internal design.

Permutit were more successful with reverse osmosis and they sold a number of fine plants to the oil industry for off-shore rigs and to the military, although it is uncertain whether the latter plants ever got further than being unpacked somewhere in North Africa. Squabbles between Permutit and PCI's reverse osmosis division resulted in neither really making a success of these markets.

Chapter 7

The Permutit "Varivoid" filter was a very successful development and well marketed. The device consists of a deep bed filter with very fine material filling the interstices of the sand bed. The theory was perhaps less sound than the marketing but it was successfully used in a number of applications where the product quality was not critical and the very high rating made it competitive. One of the most spectacular plants was that supplied to British Steel for cooling water recycle, where the filters did the same job as the clarifiers and conventional shallow bed filter plants supplied fifteen years earlier by Paterson's and Candy's.

Varivoid filters at British Steel for treating re-cycled strip mill cooling water.

"Hipol" was also a success. The idea behind this development was the replacement of relatively complex mixed-bed units as the final polisher following cation-anion demineralisation. The concept stemmed from the compact-bed technology developed by Permutit for the BZA softener. Essentially, Hipol is a small packed-bed, strong cation exchanger which is used to mop up any cations remaining from the preceding ion exchangers, and it is regenerated in series with the main cation unit. Because the Hipol unit has little to do, the unused regenerant super-regenerates it at almost no cost. The idea has been adopted by many plant suppliers to replace a final mixed bed unit.

Another interesting packed-bed device was called "Tripol" because it used three layers of resin, cation/anion/cation, separated by screens and regenerated separately. The device was a good condensate polisher but only a few were sold, to Singapore and Australia.

Reverse osmosis desalinator for North Sea oil rig, late 70s

"Scion" (short cycle ion-exchange unit) also stemmed from the packed bed technology and it has been a major success. The small inventory of special resins is regenerated frequently, providing a very competitive and efficient demineraliser. Many have been sold, however the marketing of this excellent development was affected by the moves of the standard plant activities within the group and much more could have been made of it.

Bayswater Power station, One of the Reverse Osmosis trains, part of the water treatment system supplied by Permutit-Australia. 1980s.

The Bayswater power station in New South Wales was designed for zero liquid discharge to the environment. To achieve this, the cooling tower blowdown is treated by a complex scheme involving carboxylic cation exchange to reduce alkalinity, precipitation lime-soda softening and reverse osmosis. Most of the water is recovered for re-use in the power station. The wastes from the treatment units are finally concentrated by a seeded brine evaporator to precipitate the salts. The plant was highly innovative and removes about 24,000 tonnes per year of salts from the power station's water systems.

There were lots of other developments during this period, including improvements to counter-current regeneration techniques, resin hold-down systems etc., all aimed at improving efficiency and quality, though many came too late to benefit the plants built in the big investment period.

Postscript

Permutit were perhaps the foremost industrial water treatment specialists in the world and they retained this position until the late 1960s when, like Paterson's, they began to lose their way. The acquisition by Portals in 1970 brought few advantages other than a solid group balance sheet, and the purchase of William Boby's business, which was hurting Permutit, only diverted the management and brought little benefit.

There were many technical and commercial achievements during the later years, and the neglect of their technical base during the 1970s and 80s was not immediately apparent. The company, despite being taken over, remained strong and often vibrant until the mid 80s. By then, as for PCI and most of the other

Chapter 7

treatment specialists, business was scarce and profitability poor, and in 1988 Permutit and PCI were merged. Permutit did not recover from this. Their once dominant overseas subsidiaries had been taken from them and they had lost the resin business, together with the service division and the specialist filter and standard plant activities. The merger, resisted and unwanted by both parties, saw the end of the use of the Permutit name by the main business, and led to the rapid decline of what remained of this once great company.

Frank Blight, 1970, co-author and compiler of the renowned Permutit Data Books.

8-THE SECOND WORLD WAR

At the start of the war the water treatment industry was in good shape, and business carried on as usual for a few months whilst the various ministries decided on the controls for materials and the work necessary to protect the population. Permits to buy steel and other metals soon became essential, followed by rationing of diesel oil and petrol. Like many others, Candy's built air-raid shelters for their staff and purchased diesel engines for the works as back-up power supplies to drive the shafts and pulleys which normally powered the machines from central electric motors.

Water treatment sections appeared in various Government departments and the staff responsible for issuing tenders and managing the projects were soon well known to the suppliers. The main contacts were with the Ministry of Works which dealt with ordnance factories and the emergency hospitals, expected to be needed for treating air-raid victims, and for essential industrial projects; the Air Ministry dealt with airfield water supplies; the War Office with camp supplies and mobile plant for active service requirements, and the Navy with "special" requirements.

Fairly early on the supply industry, with government encouragement, formed a water and sewage advisory group to keep the government bodies aware of the industry's needs for efficient working under war conditions. The organisation also distributed and provided advice on the various edicts issued by government departments.

Second war military water set

Permits had to be negotiated to acquire steel and other metals, not just for the war projects but for all other work. In some cases, refusal meant a delay until the war ended: for example, a plant for the St. Saviour's water supply in Guernsey was stopped in 1940, whereas a 4 mgd plant for Kingston, Jamaica was approved. Perhaps even at that early stage of the war it was expected that the Channel Islands would be difficult to defend. By contrast, the City of Coventry was able to order a 1.5 mgd emergency supply to back-up the sources within the city boundary, which were thought to be

Chapter 8

vulnerable. The wisdom of this action was born out when the devastating air raids occurred, fortunately just after the works was commissioned.

In general however, difficulties were smoothed out quickly, and the wide range of water treatment plant requirements for both civilian and military needs enabled the companies to retain most of their staff, as the work was regarded as essential to the war effort. Throughout the war, perhaps surprisingly, given the conflicting priorities, there was a steady flow of export shipments of plant, some of which failed to arrive when the ships carrying them were sunk.

The Stellar filter

When war broke out, Paterson's, Candy's and Bell Brothers were quickly involved in a joint effort to supply mobile water treatment plants for the services. In his annual review a year or two earlier William Paterson had mentioned *"a significant development of a means of purifying small water supplies,"* and it was this which had now become of vital importance to the War Office.

Prior to the start of the war, J.G.Royce, who was an employee of the Metafiltration Company, had left them to develop a filter element to compete with the Metafilter. Royce took his design to Paterson who decided to market it, and so set off a bitter legal conflict over patent rights with Professor Pickard, the owner of the Metafiltration Company. After a lengthy court case, Paterson was allowed to promote the new filter which he called *"Stellar"* because the filtered water obtained was of *"star bright quality"*.

J.A.Pickard

The military water units consisted of a trailer which was equipped with a 3,000 gallon tank supplied by an engine-driven raw water pump and the Stellar filter. The unit also had a Candy Autominor chemical dosing set for chlorine solution. As the number of units required multiplied, new factories were needed away from London, and Bell Brothers' works at Wellington in Somerset became the site for the assembly of the trailer units. In all, over 40,000 were supplied for the Allied forces, with capacities ranging from 300

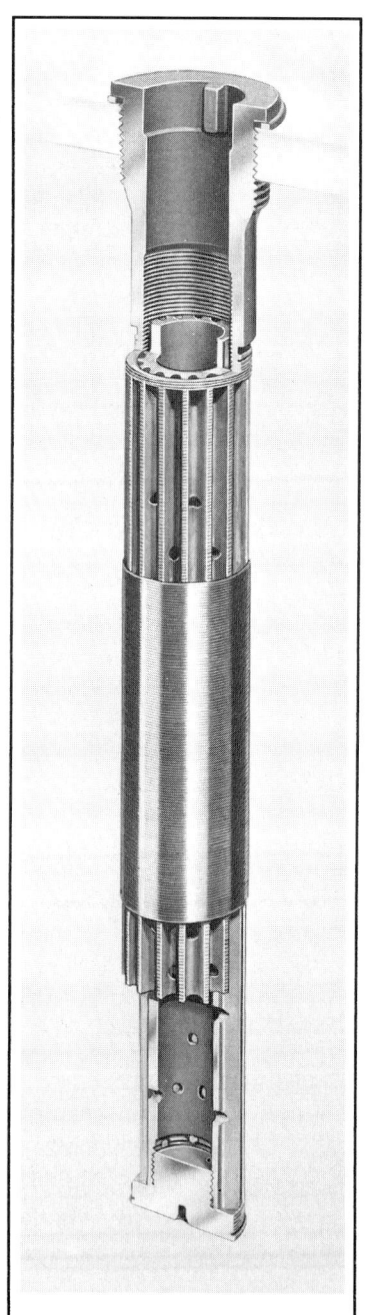

The Stellar filter element

grossly polluted sources. The Stellar-based military units continue in production to this day, albeit in various formats, including more complex versions using reverse osmosis membranes for nuclear, bacteriological and chemical warfare needs.

The Stellar filter proved to be a reliable means of achieving very high quality filtration and was widely used for filtering juices, wines and other beverages, and for many other industrial uses including cleaning the re-cycled coolant for aluminium foil rolling mills.

An interesting and very profitable application was for the recovery of gold using the cyanide extraction process. Most of the world's gold is now extracted from quartz and other gold-bearing ores, rather than the perhaps more romantic "panning," although a substantial part of the production is by recovery of particulate gold in the ore using riffle tables. The ore is crushed, washed and classified to separate the particulate gold, the gold-bearing ore and the dross. The ore is then contacted with cyanide solution to extract the gold as "pregnant liquor" which is clarified by Stellar filters. The filtrate from these is de-aerated to remove oxygen before being mixed with zinc dust and lead nitrate to precipitate the gold onto more Stellar filters where the gold slime is retained on the pre-coat. This is then calcined, pressed and smelted to produce a cyanide bullion for final refining. This much simplified description illustrates the importance of the "Stella-Meta zinc precipitation process" which for a number of years provided the South African company with a very profitable income.

New Consolidated Goldfields Ltd, Stellar filter plant.

Royce's excellent design consisted of a wire-wound septum, the gaps between the windings being sufficiently narrow so as to support a pre-coat of Kieselguhr or other material. Although the stainless steel construction was later replaced with plastics, the design remained almost unchanged for fifty years, and despite much effort, the company never designed a successful replacement. Royce died shortly after the start of the war and so did not see the success of his design. Professor Pickard continued to battle against Paterson in the marketplace and his Metafilter was always regarded as superior for filtering beer. The dispute finally ended in the 50s when Pickard retired and sold his company to his arch rival Paterson, who ran the Metafiltration Company and his Stellar business separately until the 1960s when the two were merged to form Stella-Meta Filters.

Many hundreds of Stellar filters were supplied to the South African mines, as well as to producers in Spain, Nevada, the Philippines, Sudan and elsewhere. The development of the more economical carbon-in-pulp process during the 1980s effectively ended the demand for new installations of the Stella-Meta zinc process, though a number of mines still use it.

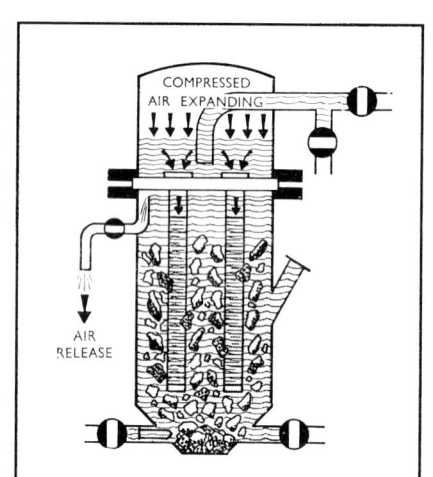

The Anderson shelter

Shortly before the start of the war, the Home Secretary Sir John Anderson wrote to his life-long friend William Paterson, seeking his urgent assistance with some form of protective device which could be issued to the public to provide protection in their own homes against air-raids. *"The only specification I gave to William Paterson...was that the material should be capable of being rapidly produced, that it should be of such dimensions and such a nature that two adults of ordinary strength without technical skill could quickly erect it and the cost should not exceed £2 per person sheltered..."*

Paterson responded quickly with a simple and inexpensive shelter which could be assembled easily in a garden. The shelter consisted of corrugated steel sheets rolled into a half cylinder which was then partly buried and covered with a thick layer of earth. Over three million shelters were supplied, and they provided substantial protection against all but direct hits and undoubtedly saved many lives. Paterson, together with Kerrison who had been associated with the project

Paterson's "Autopact" system. This used the feed inlet pressure to compress a volume of air in a chamber above the filter elements during the service cycle. By quickly opening a valve at the side of the filter, the compressed air expanded explosively to reverse the flow through the elements and dislodge the filter cake. This very simple mechanism was remarkably effective and has since been adapted by others to a variety of devices, including fat-fibre microfilters.

throughout, patented the device and assigned the patent to the nation. Some years after the end of the war Paterson was acknowledged publicly as the inventor, but only because a national newspaper had wrongly attributed the invention elsewhere. Inevitably, there were several rival claims regarding the origins of the shelter.

In 1944 William Paterson was accorded the honour of a Knighthood for his service to the country, and in 1945 when the war was over, he was able to publicise his group's involvement, saying, *"We were privileged to supply much of the necessary equipment to ensure this* [maintenance of an adequate supply to the fighting forces] *for the Army,*

Navy and Air Force in every theatre of war. Waterworks established at over a hundred military camps and Air Force depots in the Middle East, each capable of supplying from 100,000 to 2 million gallons daily, were fitted out with our equipment." He was no orator but the message is clear!

Concrete and code names

All of the water treatment companies were involved in war works and Candy's experience was typical. In addition to the military and armaments needs, there were many small contracts for pressure or gravity filters using concrete pipe sections, to treat water from rivers or lakes. These were installed at such places as Longleat, now famous for its safari park, and Tortworth Court, both large mansions that were to be used as hospitals for air-raid casualties, though in the event they were not needed.

Throughout East Anglia, the Scottish Border country, the Western Isles of Islay, Benbecula and Barra, and in other parts of the British Isles, airfields were developed quickly. Most had Candy treatment plants. They had high government priority and were given special code names that later were found to refer to the Battle of the Western Approaches, the Battle of Britain, and finally the invasion of Europe. Momentous times!

The Anderson shelter

This type of shelter was the most widely used domestic shelter at the height of the Blitz. It was built of corrugated iron sheets to provide a space about 6ft x 6ft x 6ft. It was set 3to 4 ft in the ground and covered with a minimum 15 inches of earth. The shelter could accept up to six people but normally had four bunks. Access was through the small aperture shown and which would have been at ground level. Despite its simple construction it could withstand almost any bomb blast except a direct hit. More than 2.3 million were built by September 1940.

Chapter 8

Pullen Candy retires

Pullen Candy, who had reached the age of 70 in 1941, carried on until the air-raids started in London. He then moved to Bath, and came to the office on two days a week. For the rest of the war he dealt with patents and acted as a consultant to the company. He formally retired in 1959 and resigned his position as chairman to Warwick Dufour.

Kampala, Uganda. The first four filters were installed in 1928. The works has since been extended several times.

9-RECOVERY AND THE MOVE TO PORTALS, 1945-1960

Export recovery

Once the war had ended, the companies needed to rebuild their overseas connections, as well as to complete the orders which had been delayed. An early success for Candy's was a new 6 mgd works for Launceston in Tasmania in 1948, to extend the original installations dating from the 20s.

Candy's were particularly well placed in the West African territories of the Gambia, Sierra Leone, the Gold Coast (Ghana), Nigeria and East Africa, as well as Cameroon, where they also took most of the available work. Nigeria was the largest market and already had some old Candy pressure plants of 1910 vintage, the biggest at Abeokuta. The surge of business after the war covered all regions, and important new orders were taken for Lagos, Ibadan, Kaduna and Onitsha, Sokoto, Kano, Minna, Ilorin and many other towns. Nigeria continued to be a good market for PCI until the 1980s, by which time the administration was in a state of disarray and trading became very difficult.

Flow meters at Torquay, Tottiford, early 1950s.

Many of the orders for the developing African colonial territories were received via the Crown Agents, and resulted in an increasing flow of local recruits for training in the UK, prior to returning to run the new works in their own countries. The trickle of trainees grew, and within a few years, African plant operators in parties of six were arriving for three-week training courses arranged by the company.

Chapter 9

By contrast, Paterson's continued to dominate much of the North African and Gulf markets, supplying major installations for Egypt, the Sudan, Iraq and Persia (Iran), and Paterson's companies continued to be the principal suppliers of treatment plants throughout the British Empire and Commonwealth via subsidiaries in Australasia, Malaya (Malaysia), Hong Kong, Singapore, India, Ceylon (Sri Lanka), South Africa and elsewhere. One of the many orders was an 8 mgd plant for Hong Kong, a replacement for equipment supplied during the war but presumably lost at sea.

However, except for a few notable orders, the substantial pre-war involvement in Europe declined and was never fully re-established, despite attempts in the 60s to enter the French, Italian and Spanish municipal markets. Local preference and the inability of most UK personnel to speak the country's language proved to be formidable barriers, and it was perhaps easier to concentrate on the Empire and Commonwealth.

Paterson's recovery in the UK

By 1945 Paterson's had a substantial backlog of work including an important 15 mgd contract for the South Staffordshire Seedy Mill plant (re-built by PWT in about 1992), a 3 mgd extension for Chester, a 6 mgd gravity filter plant for Worcester and a gravity filter plant to supply 2.5 mgd for the Bucks Water Board. These were all in progress by 1948. Ten new plants for paper mills were quickly booked, ranging from 0.5 to 5 mgd capacity, and these confirmed Paterson's as the premier supplier to this market.

Tees Valley and Cleveland, Broken Scar. One of the filter galleries. 1950, 13.2 mgd.

The post-war years were good to Paterson's, and in 1950 the company paid a dividend of fifteen percent plus a bonus of five percent. Over half the turnover was exported and the company had a three year order book, including the 13.2 mgd Broken Scar plant for the Tees Valley and Cleveland Water Board. The Stellar filters and chlorinator businesses were booming.

Then in 1951 with work at a record level for all the companies, the chairman of Portals joined Paterson's board, a move that began a gradual process of consolidation of the water treatment companies. Amongst other changes introduced as part of the Jubilee celebrations, a new staff pension scheme was adopted to replace an insurance scheme of twenty years standing. Paterson's also bought British Berkefeld Filters, the well-known makers of impregnated ceramic candle filters.

Bell's were also prosperous during the immediate post-war years, dealing with the pent-up demand for treatment plant for the paper, bleaching, dyeing and textile industries, and there were substantial extensions to their existing waterworks business. Bell's had always been stronger in the UK swimming pool market than either Paterson or Candy, with a turnover exceeding the others' combined pool business, and the company soon established a dominant position as supplier to the newly developed holiday camps. Their chlorine plant sales were also large compared with Candy's, and very profitable. However, this prosperity masked the underlying trend and by the mid-50s there were already signs that the Bell business was in decline.

New automatic plants

Considerable changes were about to take place in treatment plant design to meet the need for much larger works, and to cope with new arrangements for delivering and handling much larger quantities of chemicals. New chemicals such as flocculation aids, bringing with them their own handling problems, appeared on the market. At the same time a number of water suppliers were reviewing their manning practices as automated control and alarm systems became available and affordable.

Of particular note amongst these developments were two orders which

Denny, Broadside works, early 1950s. The handsome all black Lindars sequencer (front centre console) provided automatic backwash of the filters. This, with a similar unit supplied to Strensham, were probably the first examples of this type of control.

The Candy-Lockheed system was already well established as a reliable, manually controlled method of operating valves remotely, but the central automation was entirely new. With the new system, filter washing could be carried out under automatic control, triggered by a pre-set head loss, or by elapsed time, or by hand from the local filter control panels in the operating gallery if necessary.

Candy's negotiated in 1949 for the Stirling and Falkirk Water Board for their Broadside works, and the Strensham works for Coventry. Built at much the same time, these plants had many similar features, and for the first time, the gravity filters were supplied with fully automatic wash controls from a central console. There were also automatic features for chemical dosing control, with alarms in the works and repeater alarm signals in the Superintendent's house.

The new technology also spread to overseas plants and soon afterwards Candy Filters (New Zealand) supplied the first auto-wash plant for the Auckland City Ardmore plant. These early part-automated works heralded the arrival of widespread automation, culminating in a remarkable plant for Sheffield. However, reliability was patchy and many plant operators remained distrustful of the controls and over-rode them or restricted their use to periods when the works was manned.

Tertiary filtration

In 1949 the Luton Corporation Sewage Department was served an injunction ordering it to prevent the effluent from their sewage works from polluting the River Lee. The effluent was affecting fish in the river downstream of the works, and the town's councillors were ordered by the court to improve matters or face being thrown in gaol. Candy's put forward a pilot filter with a coarser than usual filter sand, rated at 200 gallons/sq.ft., which was run against a Glenfield & Kennedy micro-strainer. After about a year of trials, a 6 mgd gravity filter plant was ordered, so Candy's were back in the sewage business with a new development which was referred to as "tertiary filtration". Subsequently, three more filters were added to the plant which was converted to automatic wash a few years later.

The unusual filter house at Caithness, 1.25 mgd

The development is of interest only because it enabled sewage plants to achieve a "ten-ten" (ppm BOD and suspended solids) effluent reliably. The Luton plant never worked properly as the separate airscour and backwash system did not adequately clean the filter medium, so it gradually accumulated biomass on the sand grains. Later, Boby's introduced their Immedium upflow filters for the same duty but these were also not really satisfactory, and sewage effluent filters never worked properly until much later when combined wash downflow systems were introduced. The term "tertiary treatment" is now more widely understood to refer to the removal of nutrients.

Chapter 9

Longham

Pressure filter installations continued to flourish during this period, and Candy's installed thirty-three 8 ft. diameter filters at Rivelin (which had previously been equipped by Paterson's and Bell's) for the Sheffield Corporation, followed shortly afterwards by another seven, and the conversion to air scour of twenty-four Mather & Platt (Bell type) filters at the same site.

There were many similar works but perhaps the largest of all was for the Bournemouth Water Company at the picturesque if haphazard site at Longham. The competition to extend the original twenty Paterson filters had sparked off the first discussions between Paterson and Candy in 1932, when Candy won the contract. Subsequently, regular orders of batteries of Candy pressure filters, both vertical and horizontal, resulted in what is perhaps the largest pressure filter installation in the UK. Other sizeable pressure plants were installed at Torquay, Biggleswade, Caithness (Hoy) and Carlisle.

Kuala Lumpur, Bukit Nanas, 20 mgd, 1954.

Southern Africa

In Southern Rhodesia (Zimbabwe) and Northern Rhodesia (Zambia) where Paterson had supplied most of the treatment plants since 1928, the pattern was changing. Following the introduction of Candy's vertical flow tanks and gravity filters, most of the principal towns there were supplied with Candy equipment. Candy's also achieved a very strong position in South Africa with orders throughout the country, and with the new gold discoveries in the Orange Free State, were soon engaged in some very large plants for the mines.

As more materials became available from local manufacturers, less and less was shipped from the UK. This trend grew

Hong Kong, Tsun Wan, 40 mgd, 1955

Chapter 9

over the years, and since 1982 virtually everything has been supplied by PCI's South African subsidiary. The distance between the parent company and the subsidiary has also resulted in some of the technology developing separately; for example, the Rand Water Board's most recent plants have used fibre optic controls to overcome the problem of rats eating the PVC insulation of the conventional wiring supplied to earlier plants!

The Rand Water Board

The Rand Water Board has been a good customer for Candy's since the 1930s, when the first six Candy filters were added to the original twenty Paterson filters. Subsequently, Candy's/PCI secured virtually all the filter business up to the present time, with the exception of some experimental moving-bridge filters that were installed in the 1980s. Because of the scale of the operation it is worth recording its development, and ignore the chronology. Unfortunately, because the filters are covered, there are few interesting photos of the recent very big filter plants.

Vereeniging.
No 1 station, 1921 eight Paterson filters. 1924 ten Paterson filters. 1931-39 fifty-four Candy filters. These filters were backwashed from an overhead tank.
No 2 station, 1941-46-62 forty Candy filters, originally designed for backwash from an overhead tank.
No 3 station, 1982 seventy-two PCI filters for 900 Ml/d.

Zuikerbosch
No 1 station, just pre-war, seventy-two Candy filters.
No 2 station, 1966 sixteen 200m2 PCI filters. This was the last RWB plant fitted with double beat outlet valves. Thereafter, all the plants used butterfly-type outlet controllers with flow measurement by filter outlet weirs.
No 2a station, In the mid-1980s the RWB installed three types of moving bridge filters as a trial. PCI were unsuccessful (perhaps fortunately) with their own moving bridge offer as the test units did not wash properly, produced poor quality and have been abandoned.
No 3 station, 1972 sixty-four filters for 1200 Ml/d. PC(SA) are currently (1999) renewing the valves and automation for this plant and are about to start the replacement of the automation of the No 4 plant.
No 4a/b station, mid-80s, forty-eight filters for 600 Ml/d.
No 4c station, 1992 forty-eight 180 m2 filters for 1000 Ml/d.

Stark architecture at No.2 station, 1955 photo

All of these filters are still in service in 1999, although the very early plants urgently need re-furbishment. The chemical treatment is of interest as the raw water is treated with excess lime in the clarifiers, prior to filtration. This somewhat unusual approach, which was developed by the RWB, provides a reliable treatment for the very variable river water. The early plants have Candy hopper type settling tanks but the recent big plants use an RWB design of horizontal clarifier fitted with travelling scrapers. An interesting feature of these plants is the spiral flocculators which have a centre discharge.

Orange Free State Goldfields, Balkfontein, 1964, 30 mgd. The plant was refurbished in the 1980s.

The chemical handling revolution

The late 1950s saw a period of great commercial and technical change, and the start of the construction of a series of innovative large precipitation softening works and cooling water re-cycle plants for steelworks. Bell's continued to dominate the UK swimming pool market but were becoming less important as a major supplier.

It was a time of significant development in filtration and chemical plant automation and control technology, and the days of handling chemicals in sacks were coming to an end in the UK as bulk supplies with purpose-built road tankers were introduced. The first municipal bulk handling plant was probably that installed at Chelmsford. It appears that this may have resulted from a chance conversation between the deputy engineer and his father-in-law Harry Revill, who was an insurance inspector. Revill suggested the use of pneumatic transfer for moving dry chemicals and after some initial reluctance, British Rail were persuaded to transport Buxton lime in drop bottom L-type containers rather than paper sacks.

Lime plant, Sandford Mill, late 1950s

From this simple beginning, the chemical plant for treatment works developed rapidly. Bulk silos, chemical transfer pumps and blowers, batch weighing machines, solution density controllers etc., became standard features, with Candy's and Paterson's very much in the vanguard with a series of spectacular and innovative installations that extended the use of bulk chemical handling and introduced widespread automation to treatment plants.

Diddington. Batch weighers, "D-Mixers" and "G" pumps.

Pitsford softening plant

Two early examples of automated plants, largely foreshadowing the major works of the 60s and 70s, were Pitsford (Mid-Northants WB) and Hurleston (Mid and SE Cheshire WB).

Although very different, both these plants were the result of close co-operation and innovation between the water board engineer and the contractor's project director. Both plants were completed and commissioned around the end of the 50s. Both had fully automatic filter washing which had been introduced at Broadside and Strensham, but their innovations were in chemical storage, mechanical handling, chemical plant automation, and in the case of Pitsford, sludge drying, with centrifuges being used for the first time. The experience Candy's gained from building Pitsford led to many automated softening plants, and culminated in the spectacular works at Diddington and Elvington.

Weir Wood, East Sussex. 3 mgd. 1955

Chapter 9

Pitsford. The main pump house, a fine example of the traditional approach to waterworks design. The plant, built for the Mid-Northants Water Board in 1958 was remarkable for its innovative features. Like many of Griffiths' plants, it had to be designed before the nature of the raw water was known, and consequently included substantial flexibility in the treatment available. The plant was designed to treat 10 mgd of impounded river water by lime-soda softening. It is of particular interest for the extensive use of automated bulk chemical handling, and for the first time in the UK and perhaps anywhere, thickening of the softener sludge by centrifuges. Whilst Pitsford was not the first plant to use bulk handling of chemicals, it was the first to have full automation with all operations controlled from a central control room. At the time, the plant was probably the most advanced of its type anywhere.

The plant consisted of eight vertical flow softening and clarifying tanks with (for Candy's) an unusual chemical plant where milk of lime was converted to lime water with dilution and mixing vessels for each tank. The lime was measured by accurate batch weighers based on the systems used for concrete batch plants. An unusual feature of the plant was the client's requirement for 2" diameter glass chemical tubing for delivering the chemical solutions, which caused considerable installation problems.

Chapter 9

Musical chairs

With a very full order book and work coming in at an increasing rate, there was soon an urgent need for additional space for draughtsmen and technical staff. The whole Hanwell site, which had served the company well since 1924, had been re-zoned for housing, so in 1955/56 most of the works moved to a nearby industrial estate, and the stores went to Tonbridge in Kent. Extra office space was essential, and fortunately, Permutit owned premises at 21 The Mall, Ealing, which they were willing to sell for £17,000. The various support departments moved there, together with the industrial pumps staff.

However, the Industrial Pumps Division had always regarded itself as a separate operation, and in June 1958 it was set up as a subsidiary company, Metering Pumps Ltd, to concentrate on building the chemical pump business separately from Candy's.

Pressure versus vacuum chlorinators

With the advent of vacuum chlorinators there had been a gradual move away from the pressure chlorinators produced by Paterson's, Candy's, Bell's and others, on safety grounds, although the thousands that were in use in many parts of the world had given trouble-free (and largely safe) service over many years. Paterson's alone had supplied over ten thousand units, and their overseas subsidiaries had made many more. Bell's and Candy's had also supplied considerable numbers of their versions. However, it was obvious that the future lay with vacuum machines, and Wallace and Tiernan dominated the market for these in the UK. So Paterson's reached an agreement with Fischer and Porter of the USA to make their vacuum chlorinators under licence, and set up a new company called Chlorination Equipment Ltd (CEL). The designs proved to be less robust than the W&T machines and the products were always regarded as second best, despite heavy promotion by the parent company. CEL continued to make vacuum gas

Diddington, (Mid-Northants WB) softening plant, late 1960s. The "Blobins" and transfer compressors. The powdered chemicals were stored in bulk silos and transferred to "day" silos by "Blobins". These were vessels (at the base of the silos) which filled with the powder which was then transferred pneumatically. From the day silos screw conveyors delivered lime and soda ash to accurate batch-weighers. The measured quantity then discharged to "D-mixers" where the suspension was kept agitated, and dosed to the softeners by "G-type" metering pumps which are shown behind the operator (photo p.141). The entire plant was under automatic control.

machines and in the late 1980s the company name was changed to Portacel Ltd. The product range was then completely re-engineered and much improved.

Despite the dominance of the vacuum chlorinators, for several years PCI continued to supply pressure chlorinators to developing countries where the more rugged construction withstood the local conditions better than the more complicated and fragile vacuum machines.

Engineering hiccups

The history of engineering is littered with the results of poor decisions and the abandonment of the Lockheed valve operating system (referred to in chapter 5) was to cause much heartache. The Candy-Lockheed system was based on aircraft hydraulics and operated at high pressure, which meant that although the equipment worked superbly, it was somewhat inflexible, expensive and by the late 1950s, no longer competitive. Candy's decided to move to a low pressure system, resulting in a need for much larger hydraulic tubing and slave cylinders. The equipment worked well but the big mistake was to try and adapt a pneumatic system: despite endless modification of the seals etc., the system always leaked oil, which apart from being unsightly, was unacceptable to the

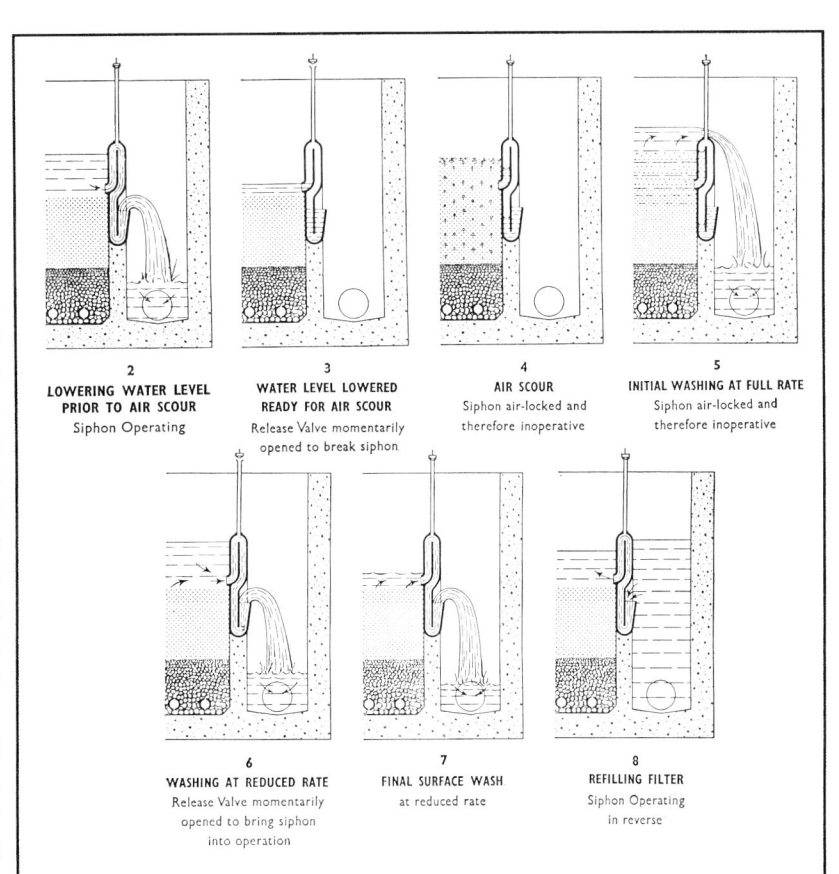

The Paterson filter siphon, introduced to counter Candy's filter technology, was an ingenious but expensive means of achieving both high and low level wash under automatic control.

High level filter washwater troughs, much favoured by American suppliers, had been scrapped by Candy in 1921 in favour of a low draw-off weir. For commercial reasons Paterson's did not wish to copy this but they recognised the advantage of the low-level washout and designed and patented their siphon draw-off system.

users. At the time, the rest of the industry used either water with consequent freezing and corrosion problems, or air, which required expensive drying to avoid freezing, and gave rise to control problems and valve slam. The obvious solution of using electric actuators was then too expensive, although it is now virtually standard throughout the industry.

At about the same time the company also decided that the Lindars sequencers were uncompetitive and so decided to design and make them in-house. A panel shop was set up which made many hundreds of systems until it was closed in the 1980s in favour of sub-contracting again.

Anthracite bi-filters

Frank Candy's compound filters were an early attempt to provide greater dirt storage without compromising the filtrate quality, but the real breakthrough came as a result of experimental work

Taunton, Maundown, showing the filter control consoles and slow-start controllers.

done at the Taunton Maundown works. This involved replacing the top twelve inches of the sand with a carefully graded hard anthracite. The difference in the density meant that a coarser grade layer could be retained on top of the filter bed to provide extra capacity for particulates and floc. The technique is now standard throughout the industry but was new at the time and it gave PCI a brief commercial advantage.

Elegant concrete cones

The steelworks cooling water treatment market was dominated by Paterson's until 1955 when Candy's were approached by John Summers Steelworks to design and provide a water recovery plant for their strip mills. These used large quantities of water for cooling the rolls, and the recycled water became contaminated with mill scale and oil. Candy's solution involved pumping the cooling water from the scale pits to sludge

The cooling water clarifiers, 80ft high, Richard Thomas and Baldwins, South Wales. Mid-1960s.

154

tanks fitted with horizontal chain scrapers and oil skimmers, and then clarification in vertical flow tanks before being cooled for re-use. There was nothing very new in this except the omission of filters, but the Summers plant was followed by others for the South Durham Iron and Steel Company at West Hartlepool, for Stewarts and Lloyds at Corby, and in 1960 for the giant Llanwern plant of Richard Thomas and Baldwin. (All these names have since disappeared with the shake-out of the steel industry in Britain.) The RTB contract included the civil works which were carried out by Holst as sub-contractors to Candy's. The installation was remarkable for the novel approach to the design of the clarifiers, and the exceptional size of the nine cone-shaped vertical flow tanks, 50 ft in diameter at the top and standing 80 ft high. Subsequently Candy's supplied a series of large installations for the Iron and Steel Corporation in South Africa, through their agents Dowson and Dobson.

Paterson Centrifloc clarifiers and pressure filters at Appleby Frodingham Iron and Steel Co. Late 1950s.

Candy's entry to the market signalled the end of Paterson's steelworks business and is an example of how the companies, although jointly owned, were allowed to compete. In later years a new generation of cooling water plants was installed for British Steel by Permutit using their patented Varivoid filters.

Portals take over

In January 1955 William Paterson retired, having been head of the company he had founded for fifty-three years. Like Candy, he hung on longer than perhaps was good for the business, even though Kerrison was the "eminence grise" actually running the company during the later years.

During Paterson's final years there had been a surge of very large orders, including in the UK, Hanningfield at 12 mgd, the 15 mgd Leeds Eccup

The signing ceremony, Guandu. E.Field-Reid representing Paterson's is third left, seated.

works and a plant for Colne Valley with a capacity of 24 mgd. The company had also been busy overseas with a 40 mgd works for Hong Kong, plants for Kuala Lumpur, Western Transvaal and a huge 264 mgd installation for Rio de Janeiro. The Rio order received substantial publicity as the Paterson contract exceeded £1 million which was a very big contract at the time.

Paterson's were very prosperous and Portals, who had a substantial presence in the paper industry, wanted to diversify and broaden their industrial base. Water seemed to be a sound second leg, so they bought a minority shareholding in Paterson's company, followed in 1957 by the purchase of the balance of the shares. As suppliers of banknote paper to the Bank of England which partly owned them, Portals were regarded as a "blue chip" company and a very attractive investor.

Rio de Janeiro, Guandu. Originally 88 mgd and later extended to 264 mgd. The filters are at the rear right of the picture.

From Paterson's side the desire to sell allegedly came from Lady Paterson who felt insecure about her future once Paterson retired. Curiously, the sale appears to have been conducted by Paterson himself, and without Kerrison's involvement or knowledge. This resulted in Portals getting a better bargain than they expected, as Kerrison seems to have thought that there was no need to inform Paterson of the financial details of the business, and had put aside substantial contract reserves of which Paterson was unaware. So Portals got a very good deal!

However, they were not familiar with the water business and only got involved in the company much later. It seems unlikely that Portals were aware that Paterson's were running into fundamental difficulties, as this was masked by the volume of work. They were not keeping up to date with changes in technology, although this might have been apparent from the age of the directors. By the early 60s it was clear that all was not well: Paterson's were more and more reliant on income from their subsidiaries rather than their own contracting activities, whereas Candy's were thriving and experiencing the start of the 60s investment boom.

Chapter 9

For some time relations between the two companies had been strained, with little love lost between the directors. It appears that the senior Paterson people looked down on the Candy directors and the Candy people regarded Paterson's directors as arrogant and conceited. What is certain is that the two were very different. Paterson's directors enjoyed a reputation as "bon viveurs" whereas the senior Candy men had an old fashioned, almost frugal view of how the company's money should be spent.

As Portals became aware of these differences and the increasingly apparent problems in the business, they insisted on removing the long standing trading constraints imposed by Kerrison, and this enabled Candy's very competent staff to blossom and take a commanding position in the UK market.

The Laverstoke Investment Trust (LIT) was set up to manage Portals' various water treatment companies, and this change resulted in the consolidation of the businesses in the early 60s. Paradoxically, the move brought little except turmoil for the following ten or more years, despite the departure of most of the Paterson senior managers, and the combined business turned out to be somewhat less than the sum of the parts. The amalgamation also opened the UK municipal market to Boby's, although this would have occurred anyway within a few years.

Hanningfield precipitation softening plant. 1952, extended to 21.5 mgd in 1958. The four Accentrifloc softeners supplied the gravity filters in the centre. Lime was supplied as quicklime and crushed and slaked in the middle building in the front. The softened water was stabilised using carbon dioxide from coke burners which also heated the building. Subsequently, the plant was extended with Candy-type precipitation softening tanks (left of the picture) in the late 60s, and (by then under French ownership) entirely re-built by Degremont in the 90s.

Portals ownership provided a very strong balance sheet which enabled PCI in later years to bid for and win a series of very big and ultimately profitable contracts. Without this financial backing it is unlikely that the company would have been able to support the bonds and finance required for these huge contracts.

The late 1950s

In 1958 the money crises and controls on imports meant few orders for Candy Filters (NZ). A very different situation prevailed in West and East Africa. With the completion of several contracts in Nigeria and with others under construction, Candy's undertook a major review of the existing installations and the future market. From this they secured substantial orders for refurbishing many of the plants, and in an attempt to hold off the increasing competition the exercise was repeated in other African territories.

At home, the famous Holborn Restaurant at 129 Kingsway was sold in 1955, and the building was demolished. By 1958 the new building on the site was completed, and it would provide a home for Paterson's until the merger with Candy's ten years later. This brought together all members of the staff, until then scattered in various premises nearby. It was a well-designed office complex with 100,000 square feet of accommodation on eight floors above a bank, with staff canteens and car park, and was conveniently placed for contact with the London-based consulting engineers, although most of these would move out of London within the next fifteen years.

Paterson's continued to dominate a number of overseas markets and they took most of the work in Hong Kong, Iran, Iraq, Egypt, the Sudan and Brazil, almost certainly due to the strength of their local agents. In the home market they obtained important contracts for the Tees Valley Water Authority at Lartington, a 10 mgd plant for Southampton Testwood, the River Dove Melbourne scheme and a 16 mgd works at Kingston-on-Hull.

Modernising the Paterson filter controls resulted in the development of the "Stack controller". This used an hydraulic/pneumatic device with balanced diaphragms to control the filter outlet valve in response to flow differential, level, and loss of head signals. Paterson's wanted to avoid using the Candy-Lockheed system, but the Stack controller was never totally satisfactory and the very large air-operated slave cylinders used for operating valves and penstocks were difficult to control and tended to slam. In later years the Stack controller developed into the PCI "AH" controller which gave way to computers.

However, the new Chlorination Equipment Ltd company was still not competing effectively with Wallace and Tiernan, and this affected Paterson's chlorine plant business as the sales of pressure-type chlorinators were by then restricted to those industries requiring a dry gas application.

In the industrial field too, Paterson's saw their market declining as they had lost the steelworks water recovery business as well as the last of the period's petrochemical water treatment plant orders to Candy's. Only the Stellar business and to a lesser extent, the Metafilter beer sales offset their industrial decline.

River Dove WB. Melbourne, 7 mgd, 1956.

Oscar Kerrison

By 1955, following the retirement of Sir William Paterson, O.C.Kerrison formally took over as MD of Paterson's. He was perhaps the last to leave his mark, having been with the company for forty-two years, and he had acted as managing director during the previous few years as Paterson approached retirement. Kerrison was primarily a businessman and was regarded as very tough. He had overseen the acquisition of Candy's and Bell's in 1934 and had always managed the relationships with Paterson's subsidiaries, though he was not often seen at Hanwell and Dufour rarely visited the Paterson offices. Nevertheless, he maintained a good relationship with Dufour over many years, and any difficulties that arose when both companies were competing for work, were apparently soon resolved. He is recalled as being very civilised and cultured and enjoyed good food and wine.

End note

So by the early 60s both Kerrison and Coulson had retired, together with

Left to right, Smalley (chief engineer) Kerrison, Burdett (chief draughtsman) Coulson (sales director) Field-Reid (sales director) about 1959.

Chapter 9

William Smalley, the chief engineer. They had lived through a period of continual growth of the company and had contributed greatly to its success. With their departure, Paterson's lost the strong management it needed for long term survival, and their successors were to preside over the merger and in practice, absorption by Candy's within fewer than ten years.

Horace Coulson

Coulson was a small, pugnacious man but he was a heavyweight who was responsible for much of Paterson's success both at home and overseas. With Eric Field-Reid he provided the company's main sales strength over a long period, and his legacy is spectacular. He was responsible (with others) for a string of major plants including Broken Scar, Lartington, Hanningfield, Langford, Colne Valley, Clay Lane and many others.

During the war Coulson, then a captain in the army, was involved in the construction of coastal defences, for which he was awarded a military OBE. He is remembered as a very pleasant man who maintained excellent relationships with his many customers. He owned one of the rare Armstrong-Siddeley cars. He retired in about 1962, but like his colleague Kerrison he should have left sooner than he did.

The small Clorocel.

Brine prepared from salt in the vessel at the back is electrolysed to sodium hypochlorite. Thousands of these small units were made for ships, trains, military water sets etc. Paterson's also developed a much larger system and sold this to a number of major coastal power stations, mainly in Italy, for treating the cooling water. However, the design was fundamentally flawed and unable to compete in the long term. An attempt to develop a new linear flow cell in the 1970s was not pursued due to other priorities.

Chapter 9

Centrifugal Balancer driving "G" pumps at Torquay, Tottiford. Late 1950s.

Typical of the ingenious devices invented by the specialist water treatment contractors was the Centrifugal Balancer, designed by Jenkyn-Thomas in the early 1950s. The Balancer was designed to use the differential generated by an orifice plate or venturi tube to provide a simple method of flow proportioning chemical feeders or pumps. The fundamental problem arises because almost all flow measuring devices produce a signal which varies as a square law, whereas the outputs of most other equipment vary directly with their speed. The difficulty had traditionally been overcome by using cams or other mechanical devices, all subject to wear and requiring the zero to be set accurately. The Balancer (a special form of centrifugal pump) overcame all of these problems by matching the venturi differential with its own square law characteristic and via a pressure relay and servo-motor, adjusted a variable gearbox driving the Balancer. The drive speed of the Balancer was thus proportional to flow and therefore could be used to drive the chemical feeders. The device was inherently self-adjusting so it was not affected by wear or zero drift, and had a built-in hydraulic feedback to prevent hunting.

The Centrifugal Balancer appeared too late and was installed in only a few works before being superseded by electronic square root extractors acting on variable speed motors.

Chapter 9

YESTERDAY

As far as 129 Kingsway is concerned, the site goes back 2,000 years and more, when early Britons fished in the waters of the Hole-Bourne and made merry on its green banks. As did their Roman, Saxon and Norman successors.

The actual site of 129 Kingsway is first identified around 1520 as "The Pightles" a part of the Crown pastureland known as "Purse Field" which ran west from Lincoln's Inn Fields. The "Pightles" was developed by Sir John Cornwallis, who leased it in 1613, and by 1650 the first frontage of High Holborn and little Queen Street (now Kingsway) had been erected. Initially residential, later on small shops appeared, and by 1840, the corner housed a variety of trades from a veterinary instrument maker, to a perfumer and hairdresser and also the National Baths.

Within a short time the National Baths had been replaced by a landmark of Victorian London- the Casino de Venise. For nearly 40 years it thrived as the Capital's best conducted dance hall complete with Turkish Smoking Salon and resident orchestra.

Fashions changed, the dance hall lost popularity and was superseded by the Holborn Restaurant, which was to enjoy international renown. Many will recall its heavily ornate style of interior decoration- antique marble dados, Venetion enamel mosaics, Derbyshire alabaster ceilings, Rouge Incarnat pilasters. And remember too, the famous "Long Bar"- one of the best known rendezvous in the English-speaking world.

The Holborn's reputation was based on good food at economic prices. A menu of 1884 lists a seven-course dinner (Potages, Poissons, Entrees, Releves, Entremets, Pouding, Glace)- all for 3s and 6d!

The policy found favour, for when the grill room was added in 1885, it claimed to dine 2,000 persons at once.

In 1955, the building was sold and thereafter demolished.

10-PATERSON CANDY INTERNATIONAL 1960-1970

The 60s ushered in a time of such change in the social and industrial make-up of the United Kingdom that it is necessary to pause for a moment and take a long view of what happened in the municipal market over the next twenty years. During this period the demand for water in England and Wales increased from 2400 mgd in 1960 to 3600 mgd by 1984 whilst the technology changes that started in the late 1950s entered almost all the major schemes. The ravages of inflation called for imaginative financial solutions, but above all there was a huge increase in the demand for plant that wasn't to be seen again until the 1990s.

Netley Mills, West Surrey W.B., 1 mgd. This amusing "round-house" filter arrangement caused some headaches with the flanged cast iron piping.

Major changes in the UK

By the beginning of the 1960s major changes were taking place throughout the UK that were to have wide ranging effects on water treatment plant contractors and designers. The last vestiges of post war deprivation had disappeared and material prosperity was rising throughout the country. New houses were being built at an unprecedented rate and domestic washing machines were becoming commonplace, as were garden sprinklers. The first supermarkets were beginning to appear while labour generally was becoming more costly as the overall standard of living rose steadily throughout the country.

As a consequence, the demand for water accelerated. Small parochial water authorities joined together to form larger units, the regional water boards. Many of the smaller (and higher quality) water supply sources were abandoned in favour of sources typically capable of providing tens of millions of gallons a day, rather than tens of thousands. Such sources tended to be on the lower reaches of the larger rivers, so were more highly polluted than the sources they superseded. Environmental pressures prevented the construction of upland impounding reservoirs from which the public had traditionally been excluded, on the grounds that large clean water sources were inviolable. Instead, the major impounding reservoirs became recreational lakes and flow/regulating/balancing sources, to reduce the peaks of wet weather flow and increase the troughs of dry weather flow. In short, the water supply engineers could no longer keep the impounding reservoirs for their exclusive use.

The combined effect of all these influences was that the water supply authorities (normally very conservative-minded bodies) became receptive to plant designs requiring little or no manual labour, of generally far greater capacity than previously, and capable of producing high grade potable water from sources polluted to a degree that before the war most engineers would have gone to almost any length to avoid them.

Candy filters at Tewkesbury. 20 mgd. early 60s.

The growth in water demand continued throughout the 1960s and into the next decade. By the middle of the 70s the new Regional Water Authorities (RWAs) had been formed, bringing with them top-heavy and complex administration. From the water treatment plant contractor's viewpoint the largely all-powerful Chief Engineer (and Manager) or his New Works Engineer, was side-lined, and many experienced and capable men were retired early, to the industry's loss. They were replaced by excessively large committees, fuelled by competition between "Division" and "Headquarters" with frequent tension between the two. Design by committee became the normal approach, and this protracted and frustrating change sometimes slowed down the design and execution of new works. Companies like PCI tended to lose from these new arrangements as the personal relationships disappeared and the market opened to new competitors. At the same time inflation and stop-go economics were rife, the latter to such an extent that on one occasion all of PCI's UK contracts were stopped for six months!

Hong Kong, Shek Pik. 35 mgd. Early 1960s

Chapter 10

The increase in water demand then slowed down and eventually almost ceased; nevertheless for two consecutive decades during the 60s and 70s the capacity and complexity of water treatment plants grew at a rate that had never been seen before. These plants called for an overall design capability to cope with chemical storage, mechanical handling and automation on a scale that was undreamed of in UK waterworks practice. At the start of the 60s, Candy's (then PCI) were the best equipped of the UK contractors to meet this need. Other firms, notably Degremont-Laing, came to the fore later on, but for some fifteen years PCI dominated the supply of public water treatment plants in the UK. The leading exponent of the new approach was Griffiths, and to a lesser although significant extent, Aitken. There were also some half dozen or so younger men coming on in Paterson's and Candy's who were to continue the approach when these two left the scene at the end of the 60s. The period from the late 50s to perhaps the mid 1970s was one of the most brilliant in the company's history.

Liverpool, Huntington. View over the Accentrifloc clarifiers. 72 mgd. 1960s

Inevitably, mistakes were made. Much equipment designed initially for industrial use was adapted for waterworks use, not always satisfactorily. In fact such adaptations were probably the cause of the largest number of problems. One high quality instrument widely used in aircraft proved unreliable in water treatment plants. It was not appreciated that being designed to withstand constant vibration, the lack of it could be the source of problems!

The RWAs themselves were slow to learn that although automation, mechanical handling and sophisticated instrumentation could reduce drastically the number of staff required, those remaining needed to be much more highly skilled than previously.

In the 1960s the common view was that precipitation softening was an attractive approach to river water treatment, possibly as much to assist purification as for the domestic benefit of soft water. The consumption of chemicals, mainly hydrated lime and granular sodium carbonate, was enormous, and it produced a corresponding

ICI Severnside, precipitation lime softener and filters. Early 1960s.

volume of sludge that created a serious disposal problem for many works. In some cases excessive raw water chlorination was adopted; a dubious practice from a water treatment point of view and undoubtedly damaging to equipment. It is probable that this over-reliance on chlorine sprang from an inherent suspicion of surface water directly abstracted from major rivers.

Some lessons were too well learned. Many plants were designed and built in two stages, with stage two usually doubling the output. More than once, as soon as stage 1 was commissioned, the plant was running above its design capacity and stage 2 had to be put in hand immediately, instead of five or ten years later. Certainly in one or two cases the contractor never left the site between commissioning stage 1 and equipping stage 2. The result of these experiences was that by the 1970s some plants were being grossly over-designed at stage 1, resulting in the demand at start-up being perhaps ten per cent of design. In these circumstances instrumentation and flow control systems rarely functioned satisfactorily.

MWB, Coppermills, 154 mgd pre-filters. late 1960s.

One 1970s plant in the north-east was designed for four stages of development so that the ultimate output would be four and possibly five times that of stage 1. What was overlooked was the fact that the equipment, particularly the controls and instrumentation allowed for at stage 4 was of the same vintage as stage 1 and therefore most unlikely still to be available.

Fifty years earlier, the bulk of the control equipment and instrumentation was made by the contractor and was much simpler. From the late 60s onwards, virtually all such items were procured from specialist suppliers and were subject to increasingly rapid design change, and obsolescence.

The clients

At the start of this period there were some 150-200 statutory water supply authorities in England and Wales. In Scotland, water was the responsibility of local authority departments which were later formed into area water boards. Twenty-five percent of water in England was supplied by water companies in 1960 and the same applied in 1980.

Chapter 10

The chief executive was invariably a chartered civil and water engineer, who frequently employed a New Works Engineer, similarly qualified, in charge of a New Works Department. Many major new schemes and treatment plants were designed in co-operation between the New Works Department and the specialist contractors without recourse to consulting engineers. Later, consultants became more widely employed for water treatment schemes and many of the clients' New Works Departments were deliberately run down or dismantled, prior to the formation of the RWAs in 1973.

Major changes came in with the RWAs. Their boundaries largely coincided with those of the old River Boards, and followed the catchment areas of the major rivers. Each RWA took in water supply, sewerage and sewage disposal (the latter woefully behind the times and still inadequate in many areas, twenty-five years later), together with river management. They were also the policemen of water course pollution, an anomaly that was not resolved until the industry was privatised in 1989, and the National Rivers Authority was set up as an independent body.

The Elvington works is part of the Yorkshire Derwent scheme and supplies the City of Sheffield. The plant was conceived in 1958 to clarify and soften a coloured surface water, with an ultimate capacity of 25 mgd. The plant was the first fully automated works anywhere designed to operate unmanned at night and at weekends. There were two parallel streams, one to clarify and the other to soften the waters to be blended and filtered. This was Griffiths' approach for producing a stable water from lime softening, and the design provided considerable flexibility to deal with a widely varying raw water. At a time before solid state devices and computers were available, Elvington had a remarkable degree of automation, and the softening process was controlled by automatic titrators developed for the project by George Kent Ltd, although these were never reliable.

Sheffield, Elvington, view of the chemical house across the softening tanks

The plant was extended in 1966 and again in 1977 to 45 mgd, and in the 1990s it was substantially modernised and the lime-soda process was replaced by partial softening with caustic soda.

Elvington was built at the height of the Cold War and the filters were covered with a wooden structure, allegedly to keep out nuclear fallout!

167

Chapter 10

A running start

The 1960s started well for both Paterson's and Candy's, and both companies had a core of very competent engineers. Both had a substantial backlog of work and the promise of a period of major orders. British influence over much of the world gave them a strong advantage and enabled them to secure some big contracts. In the UK and overseas the companies were generally highly regarded by the water suppliers, and their treatment expertise was viewed as second to none. This underlying strength enabled Candy's/PCI to flourish and to take advantage of the huge amount of work on offer during the decade, and at the same time introduce much new technology.

Ion-exchange follies

Although Candy's were best known in the municipal sector, they had a substantial industrial business at the time, and they bid for and won a contract to supply a large automatic mixed-bed ion-exchange plant for a paper maker in Scotland. The project went wrong as a result of inadequate process knowledge, and the plant suffered from fundamental bottom distribution problems because it was built with a porous ceramic floor which scaled with calcium sulphate and could not be cleaned. This design error was surprising given the deep understanding of filtration technology in the company, and the bottoms were replaced by a very expensive "Neverclog" floor with special support nozzles, designed by Jenkyn-Thomas. The replacements worked very well and a second plant was ordered shortly afterwards, but the venture into the ion-exchange market never seriously challenged Permutit.

Ind Coope brewery, Wrexham. Filters and de-alkalisation for brewing water. This fine plant was one of the few Candy ion-exchange plants. Early 60s.

UK Successes

Perhaps somewhat surprisingly, given the disruptions caused by the office, works and stores moves, and the amalgamation of the companies, Candy's enjoyed a very successful decade of municipal contracts. This was in no small measure due to the single-mindedness of Griffiths and the other project engineers as well as the minimal impact the overall changes within the company had on the organisation at Ealing.

The advent of the automated works ushered in by the Pitsford plant suited Candy's approach and Griffiths and his colleagues built on this to secure a series of spectacular and complex plants, including those for Cardiff at Llandegfedd, the Mosswood works for Sunderland and South Shields, Diddington, and the controversial plant for Nottingham at Church Wilne, built to treat the very polluted water from the Derwent. The very advanced and complex plant at Elvington was also built in the early 60s, and the automation for this and the Diddington works proved to be very demanding for the company's relatively new electrical team. Fortunately, perhaps, these contracts did not include the civil works.

The early 60s also saw the completion of a number of very large works such as Coppermills, Huntington, Hanningfield, Clay Lane, the River Dove scheme; and overseas, Johore River, Sha Tin, Kirkuk, and the huge plant for Rio de Janeiro, as well as many others. But as the decade progressed and the Paterson order bank declined, work shifted almost entirely to Candy's.

Much of the success resulted from a long association with both the clients and the consultants retained for the projects, an approach which was to continue until the re-organisation of the water industry. By then, Griffiths' relationship with the other directors had deteriorated and he resigned at the end of 1966 to join Binnie and Partners.

Diddington

The main control panel, designed shortly before the advent of the first solid-state devices. Some 5,000 Post Office relays were housed in a space under the panel floor. This plant had a degree of complexity which severely taxed Candy's automation skills. The controls were designed to operate with two parallel power grids for security, and following a power failure all machines and other power consumers were separately timed to restart in cascade, a design nightmare for the mechanical timer and relay systems then available. This sort of nonsense, imposed by the consultants, unfortunately affected the company's approach and competitivity for some years.

Whilst the Lindars sequencer set a new standard in filter automation, its successor, designed in-house, introduced new features. The Candy "Queue" system washed filters in their order of priority by headloss and reviewed this as each was washed. This was achieved using timers and relays, no mean feat in those pre-computer days. The first "Full Queue" sequencer was installed at Bolton Wayoh and became the company's standard for the next ten years.

Chapter 10

Metering Pumps Ltd

The "M" type chemical pumps originally designed by Simmons before the Second War were still in production, together with some newer models to extend the range. However, the need for in-house manufacture which had grown from the non-availability of chemical dosing pumps earlier in the century, no longer applied, and several commercial makes were available to all the contractors. Metering Pumps Ltd had effectively been independent of the main business for some time and with the various workshop moves, production of the pumps was transferred to the under-utilised Bell's works at Manchester. Not long afterwards the business was sold to MonoPumps and PCI ceased any manufacturing. This meant that the workshop became just a jobbing shop, more or less completing the cycle back to where it started about sixty years earlier.

21 The Mall

When the adjacent offices in No. 22 The Mall, Ealing, became vacant, a property company came forward with a scheme for re-developing the whole site to meet the company's needs. No. 21 as the site was then called, became Candy's home at the end of 1962.

Mid-Northants WB, Great Ouse Scheme, Diddington, the filter gallery. Note the servo-motors added to the slow start units to operate the 15 inch Modules. This sort of modification signalled the limit of Pullen Candy's Module.

Paterson Candy International

A precursor to the merger of Paterson's and Candy's was the removal of the trading constraints - "to prevent over-trading" - imposed by Paterson's management on Candy's. This enabled Candy's to expand rapidly in the early 60s to meet the market needs in the UK. Quite apart from the apparent business logic, this was one of a number of factors which led to the amalgamation of the companies following the controlling purchase by Portals. At the time, although Paterson's had substantial work-in-progress, they were struggling to be profitable and this, coupled with the retirement of Kerrison and other strong managers, led Portals to merge the two companies.

Chapter 10

The formal amalgamation was preceded by a transitional agreement between Paterson's and Candy's on work sharing, that provided for all export work to be handled by both companies under a joint commercial name, Candy Paterson International. There would be common overseas agents with the territories allocated between the two companies on the basis of their local commercial strength and this arrangement was implemented but the name was changed to the more fluid Paterson Candy International.

In December 1965, the Candy Filter Company was formally re-named, the capital base re-structured and the assets, liabilities and work in progress of the Paterson Engineering Company were transferred to the new PCI. With the change, Warwick Dufour handed over to Leo Rabeneck who became MD of the new company.

Nottingham, Church Wilne, 9.8 mgd, mid 1960s.

Despite the upheaval of the merger and the inevitable power struggle at the top, the companies managed to secure important new orders although there was a price to be paid, and many of the Paterson contracts suffered serious disruption and delays which must have sorely tried the patience of a number of good friends. There was much confusion, in-fighting and many pointless staff moves and losses to the competition over the next five years, as the offices and works were re-organised in a somewhat unplanned way.

The initial year of PCI was not profitable as the combined overheads were inevitably too high, a problem which Rabeneck delayed tackling until 1968, by which time it was very serious. However, he then brought the company back into profit where it remained until his departure in the mid-70s. When he left, the overheads again got out of control, masked by large contracts from

Cardiff, Llandegfedd. The elegant all-white control room. Mid-1960s.

which too much had been taken (appendix). Profitability returned with the Karkh contract and this supported PCI until the late 80s.

The company's survival of the problems resulting from the merger was due mainly to Candy's sustained success and growth over a number of years, both in the municipal field and with industrial work. By contrast, Paterson's had relied increasingly on profits from subsidiaries, service charges, etc., and were not making sufficient profit from their contracting business.

The Loch Eck works, late 60s, showing the unusual covers over the settling tanks.

At about the time of Candy's move to Ealing, Paterson's also decided to re-locate their offices from 129 Kingsway, and they drew up plans to lease purpose-built premises in the new industrial complex at Basingstoke. It appears that the overall plan included moving the Candy business there, although this was kept very secret. However, during the initial merger discussions, Dufour (who was to become chairman of both companies) considered the plans to be far too ambitious and he halted the project and bought Winchfield Lodge, a large house near Basingstoke, to accommodate the staff who had agreed to move. Perhaps he realised that the move would be disastrous for Candy's just as it turned out to be for Paterson's. At this late stage, Portals "offered" their Laverstoke Mill site which had buildings that would be empty in the near future and could be adapted for the Paterson staff, and the plan was again changed.

The need to rationalise the various works and stores owned by both companies led to a new works at Southall, with stores at Tonbridge, but this move turned out to be transitional, and the PCI works and stores ended up at Laverstoke towards the end of the decade.

How all this confusion arose no longer matters but it caused huge disruption as contracts under design were moved first from Kingsway to Winchfield Lodge and then to Laverstoke, with substantial losses of key

Sunderland and South Shields Water Co., Mosswood. 23 mgd. 1966. This aerial photo illustrates the very functional approach for which it gained a design award.

staff on the way. The Laverstoke site later became the offices of the Industrial Division of PCI, although by then there was little work in hand and a depressed market. Fortunately, most of the Candy contracts continued without too much upset, and the key municipal staff at Ealing got on with the job of securing some spectacular successes which kept the company going.

Paterson's Stellar Filter Division was not included in the amalgamation of the two companies, but was merged with the Metafiltration Company to form Stella-Meta Filters Ltd (SMF), and based at Laverstoke. SMF later became a division of Permutit for a few years before being separated in the late 80s as a company, which in the 90s became part of PCI Membranes Ltd.

Clatto treatment plant, Dundee. Early 70s.

Leo Rabeneck

Leo Rabeneck was an unusual man to find in an engineering company. Surrounded by legend, he was a White Russian who spoke seven, some say nine, languages and knew the best restaurants in all the major cities of Europe. He certainly spoke German, French, Spanish, Italian and Russian fluently, and for more than one international congress he provided the simultaneous translation for the Russian speakers. He was charming, civilised and excellent company but also adventurous and enterprising in business, sometimes taking risks which with hindsight might seem foolhardy.

Unlike his colleagues at Candy's, he did not attend university but took a City and Guilds qualification which provided his introduction to Candy's during vacation work in the test plant. He joined the firm in about 1937 and like his colleagues was quickly exposed to most aspects of the business. In 1947 Rabeneck went to India to take over from Aitken as MD of the local company, and returned to the UK by 1960 to join the Board, although he continued to supervise the links with the Indian company. The next few years saw him understudying Dufour whilst dealing with industrial projects, personnel matters and publicity.

Leo Rabeneck

Chapter 10

In 1965 Leo Rabeneck took over as MD of the newly constituted Paterson Candy International and brought his own style to the business. During the late 60s and early 70s he managed the company very well, juggling carefully husbanded reserves to pay for the consequences of the rapid expansion of the 1960s and the filter floor problems. At the same time he managed the development and successful introduction of the new FB clarifier. Without him the company might have disappeared from the industry. In 1976 he moved to Portals Water Treatment's central group as overseas director, as part of a management rotation scheme. After a brief stay in Singapore, he died prematurely in 1981.

The "Declared Contract"

One of the mechanisms employed by PCI to obtain a major part of the work in the 60s construction boom was the "Declared Contract", a negotiated contract idea introduced by Rabeneck to shorten the bidding period. It was successfully applied to many new schemes including several turn-key works built in joint venture with Holst's. In essence, the company provided an agreed method for costing the contract, based on detailed designs done by PCI, and gave the purchaser the opportunity to check PCI's records to satisfy himself that the basis was equitable. What was unusual was that the formula applied at the tender stage and once the scope and price had been agreed, PCI (and Holst's) took the design and purchasing risks, so it was not a cost-plus contract, except where agreed extras arose. In the 1990s a variety of negotiated contract formulae appeared as the newly privatised utilities rushed to begin huge programmes, and with a few notable exceptions, PCI's version has fallen into disuse.

East Surrey Water Co. Bough Beech. 6 mgd. Late 60s.

Inflation and "Split Contracts"

The financial problems arising from retentions or incomplete contracts had concerned the company for some time. In particular, the site construction of some overseas contracts was subject to delays arising from a variety of causes often not of the company's making, so the idea of splitting the contract into design, supply and erection came about. This device permitted the company to take profit on the

174

early parts as they were completed, leaving a provision for the erection costs to be expended when they were incurred. The approach entered the company's practice in the late 60s and in general it was operated sensibly, given the frequently extended contract periods, although there was always the temptation to take all the profit prematurely and leave the site and warranty costs for the future to deal with.

From the late 60s many of the UK contracts included an inflation clause usually based on the BEAMA formula which could and did double the value of the contract during the very high inflation of the early 70s. Most overseas contracts, however, were more precarious, as few clients would accept anything except a fixed price. These projects needed a strong nerve at the tendering stage to ensure that future inflation was allowed for in the pricing.

Paterson Candy Holst (PC-H)

Both Paterson's and Candy's had undertaken design and construct (packaged deal) contracts for many years. The attraction to the client was the saving in time compared to the conventional approach of separate contracts for the M & E and the civil works. Against this was the lack of opportunity for the client's in-house staff to develop their experience in planning, designing and supervising major capital works, and for this reason a number of engineers preferred the traditional approach.

The basis of the design and build approach was that the process contractor took the civil contractor as a direct sub-contractor, and so assumed the financial risk for what was usually a much larger element than his own supply. Almost no water engineers would consider the process contractor other than as the main contractor, and to provide for the inevitable cost over-runs both

The Glendevon works set in the Ochill hills about 40 miles north west of Edinburgh. Capacity 20 mgd of direct filtration onto sand/anthracite filters. Completed 1978.

Paterson's and Candy's added a fifteen percent provision to the civil price; lesser amounts invariably resulted in burned fingers. However, it was essential to work with a civil contractor who had his own competent in-house designers for water retaining structures, and there were three firms who normally bid to PCI, with the winner being retained for the packaged offer.

In the 70s two influences emerged to upset this not entirely satisfactory situation. Firstly, the running down of the water suppliers' New Works Departments in the year prior to and immediately following the formation of the RWAs significantly increased the packaged-deal market (but correspondingly reduced the amount of conventional work). Secondly, the arrival of Degremont-Laing heralded a company with a major competitive edge compared with the old main contractor and sub-contractor approach.

For PCI the situation came to a head in 1973 over the tender for the Glendevon works, as the project included a fair-sized reservoir. Having recently successfully completed the extensions to Broadside with Holst's as the civil sub-contractor, it seemed logical to extend the relationship and form a joint company for the Glendevon scheme. The key to the success of Paterson Candy Holst was the 50-50 basis of the agreement, an arrangement that can only work if there is close co-operation and understanding at board level in both companies as well as in the design offices. Holst's Watford office had a quite unusual proportion of designers who were members of the Institution of Structural Engineers and the combination with PCI's process and system engineering was unmatched.

Barcombe Mills, the chemical house. 11 mgd. This plant was the first supplied with the then very new solid-state control equipment. PCI made the commercial error of trying to commission the automatic controls and succeeded in connecting mains voltage to the 24v DC supply, to the advantage of the panel supplier!

PC-H enjoyed a very high success ratio - around one in two - and the order for Glendevon was followed by many others including Barcombe Mills, Juas, Wayoh, Portsmouth, Hardham, Pembury and Glenfarg. The basis of Paterson Candy Holst was of course, the trust between individuals in both companies and with their retirement, the relationship declined and ended with an acrimonious dispute over work at Newport's Court Farm plant.

Bristol, Purton, 24 mgd precipitation softening plant. Ordered 1970.

In the 1990s the 50-50 joint venture was successfully revived with other civil contractors for some specific projects, including the Walton floatation plant and the Overton works at Greenock in Scotland

Chapter 10

The Wind of Change

Overseas, Harold Macmillan's Wind of Change was blowing through the British world, with a profound effect on the fortunes of the companies. In many countries, much of the work now had to be done locally, and this reduced the involvement of the parent companies, forcing them to find new markets. Throughout much of Africa, the Near and Far East, allegiances started to change and the commercial rectitude which by and large had underpinned the previous administrations gave way to a new order to which PCI would struggle to adapt.

Suva, Fiji. 4 mgd. 1960s.

Much of both Paterson's and Candy's overseas coverage was through the traditional agencies, an inexpensive arrangement which depended on the enthusiasm of the local organisation and the support provided from the UK but this approach was becoming increasingly unsatisfactory. Australia was a case in point, where Candy's arrangements had not worked for some time and Dufour planned to start a local company. However he postponed this and instead appointed a new agent, hoping that this would lead in due course to financial control. In the event, PCI did not have a local presence until the early 70s when Portals acquired Boby's, and William Boby (Australia) joined the group. By then the UK input was limited to some design and the provision of free technology, which brought little profit to PCI.

Elsewhere, change was also needed. Both Paterson's and Candy's had companies in India, as well as the local Jewell Filter Company. It was clear that they should be amalgamated, though each had a separate area of influence. The Jewell company was closed and a senior manager appointed to run the remaining two companies, but final amalgamation was postponed due to resistance from the Indian authorities. It was becoming increasingly difficult to re-patriate profits, so in 1969 the companies were sold to Gannon Dunkerley, and became competitors to PCI for a while in East and Central Africa. In 1981 Paterson Engineering (India) was wound up; Candy Filters (India) became bankrupt in 1988, bringing to an end the direct interest Paterson started in 1920. From then on, PCI

Chapter 10

was to be little involved, other than with two contracts for Bombay, both of which were financially disastrous.

Paterson's, Bell's and Candy's also had separate agents in Malaya (Malaysia). In fact, only Candy's were doing much business there, although Paterson's had two resident staff. In 1962 PCI (Malaysia) and PCI (Singapore) were formed in conjunction with Harper Gilfillan, Candy's agents. This change brought with it much greater local autonomy and less involvement from the UK, particularly for the smaller schemes which were designed and built locally. Then in the late 1980s, the Far East companies were detached from PCI, to trade as independent organisations. Similarly, the New Zealand company, which had been re-named Paterson Candy (New Zealand) and had maintained a close relationship with the UK until then, was allied to the South East Asia group as part of the re-organisation in the 80s

In South Africa, Candy's had long and successfully been represented by Dowson and Dobson. Paterson's had also been very successful through their agents, Blane and Company, and it proved difficult to find a common arrangement. In 1967 Blane's sold their shares in Paterson (South Africa), and PCI (South Africa) was formed and traded successfully until the 1980s re-shuffle put them together with the local Permutit company, a move that was to prove as big a mistake as the merger of PCI and Permutit.

Against this background of change, the normal business of trading continued. Opportunities in West and East Africa began a period of success for Candy's, particularly in Nigeria where many substantial orders were booked, including a fine works for Ibadan. Candy's also expanded into the West Indies, taking much of the available work.

The activity in West Africa high-lighted the need for very simple small treatment plants for rural communities, and so the Waterman range of packaged plants was conceived. These very basic units consisted of an engine-driven raw water pump, a pressure settling tank and a filter with automatic backwash from a compartment in the overhead storage tank. The chemical plant used very simple displacement-type dosing equipment and controls. The first order was for a batch of sixty plants for Ghana and many others followed. The simple but very practical design did not require any electricity and was soon imitated by others. The Waterman provided PCI with a useful income and few contract problems for several years.

Chapter 10

Export slowdown and cash worries

But by the end of 1966, the overseas business was slowing, and coupled with the problems of substantial retentions on many contracts, and of managing the transferred Paterson work, the company once again began to have cash problems. At the same time, the industrial market dried up and there was little work for the new industrial division at Laverstoke as the main industrial activity in the UK was for the massive power programme where Permutit had a commanding position. In 1968 staff numbers had to be reduced, with the bulk of the cut falling on the ill-starred Laverstoke office.

1970 saw a successful turnaround and the company was again profitable, with a substantial backlog of work and good progress in clearing the mess resulting from the amalgamation. Ealing had gained some very experienced staff from Paterson's and sales were obtained from the Middle East, Chile and in the UK. The decade had brought in major changes for the company. Dufour, Griffiths, Thomas and other experienced men had left or retired, whilst none of the senior managers and few of the experienced engineers and draughtsmen from Paterson's remained.

Hong Kong, Sha Tin. 90 mgd. Mid-60s.

The French and other adventures

The early 60s saw associations with El Car in Italy and Cadagua in Spain. The Italian connection resulted in a number of industrial and municipal plants in Italy and elsewhere, but little worthwhile work resulted from the link with Cadagua. Although these ventures were entertaining, neither resulted in much profit for PCI and both were ended in the 1970s.

Leo Rabeneck had long enjoyed his contacts with France. Early in 1965 he set up a joint venture with Wanson, a

CP plant, West Africa. PCI supplied many of these simple, pre-fabricated plants

Chapter 10

Belgian company whose business was mainly in industrial heating and packaged boilers, though they also had a small industrial water treatment activity in France and Belgium. The co-operation, which was somewhat unfocused and under-resourced, pursued both industrial and potable projects and succeeded in booking some work, although this turned out to be under-priced. Within three years Wanson's became uncomfortable with the arrangement as the contracts secured were very large by their terms and did not really fit their main business. So the co-operation was ended and PCI formed a company jointly with Progil-Sateb, called Compagnie Internationale des Eaux (CIE). The venture met strong commercial opposition from Degremont and was not successful. CIE traded unprofitably for a few years before PCI wrote off their investment in 1973.

The idea of establishing a presence in Brazil arose following the completion of Paterson's huge plant for Rio, and this occupied the company for some years. Finally after a brief and inadequate study, PCI (Brazil) was formed in 1972 jointly with ECIL, who were Paterson's agents. The adventure was poorly supported, wrongly targeted, and PCI's interest was sold after only three years, the local organisation having made continual demands for funding.

Improving productivity, a cartoon from the House magazine September 1976.

There had probably been little real opportunity for the business, due to the exchange controls, but it seemed a good idea at the time.

Another enterprise which went nowhere was the foray into Saudi Arabia in the 80s, which was intended to represent all the contracting companies in the group. The venture did not have good enough links to access the major schemes and it lacked an adequate local service organisation essential to support the small and medium-sized jobs. It was a brave attempt but in retrospect, as with the other ventures, it was not sufficiently focused or resourced and was abandoned before it got established.

PCI Membranes

In 1968 as part of Harold Wilson's "white-hot technology" initiative, the Government launched a series of technology ventures, including four desalination projects to be managed by the United Kingdom Atomic Energy Authority, Harwell, for which they sought industrial partners. The most significant of these was the multi-stage flash distillation project with Weir-Westgarth, who invented the idea. Less successful were the freezing process with Simon Carves and the

Chapter 10

electro-dialysis partnership with William Boby Ltd, that later became available to the Portals group through the acquisition of Boby's.

Of more interest here was the collaboration between PCI and the UKAEA to develop reverse osmosis for water desalination. This partnership took the company into a number of food and pharmaceutical markets to treat an astonishing variety of liquids. The initial co-operation with Harwell centred on using Portals' paper technology to produce a paper-based tubular membrane system. However, the link between paper and producing the tubes had no practical logic, and the paper was soon replaced in favour of stainless steel which owed its origins to the world copper shortage at the time. This quirk of the market resulted in stainless steel tubing being developed as a substitute for copper for domestic heating systems, so it was in mass production and very competitive for a brief time.

The initial development work on reverse osmosis inevitably took longer than expected, so in the early 1970s an agreement was made with Dupont to market their Permasep hollow fibre devices, which gave PCI an entry to the brackish water markets of the Middle East and elsewhere. As the development of the tubular system progressed, the commercial emphasis moved to the more profitable food and pharmaceutical markets, although there were some painful lessons to be learned about the requirements and standards, and it was not until the mid-1980s that the subject was sufficiently understood.

The non-water markets are generally fairly small and of finite size so it was essential to identify the size and nature of each before expending much

The B1 module consists of 18 half-inch diameter stainless steel tubes fixed between tube plates and enclosed in a stainless shroud like a tubular boiler. The end caps are available in two formats - to connect all the tubes in series, or all in parallel. The membranes take the form of porous tubes fitted inside the stainless tubes. The pressurised feed liquid is on the inside of the tubes, the permeate passing through the membranes and the holes in the supporting stainless tubes for collection in the shroud. This simple and elegant device resulted from PCI persuading the manufacturers of the stainless steel heating tubing to make a precision version rolled from punched high grade strip. The B1 module has spawned a variety of tubular devices, including throwaway cartridges, smaller tube units and modules with more tubes. The tubular design retains a valuable place as a high value niche market device.

effort on it. Applications successfully tackled ranged from concentrating whole whey and tomato juice, to fractionating antibiotic broths or lignosulphonate effluent. Some spectacular plants have been built over the last twenty-five years. That at Stora Nymolla in Sweden illustrates how far the business has moved from its R&D origins.

Chapter 10

The business is still very active in these specialist markets but it also has a successful business supplying Nano-filtration systems for treating coloured waters for potable supply. Although this elegant idea first appeared in the late 60s, the technology to make it work was not to become available until over twenty years later.

In 1999 PCI Membranes remains part of the Thames Water group.

An overall view of the plant at Stora Nymolla AB pulp and paper mill in Sweden. This is the largest tubular membrane plant in the world. The ultrafiltration plant reduces 300 tonnes/hour of bleach effluent to 6 t/h. It consists of 1784 PCI 3.6m long B1 modules and has a total membrane area of 4740 m^2. 1990s.

11 - THE BIG CONTRACTS 1970-1988

Permutit joins the Portals Group

By the end of the 60s, Permutit's formerly strong management had retired, there was less work available, and the technical strength that had provided the foundations of the company was beginning to age and was not being maintained properly. This provided Portals with an opportunity to buy the company and its overseas subsidiaries in 1970, partly to close down a municipal competitor that was hurting PCI even though its market share was small.

Permutit was still a world class company in the industrial field, with a worthwhile presence in the smaller end of the sewage market, which complemented PCI's business, so there were good prospects for consolidation. They also had strong subsidiaries in Australia, South Africa and India. The direct consequences of the purchase were minimal until the 1980s, although it inevitably opened the municipal market to new competitors, just as the merger of Paterson's and Candy's had done five years earlier. Apart from some marketing rationalisation, the two companies then co-existed uneasily until the merger in 1988.

Strathclyde R.C., Afton treatment works. 5.5 mgd. The plant illustrates a trend in the 80s for all-steel construction. In service 1991.

On-going cash problems

1970 ended with a number of new orders including an extension for Diddington, a substantial new works for the Bristol Water Company at Purton, and the Upper Pierce Scheme for Singapore. There were also extensions for Portsmouth, Hanningfield and the River Dove works, built by Paterson's in the early 60s.

Although the order book and invoicing were very strong, 1971 opened with the need to address the serious cash problems resulting from retentions on a number of contracts in the UK and overseas. Bob Williams, who was PCI's contracts director, travelled extensively, visiting clients in India, Sri Lanka, Malaysia, Singapore, Thailand, Hong Kong, Australia, New Zealand, Fiji, Trinidad and Brazil. This was partly as a farewell tour before he retired but also to try to resolve the problems and close some of the contracts. The list of countries indicates the scale of the difficulty, but he was successful in many cases. He was also able to negotiate a final payment for the sale of the Indian companies, ostensibly to cover royalties and on-going advice, and against all expectations, these moneys were ultimately received. This was his last duty prior to retiring, and he declined a suggestion that he might spend the next two years trying to clear up the mess that Bell's had got themselves into. (Bell's had become involved with the domestic swimming pool market with the inevitable problems of servicing this low value business. Their main waterworks activity had declined, their overheads were much too high, and the end of the company was imminent).

In spite of Williams' success in collecting cash, PCI's financial problems were very deep-seated. Some of the new contracts such as Upper Pierce simply added to them, although they also brought in much-needed cash which enabled Rabeneck to keep the company going.

Interesting patterns made by the walkways over the scraped tanks, British Steel cooling water re-cycling plant. Supplied by Permutit 1980s.

Boby's absorbed

The purchase of Boby's business via Permutit in 1972 brought a number of incomplete contracts. The municipal work was passed to PCI and the industrial contracts were assumed by Permutit. It appears that there were already concerns about the cost estimates and the purchase price was immediately written off as goodwill. These worries proved to be soundly based, although part of the trouble may have resulted from old hands re-designing the contracts. The acquisition brought some useful Graver technology as well as an excellent subsidiary in Melbourne which complemented Permutit's Australian business, but ultimately, little else, and the staff who left strengthened Dewplan and other competitors.

Chapter 11

The Regional Water Authorities - the beginning of a new era

Just as the dismantling of the British Empire in the 1960s had ushered in a period of rapid change in much of the world, the formation of the ten Regional Water Authorities in 1973 was to make profound changes in the home market. PCI underestimated just how much this would affect the business and failed to adapt vigorously enough to resist the competition from abroad, in particular, from France. Many old friends were swept away and the new organisations saw the relationship with the contractors in a different light. Whilst the change was gradual and uneven, the technical position of companies like PCI began to erode as the water companies increasingly took the design lead. Thin trading in the UK at the beginning of the decade resulted in cutbacks in investment in development and training, which, coupled with poor management decisions, had a profound effect on the future. At the time, some spectacular (and ultimately very profitable) overseas contracts distracted the company from seeing the importance of the fundamental changes at home.

The period also saw the introduction of much more commercial control on tenders, essential because of a changing attitude by clients everywhere, and the introduction of very onerous conditions of contract by some of the Water Authorities. Whether these changes produced any worthwhile gains for the purchasers is debatable but thereafter the emphasis in the market moved strongly towards the contractual aspects, to the detriment of the technology. Previously, the emphasis was usually on building a good works. In the new climate, much time was spent on contract conditions and the enforcement of performance and penalty clauses, and less on efficient design and engineering. PCI found this change difficult, having enjoyed a much more gentlemanly relationship with their customers in the past.

NZ Ammonia plant with Mount Egmont in the distance. Supplied by Permutit/ PC NZ. 1980s.

Chapter 11

Downturn in the UK

The effect of the general recession of the early 70s reached PCI after much of the rest of industry was feeling the pinch, but by 1973 the work in the UK had started to dry up. Few orders were available to share between too many suppliers, and such bids as there were, were sharply priced. Coupled with the recession, the oil crisis and the industrial problems in the UK started to make life very difficult, and the management was pre-occupied with cash problems. The third extension of the Elvington works provided some good news but the UK market remained very flat for the next few years.

1975 - Sewage again

1975 saw the start of a number of changes. Bell's works at Manchester were closed and some of the staff moved to Ealing. The Brazilian company was sold, and Burville Candy, Pullen's only son, died in Australia, so ending the male line.

Overseas, PCI's subsidiaries also reported trading difficulties, with the exception of El Car in Italy, and negotiations were completed for an investment in Cadagua in Spain.

Tilbury sewage works, with the power station behind. Two stages each 9.9 mgd. Each has a "Deep Shaft" 5.7 m dia. x 60m deep, designed to treat mixed domestic and strong industrial waste. The plant has proved to be very resilient to load variation.

In these difficult times PCI launched a new sewage division, based on a product range from Envirex, and they recruited a number of people for the new business, all of whom underwent an extended training programme with the American licenser. On the process side, PCI linked with ICI to promote their revolutionary Deep Shaft process, and built a pilot plant for them at their Wilton site. This provided much process design information for the company and the technology for building a very large plant later at Tilbury, on the Thames estuary. But the sewage market proved hard to enter. There were few plant starts in the UK and delays to many projects in the targeted markets overseas. As far the products were concerned, PCI did not make any of the equipment and were competing with relatively low-cost companies in the Midlands who did; much of the American equipment turned out to be dated and very heavily built. PCI's strengths lay more in designing treatment plant and less in selling industrial goods to customers who, by and large, knew what they wanted. Despite a substantial order for Holdenhurst (Bournemouth) based on Envirex products, by 1978 the pressure on overheads necessitated a general cut-back, and spelled the end of the division as a separate entity.

The remaining sewage staff were integrated with the main sales group, with the emphasis on specific, engineered contracts rather than the Envirex products, which were quietly dropped from the company's activities.

One of the bright moments of this difficult period was the development of a new floatation clarifier, bringing PCI into this growing sector of the market. Few people in the company could have imagined the extent to which this new technology would take over the home market in only a few years.

Permak sewage treatment plant, South-West England.

The "FB" clarifier

Griffiths' hopper tank had served the company well for several decades and had been used in many very successful works. However, by the late 60s it was already very expensive to build and unsuitable for large units due to the very deep structures needed. PCI tried various means to extend its life but really had no competitive clarifier to offer to the market. The alternative was the Paterson Accentrifloc which was a very robust and effective clarifier but was very expensive to build, and being circular, occupied lots of ground. The problem was brought to a head by the arrival of Degremont in the UK market in the late 60s, and in particular, the loss to them of the contracts for settling tanks for Iver and the Plymouth Crown Hill works. In both cases, PCI's reputation and links to the customers were not strong enough to counter the advantages of Degremont's Pulsator clarifier.

The flat-bottom or "FB" tank was conceived in the early 70s, although the idea perhaps derived from a much earlier tank built in-house by Northumbrian Water. PCI's contribution was to understand the underlying technology for coagulation and mixing, inlet distribution and sludge removal. Inevitably, there were some false starts with the

Chapter 11

FB, and the first plant in service was equipped with plastic distributors which distorted in the sun prior to start-up and did not work at all well.

But, as with the new suspended filter floor, the FB was soundly based and it rapidly demonstrated an ability to deal with a wide range of natural waters. The concept was very simple, and because the structure was a box, it was economic to build, with the water inlet and outlet channels used as structural members as well as distributing the water. The new knowledge about mixing and sludge removal turned over many views long held in the industry and enabled the tank to be operated at much higher ratings than had previously been imagined, giving PCI a competitive clarifier once again. The new mixing and sludge control technology was not related just to the FB but was applicable to all clarifiers, and this provided PCI with a series of negotiated contracts to re-visit many of the existing Candy hopper tank plants and uprate them by factors of two to three.

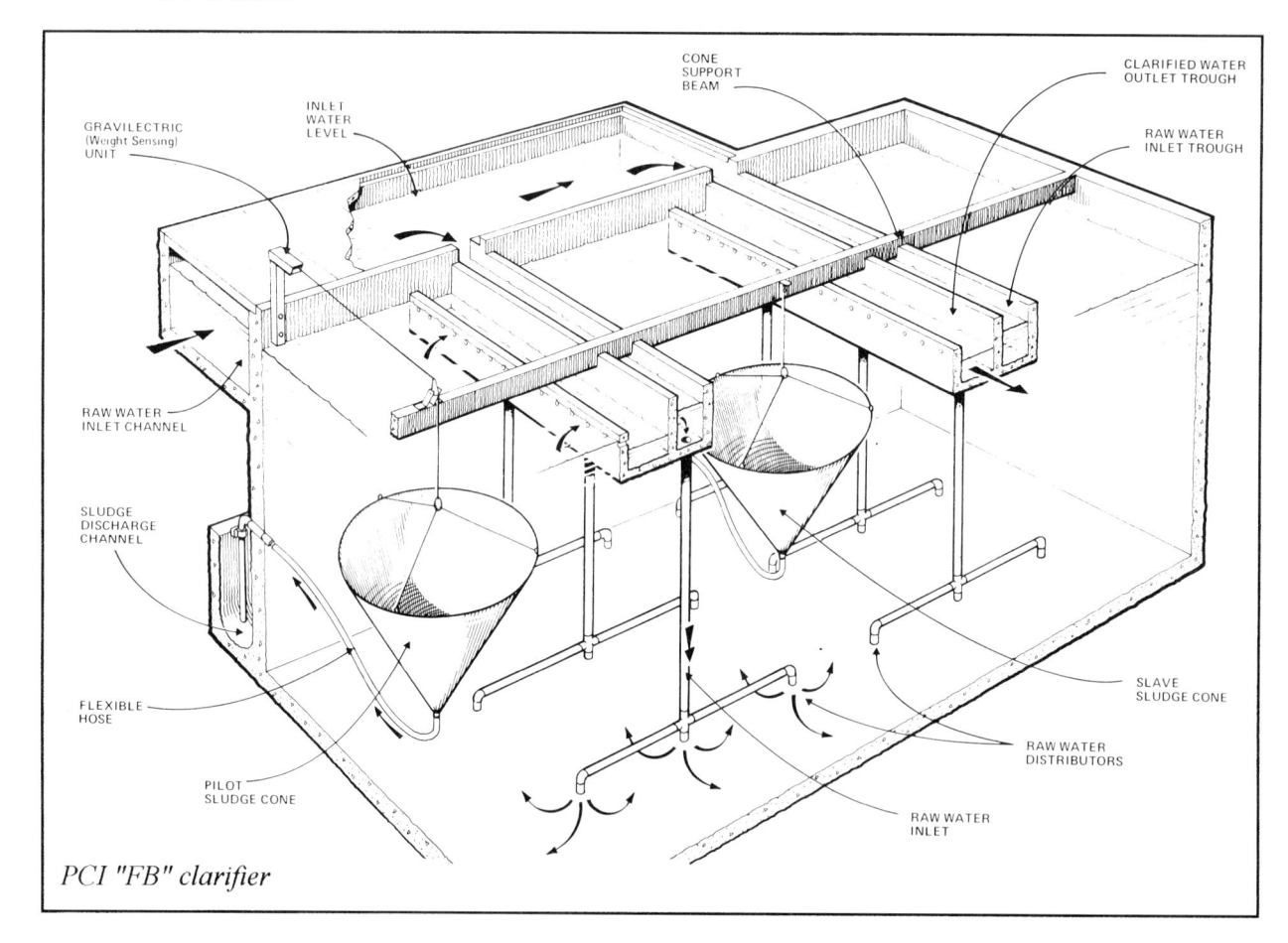

PCI "FB" clarifier

Chapter 11

The home market in the late 70s

Though the glamour schemes appeared to be abroad, and trading conditions in the UK were difficult, the home team was not idle, booking a large ozone plant for the Barmby Marsh works in 1976, as well as floatation plants for Bolton Wayoh and the Shetland Isles. 1977 saw orders for Chellow Heights, Bradford, the start of the Hardham scheme which had very complex computer controls, and the 20 mgd Glendevon scheme with PC-H. The very attractive Lumley works for the Sunderland and South Shields Water Company was completed that year, as was the Broomy Hill plant, both winning awards for their architectural design. There were extensions for Farlington, and others.

The end of the decade continued to be hard although some nice orders were taken, including the PC-H order for Glenfarg. There was also work for the existing plants at Mythe (Tewkesbury), Barsham, Broken Scar, Bristol Purton and elsewhere, but by this time the company's attention had moved to the big overseas projects. As the 1980s opened, the UK market was more concerned with refurbishing plants and updating the controls and automation of existing installations. PCI modernised several old contracts and supplied automation to Clay Lane, Weir Wood, Sandhouse and Bough Beech, but the proportion of home contracts during this period was relatively small.

A close-run thing

The expansion in the late 60s brought orders with much larger filters and more importantly, higher wash rates than the company was used to. Candy's lateral floor was based on short earthenware pipes that were butt-jointed and set in concrete. These were superseded by plastic lateral pipes as the new materials became available, and they worked well when they were properly laid. However, the advent of bigger filters and the higher wash rates demanded by some consultants resulted in the laterals becoming longer, and the increased hydraulic loss during backwash could not be dealt with adequately by the

Sludge cones being installed in an FB clarifier. The PCI "Gravitrol" system was spawned by the development of the FB and was the core of the optimised sludge control systems put in by PCI. In essence, a sensitive mechanism weighs the sludge collection cone and its contents and at a pre-set value discharges the sludge. This very simple and elegant device permits the very thin sludge in the clarifier sludge blanket to thicken by settlement in the cone and so minimises the water wasted when removing sludge from the clarifier. A single Gravitrol unit can be used as a pilot to control the discharge from other cones on a rotational basis.

Chapter 11

nozzle loss. As more and more filters were installed the incidence of backwash problems and failures increased, and by the mid-70s the problem was very severe.

The cause was quite simple, and it came about as a result of a cavalier approach to the expansion of filter wash rates, which were extrapolated without proper checking in the laboratory. The high wash flows in the laterals caused instability and destroyed the distribution of the wash. With hindsight, it is easy to see what went wrong and to blame individuals for making unprofessional changes to long established filter technology. At the time, in the hurly-burly of a rapidly expanding market and changing technology, confusion and errors were more readily understandable, though they were surprising, given the company's tradition of fine hydraulic engineering. Clearly, Pullen Candy's design had been pushed well beyond its limit, and as the list of problem contracts increased, the company's resources were stretched to near breaking point. In the less tolerant climate that pervades the industry now, the outcome might have been very different. As it was, Rabeneck kept his nerve and by careful use of his substantial and prudently hoarded contract reserves, he gave the technical staff time to resolve the fundamental problems.

Melbourne, Sugarloaf. 100 mgd. View over the clarifiers showing the tubular settled water collectors.

Variants of the type-A floor were developed using PVC laterals in place of the earthenware pipes, together with a whole range of nozzles. These helped with many of the problems, although in the middle of this mess and prompted by competition from Degremont, the company tried using a version without packing layers, which introduced yet more problems when sand got into the underdrains and blocked the nozzles.

Although intermediate solutions were tried, mostly based on modifying the nozzles, the final solution was a plenum chamber suspended floor. To many of PCI's older staff this was nothing short of revolutionary. Other companies, particularly Degremont, had used a suspended floor for some years but inevitably the concept was seen as somewhat alien within PCI, and many of the senior staff were unconvinced that combined wash was superior to separate airscour. This is ironic, given that Pullen Candy had developed a combined wash floor forty years earlier.

Chapter 11

By about the middle of the decade, a new suspended floor was conceived, called the "Aylesbury Floor" as it was intended for a scheme for Aylesbury. PCI didn't win that contract but they went on to do the necessary work to understand the exceedingly complex behaviour of the water and air in the plenum chamber below a suspended floor. The resulting design was virtually complete in time for the massive Karkh contract, and it was thoroughly tested in a half full-sized model at Laverstoke. It had been a close run thing but the company then had a filter bottom which is perhaps the definitive floor to date.

The 70s were a period of extreme financial difficulty that seemed to get worse as the decade progressed. Government incompetence led to the general downturn in the UK and caused the postponement or cancellation of many schemes, at a time when the company was wrestling with technical problems whilst developing the new technology essential for remaining in business. Leo Rabeneck juggled the company's finances to weather the storm of the effects of the merger, the technical problems, and the dreadful inflation which resulted from the oil crisis in the early 70s. Through these difficult times he took the business back into to profit, until he left PCI in 1976, when the company's finances deteriorated once again

The end of 1979 brought a small turn-around, and the 1980s started with PCI once more well in control of its technology.

Oyo state Nigeria, Oshogbo-Ede works under construction with the impounded river beyond. 35 mgd. 1970s.

Overseas

Although the company's emphasis had moved to "the big schemes", PCI continued to do smaller projects. As well as helping Boby Australia to secure a major order for Melbourne, there were orders for Nigeria, and in 1977 a very large filter plant was built for the Rand Water Board, although it was supplied almost entirely by the South African subsidiary. Filter floors were delivered for Riyadh, and treatment plants for

Chapter 11

Iran, Ethiopia and elsewhere. In 1978 PCI (NZ) celebrated 50 years of fine service and achievement.

Of particular interest was the sale of an ozone plant for Abrera (Barcelona) in Spain, which at 45 Kg/hr was one of the largest anywhere at the time. The company hoped that it would lead to other orders, but the technology which was licensed from Germany failed to become a world leader. Apart from the Broomy Hill plant in 1979, PCI sold few ozone plants until the 1990s.

The big contracts

The scarcity of work led the company to concentrate on the glittering big contracts, lured by the relatively huge sums involved, and perhaps not fully understanding how long these schemes might take to bring to fruition, or the high failure rate. The learning process involved several expensive false starts, but the verdict after twenty years is that overall the policy was very successful, and the few big schemes made much more money than the mainstream business. The funding for these schemes often had to be arranged by the contractor. They were turn-key contracts that generally covered a much wider scope than the traditional and perhaps, more orderly work. New commercial skills were also needed, along with access to the banking world to arrange the finance packages, and to governments for the guarantees the bankers needed. Over the next ten years PCI secured several very large contracts in this way.

Ankara, stage 1, late 1970s and doubled to 248 mgd in the early 90s

Ankara

The Ankara contract started life as a conventional tender for the mechanical supply for a very large but technically straightforward treatment plant for the city of Ankara, the capital of Turkey. The order was won in 1977 against hard international competition but the contract ran into funding problems almost immediately, not unusual in Turkey, and ground to a halt. It took two years until PCI was able to put the financial package in

Chapter 11

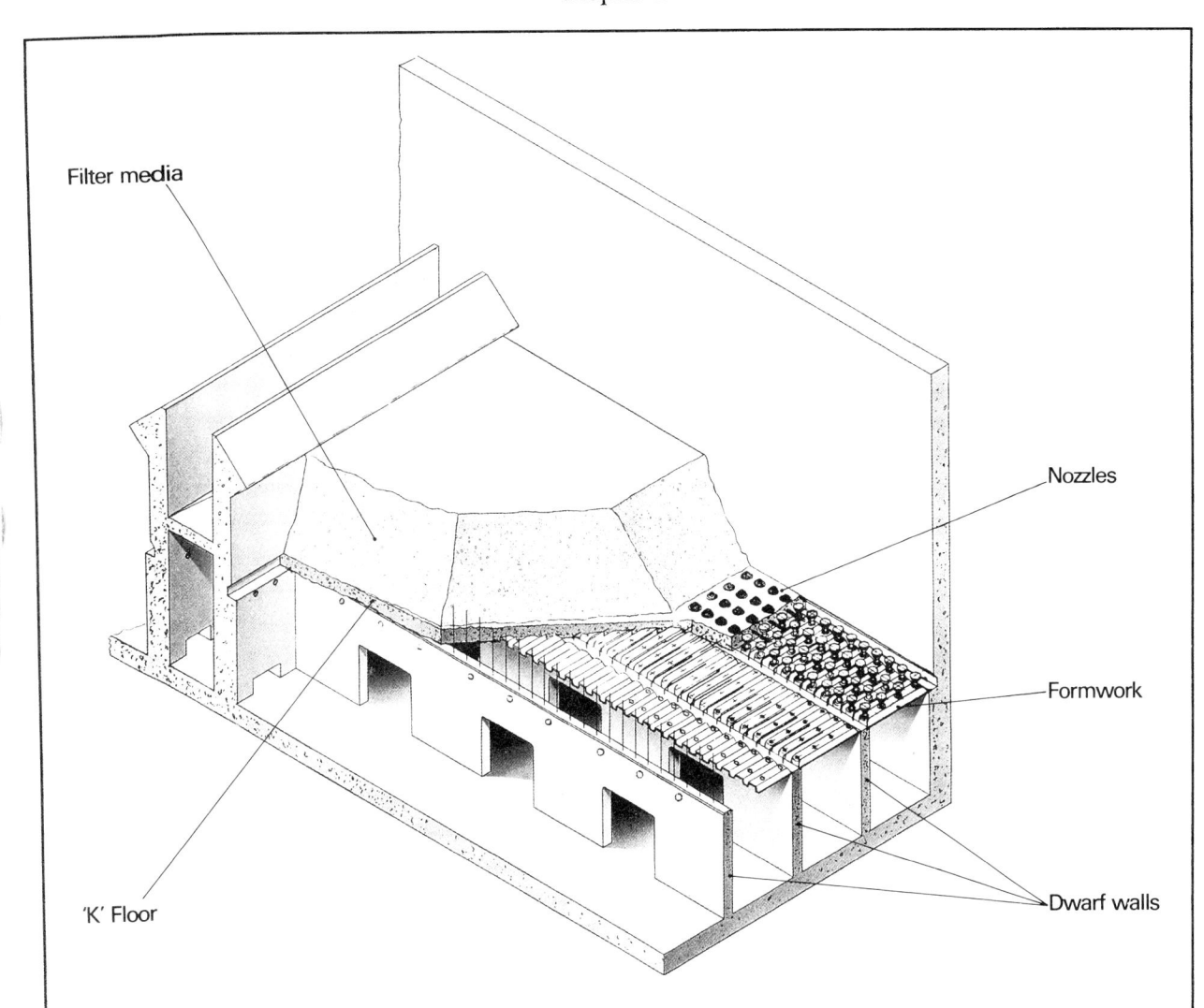

K-floor showing half of a double filter.

The K-floor consists of a monolithic suspended floor supported on dwarf walls (or in a few cases, columns). Distribution of air and water for combined wash is achieved by a complex but ingenious nozzle with very fine slots so that the filter sand can be placed directly on the floor. Apart from its very substantial flexibility with regard to air and water flow rates, the nozzle is designed to provide up to two inches (50 mm) in-situ level adjustment to cope with the vagaries of site levels. Once cast, the floor is immensely strong and an earthquake-resistant version was also developed for the Californian and Japanese markets. A variant with a sloping floor is available for granular carbon (GAC) filters so that all the carbon can be removed automatically, and this has been used for the Thames Water plant at Walton as well as some other sites.

Chapter 11

place through the British Government, enabling the largest plant in Europe to proceed, and in so doing, sowing the seeds for the huge Izmit scheme of the 90s.

The K-floor

The Karkh project for Baghdad brought PCI's weakness as a filter manufacturer to a head, as the company did not have a proven floor design that would be acceptable for the very large filters required for the project. So a licence was taken for a Graver (Canada) design to buy time to complete the development of PCI's own suspended floor. Crucially, the licence also provided access to commercial references that were essential to support the tender, although the K-floor actually used little of the licensed technology. The K-floor is now the company's standard filter bottom, following the tradition of the excellent filter technology established by Pullen Candy in 1921 with his type-A floor. The type-K has been widely specified by consultants throughout the United States as well as being installed in many plants around the world.

The PCI type-K filter under construction. The left side shows the underfloor details. The washout bay is in the centre and the right hand side has the nozzles and reinforcing bars installed, ready for final concreting.

Chapter 11

Karkh

The order for Qualat Sukur in Iraq (booked in the mid-70s) was significant in that it probably opened the way for the Karkh contract. There was certainly no other reason to take it. At £4m it was substantial, but PCI's margin was wafer thin: their role was that of management contractor for a scheme that included a treatment plant, sub-let to PCI's Malaysian company, with the civils by a local Iraqi contractor, the tanks from Spain and the cast iron pipes from Italy. It did not go well. When the pipes were delivered, they failed at the threaded joints and had to be re-sourced, and the civil contractor proved incapable of building water-tight structures. It was a miserable experience but by persisting, PCI found themselves well positioned for "the big one".

The Karkh contract was in every way colossal; it is still one of the largest treatment plants ever built, with a capacity of 300 mgd, and covers an area about twice the size of Hyde Park. The order, booked in 1981, is by far the largest taken by PCI in any of its guises, and before completion, was extended by the addition of a two year operation and maintenance contract.

For such a huge scheme, the work went particularly well and ran to time despite the Iran/Iraq war (PCI site staff recall seeing the vapour trails of the incoming rockets aimed at Baghdad). But storm clouds were on the horizon and although the work was

Karkh, panoramic view of part of the site during construction

The statistics are impressive by any standards, with twenty-four huge scraped pre-settling tanks designed to remove over 40,000 tonnes per day of sediment from the raw water when the Tigris is in spate - enough for about 1.5 km of 6-lane motorway - and most civil contractors would be proud to be able to move anything like this! The works is designed to treat 1,300 Ml/d or about 300 mgd. Eighteen 51m diameter Centrifloc clarifiers take the supernatant from the pre-settlement tanks and supply sixty 150m^2 filters. From the three treated water reservoirs, eight 2,200 kW pumps supply four local reservoirs around Baghdad. There are 23 overhead cranes, gas turbine generators to supply 16 MW of power - enough for running at half capacity - whilst the chemical plant can store 3,600 tonnes of aluminium sulphate, 1,200 tonnes of hydrated lime as well as large quantities of polyelectrolyte and chlorine. And so it goes on.

complete by the outbreak of the Gulf war, PCI still had a number of staff in Iraq. They and their families were interned and used as part of the human shield to protect some of Iraq's sensitive installations. Following UN intervention, they were all released, except for the resident branch manager who had been arrested earlier and spent six years in the notorious Abu Ghraib prison, much of the time in solitary confinement.

Karkh. Filters as far the eye can see

Despite being an obvious target, the works was not damaged by the western allies, though it suffered seriously from a lack of spare parts and adequate maintenance. In about 1992, two PCI (by then PWT) staff visited Iraq under the auspices of the Red Cross to advise on repairing the generators at the Baghdad supply pump-stations. By then, the main power supply had been disrupted by allied bombing and the water supply to the city was affected.

Karkh, one of the pump houses.

Nigeria: Calabar, Gongola State and Benue

The 60s, 70s, and early 1980s saw much activity in Nigeria, and PCI was very successful, taking much of the available work to

Karkh. One of 24 scraped pre-settlement tanks.

Chapter 11

Benue before..

continue the pattern of the previous seventy years.

Perhaps the most important project of the period was a scheme for Calabar State which called for up to fourteen pump stations and treatment plants to be built on both sides of the Great Cross River, including a large plant for Calabar city. The discussions started in about 1974 and by 1979 it looked as if they could be turned into an order. However, at the last minute the German funding was withdrawn and PCI, by then well practised in the subject, had to arrange alternative finance in the London money market.

The Gongola project consisted of five town and thirteen village schemes to supply about one million people with abstraction and treatment from over one hundred sources. This led to the Benue contract, worth about £21m in 1983, for the turn-key supplies to a network of twenty-four townships and villages. Both projects included completing the demand and design studies, the boreholes and earth dams, as well as the treatment plants and distribution systems. All of the works were small with capacities ranging up to 0.2 mgd but there were a lot of them.

PCI arranged the finance package for the Benue scheme, syndicated amongst nine banks, but like many projects of this nature, things did not go to plan. The civil contractor had to be replaced mid-contract, and his work was taken over by PCI staff who set up a direct labour force with thirteen ex-patriate supervisors, purchased the necessary machinery and completed the construction. During a period of political and economic upheaval some 12,000 tonnes of materials were shipped through Makurdi and delivered to the sites over the frequently impassable

Benue after. The photo shows a typical village scheme consisting of a CP clarifier (right rear) filter and simple machine and chemical house. Late 1980s.

Chapter 11

roads. Despite the risks involved, and although the programme was heavily delayed, the financial outcome was very good.

The Benue project, together with the other work in Nigeria such as the 36 mgd plant for Oyo State, required the company to set up a local subsidiary in 1983. This provided a base until the mid-1990s, by which time the political and economic situation had deteriorated to such an extent that it was no longer worth being there.

The Los Angeles Aqueduct Scheme

The development of the K-floor in the late 1970s provided PCI with a world-beating filter bottom. This was recognised by several American consulting engineers who opened access to a number of treatment plants in the United States, although PCI had to learn some new tricks to cope with the particular nature of the American contracting system. A network of agents was appointed and a series of orders for K-floors was secured; however because the PCI floor was almost always replacing a competitor's pre-specified design, the structures often didn't suit the dimensions of the K and odd sizes had to be designed.

The spectacular success in taking the order for the huge LA Aqueduct scheme followed a major sales effort to convince the purchaser of the robustness of the design. The earthquake conditions in the area (the works is situated more or less directly over the San Andreas fault) required PCI to design a special version of the floor.

The LA Aqueduct scheme. View over the filters.

The basic monolithic concept lent itself to relatively easy re-design, giving PCI a major advantage, and the plant subsequently survived a major earthquake whose epicentre was only five miles from the site.

12 - EPILOGUE 1988-1996

PWT Projects, Thames Water, The Gulf War

By 1988 both PCI and Permutit were struggling to make a profit after a period of very high inflation and poor trading in the UK. The profits from Karkh and other very large contracts had been taken, and a merger seemed to be the solution to save costs in the contracting businesses. The combined company was renamed PWT Projects Ltd and moved to the Permutit premises in Isleworth. The new organisation started badly, and initially struggled to get orders and cope with the inevitable internal differences in approach to selling, design, and project management. PCI brought with them a backlog of bad and unfinished contracts, and Permutit had very little work and faced a depressed industrial market.

Thames Water, Walton. 52 mgd CoCo DAF and activated carbon, plus ozone, for part of the supply to London.

The move coincided with the start of the privatisation of the water utilities in the UK and in 1989, Thames Water conditionally purchased a number of specialist companies from Portals, including PWT, thinking that this would provide them with an international marketing organisation, and perhaps a captive contractor to deal with part of the massive programme envisaged under privatisation. The due diligence carried out by Thames revealed the extent of PWT Projects' financial problems and resulted in a

Damanhur, Egypt. 11.3 mgd. This and its sister plant for Idfina were booked in the late 80s in joint venture with a local civils partner. The partnership soon failed and PCI/PWT took over the work using direct labour. The site conditions in the Nile delta were dreadful but the finished works is a fine tribute to the company's engineering quality.

bitter and protracted sale that diverted the company's management for the best part of a year. The new company needed to make massive provisions for losses and bad debts and started 1990 in very poor shape, with the internal organisation problems unresolved and very little profitable work. Then in 1990 the Gulf War threw the Middle East into chaos, leaving firms such as PWT to cope with suspended contracts, delayed projects, and worst of all from a management point of view, staff and their families held hostage in remote parts of Iraq.

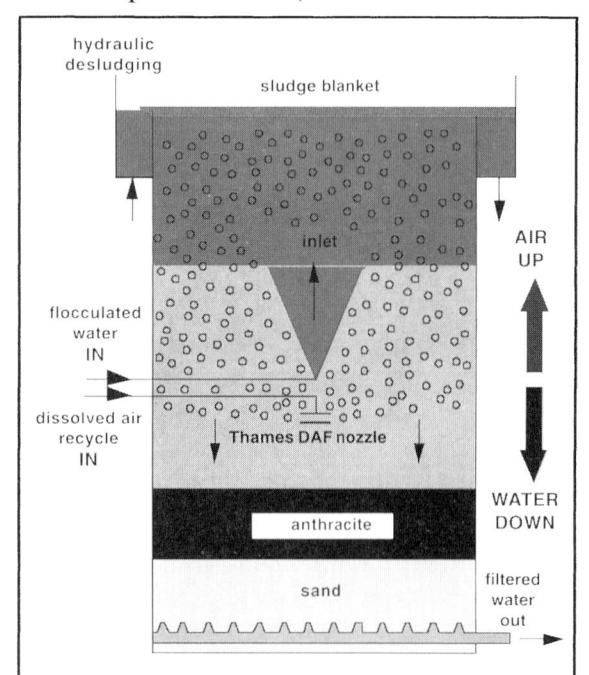

Jebel Ali re-carbonation plant

PWT's ingenious countercurrent and very compact CoCo DAF design combines floaters and filters in a single process unit, which requires reduced flocculation time upstream, due to the intimate contact between the flocculated water and the rising air blanket.

The Thames management responded well and was very supportive at first, injecting cash to meet the deficit and providing work under their "Enabling" programme. This novel approach to contracting established a general basis for negotiation and agreement of prices so the Thames contract managers could issue fast-track work to the pre-selected contractors, with the minimum of pre-contract discussion or design. The method, although very bureaucratic and sometimes expensive, was very successful and enabled a large number of contracts, some very complex, to be completed more quickly than was possible by traditional methods. Typical of this was the new 120 Ml/d works at Walton, built turn-key in about three years, whilst incorporating a novel counter-current dissolved air floatation system as well as a new design of activated carbon contactor, both of which had to be developed "on the hoof" by PWT.

Chapter 12

The flood of new work was a welcome change, but paradoxically, the rapid expansion of the UK market post-privatisation was to result in major problems for the traditional specialist contractors. A host of civil engineering contractors (and overseas competitors) rushed into the market, willing to take almost any risks at little or no bid margin, and relying on their buying power and positive cash flow to make up for it. After five years, much of the new water and sewage infrastructure in England and Wales was in place, but by then, most of the traditional specialist contractors were in difficulties. They had to shed staff with the attendant loss of experience, and perhaps more seriously, they now had a limited ability to compete effectively overseas after several years of negotiated work at home. In retrospect, the privatisation of the UK water suppliers (a change not followed by any other major economy) was a substantial cause of the rapid relegation of the UK specialist water treatment contractors after ninety years of dominating the world market, but this might have happened anyway.

There were some bright moments. After a long and expensive build-up, a consortium formed originally by PCI with local contractors Guris and Gama, and later Thames Water, secured a massive BOT (build, operate and transfer) project to supply water to the city of Izmit in Turkey. This impressive project included completing a dam, building a large treatment plant and laying over a hundred miles of major water mains (some parts were big enough to drive a small car through) across difficult country with two large pump-stations. The scheme required years of negotiation as well as the setting up of major international finance packages. The negotiations spanned the sale of the company, which became Paterson Candy Ltd, and kept responsibility for the Izmit treatment plant, the pump-stations and the supply and installation of the pipelines, as a sub-contract to Thames Water.

The 105 mgd (480 Ml/d) treatment plant at Izmit. The works has 6 FB clarifiers and 20 K-type filters.

The scheme was originally designed by the DSI in Ankara and was under construction as a Turkish Government project, although much delayed, when the consortium became involved to try and find international funding as a BOT scheme. The water supply was originally planned for Izmit and the industrial town of Gebze, with a substantial portion reserved for Istanbul, but in the event, local disagreements resulted in the cancellation of the Istanbul involvement. The order was secured at the start of 1995 and was putting treated water into supply by mid-1998, no mean achievement given the political complexity of the scheme.

Chapter 12

During these years the industrial division continued to struggle, not having the cushion of the Thames work, but it secured an impressive and valuable contract for a re-carbonation plant for the Jebel Ali distillation plant in Dubai. However, notwithstanding this and a number of other good orders, the merger with PCI resulted in the end of the original Permutit Company which had once dominated the world industrial market. At the time of the amalgamation in 1988, the standard plant and specialist filter and membrane divisions were hived off, and the great name of Permutit, together with those of Candy and Paterson, disappeared from contracting. In 1994 Thames decided to sell the ailing Permutit standard plant business to US Filters (by then the owners of Permutit NY) and in so doing, re-united the Permutit name under a single owner.

Sharjah sewage works, UAE.

The purchase in 1993 of Simon Hartley, a sewage treatment specialist, was intended to strengthen PWT's position in the sewage market as well as adding useful products to the group portfolio. Instead, the contracting side turned out to be another disaster as the true position of the technical dereliction and bad contracts of that once flourishing company were uncovered.

Although the Thames work was to dominate the company's activities until the mid- 1990s, major effort was put into securing other work in the UK and aid-funded work in overseas markets such as India and Pakistan. Perhaps predictably, the privatisation of the UK municipal water and effluent treatment market had resulted in much petty rivalry between the newly privatised utility companies which, coupled with French ownership of several of the ex-statutory water companies, meant that in practice, much of the traditional UK municipal market was no longer accessible to PWT. To make matters worse, many industrial schemes were

Thames Water, Silchester sewage works. View over the "SAFe" submerged aerated filters. This very compact design produces a high quality effluent.

Panjrapur, Bombay (Mumbai) 100 mgd. Completed mid-90s. A fine plant after much heartache!

delayed or cancelled, and as the Thames work ran down, so the company again found itself short of work, which further strained the by then difficult relationship with the Thames management.

In common with most of the water utilities, Thames had not had many successes amongst their acquisitions. By the mid-1990s they had had enough, and started to divest themselves of almost all their water treatment subsidiaries. In retrospect, it was perhaps too much to expect that there could ever be a successful marriage between a geographically-based utility operating as a regulated monopoly, and a group of contractors exposed to the vagaries and risks of the international market. Despite genuine efforts at the start to understand one another, the businesses and their management needs remained fundamentally incompatible.

Paterson Candy Ltd

On the 2nd of October 1996, Thames Water transferred ownership of the successors of Frank Candy and William Paterson to Black and Veatch who re-launched the company as Paterson Candy Ltd.

End note

Black and Veatch, with headquarters in Kansas City, Missouri was founded in 1915 as a partnership, only converting to corporate status in 1999. The corporation is now one of the largest and most diversified engineering and construction firms in the world with a proud record of over 30,000 projects completed for more than 6,100 clients worldwide. The corporation maintains over ninety offices across the world with a staff of more than 9,000 professionals spanning a wide range of disciplines including environmental, civil, electrical, structural and mechanical engineering as well as construction, science, economics, planning, architecture and finance.

Chapter 12

Black and Veatch is organised as five businesses- Infrastructure, Power, Process, Telecommunications and its IT (known as the Solutions Group) and Buildings. In turn, each comprises divisions and subsidiary companies to match the corporation's specialised capabilities to specific client needs.

The Infrastructure business provides a complete range of planning, design construction management, and design-build services for virtually all areas of infrastructure engineering. The Power business is the wordwide leader in project awards for electricity generation as it has been for the past ten years. The Telecommunication business also covers electrical and telecommunication services and allied fields, whilst the Solutions Group offers high tech. innovation engineering in the information technology field. Black and Veatch Pritchard is the Process business, specialising in gas processing, petroleum refining, petrochemicals etc.

Simly treatment works, Pakistan.

Paterson Candy Limited forms part of the Infrastructure group and is once more trading successfully, both in the UK and its traditional markets overseas.

Luton, East Hyde, STP, sludge digestion plant. Late 90s.

Chapter 12

British Nuclear Fuels, waste recovery plant.1997.

Appendices

A. Extract from Bob Williams' final notes, October 1982

"Some notes on research difficulties and rewards - Polarite then and now"

By the beginning of 1980 I had collected together my own diaries, photos and papers, as well as historic pamphlets and illustrated plant descriptions and started jotting down ideas on the form the history would take.

There were discrepancies in dates and there was a "dark age" period of a few years before and after the turn of the century. I had found three dates given for the original company formation. That of 4 November 1906 for the Candy Filter Company was correct. Little realising the difficulties and frustrations ahead, I decided that I would find details and proof of Frank Candy's ancestry, early life and achievements to provide continuity of interest and build up a picture of the man and his work. Finding the date of his birth was my number one priority - a simple task one would think until I found that his birth was not registered, like many people in that age. There were no relatives who knew, no notice of his death in national or local papers or records in Torquay where he lived and died. I found the house, now a hotel, where he spent the last twenty years of his life, but no information. However, The Town Hall records of the old cemetery led me to two graves with the names and ages of Frank Candy and his wife on one headstone and of their two daughters on the other. With a strange feeling of respect, being an interloper, I learned from the faint wording that he was 92 when he died in 1934 and his wife and daughters were all in their eighties.

There were several similar frustrations, but there were the exciting bonuses when completely unknown material came to light and filled in blanks in both knowledge and time span. It is worth listing a few examples.

1. Some people named Candy, living in the Birmingham area, were researching details of the south-west Candy families and sent a letter to Burville Candy, grandson of Frank Candy, care of PCI. This letter was forwarded to him in Australia and then on to New York, where Burville was spending some time with his niece Jane Lloyd. He died there some months later but the search of his papers produced the family tree and a copy was sent to me. It provided the details of the farming background and other interesting information about the family.

2. My knowledge was further enhanced when I was able after a long search, to trace Frank Pullen Candy's step-daughter, Mrs Bridges. Our first meeting had been at the new Shrewsbury waterworks in 1934 when Mr Candy with his wife and step-daughter arrived there for an inspection of the recently commissioned plant. It was her help that enabled the early years of Frank Candy as the young auctioneer and surveyor, his marriage, the interest in geology and his return from London to the Newton Abbot district, to be recorded.

Appendices

3. During 1931 I carried out some experimental work at the Paignton waterworks on Dartmoor near Holne. Here I learned of a Candy brick and pottery works near Newton Abbot and was told that it had been founded by a Candy of the same family. My recent research confirmed that it was in fact founded by Frank Candy and I was able, through the kindness of the managing director Mr Putz, to see the factory and some of the old buildings of the original works. I was shown the early details of the shareholdings and capital and given photographs made from an engraving of the works.

4. My visits to the old company records at Kew unexpectedly provided exciting finds, completely unknown within PCI, including the names of Candy's partners, the agreement and very full articles of association, the agreement for mining the material to make Polarite, together with the signatures of the people concerned and finally, the demise of the company in 1900.

5. Within PCI it was often asked what Polarite originally was, as a crushed manganese ore of very small particle size and including plenty of dust and difficult to handle, was now used. The patents for Frank Candy's Polarite are available and he obtained the material near the Brecon Beacons, then a lonely part of South Wales, so he carried a small revolver, purchased in Paris, when doing a lone survey. I am informed by Mrs Bridges that during the second world war, Pullen Candy, then living in Bath, surrendered the revolver to the police under a government order.

Before leaving the subject of Polarite it will be seen from the International Water and Sewerage Purification Company letters that the telegraphic address was "CIMOLITE" and this remained with the company until the formation of PCI when the Paterson "CLARIFY" was adopted. I am not sure why this happened, or how "CIMOLITE" was formed, but I feel it would be in keeping with Frank Candy's character that it was made from "Candy International Makers of Polarite"!

6. In 1901 Frank Candy received from the Leighton Buzzard Town Council a rather handsome certificate bearing testimony to the Polarite filtration system working in the town. From this I learned of the existence of the International Purification Syndicate and from other sources, information about the considerable number of waterworks contracts in hand between 1900 and 1906.

7. From 1887 to 1927 medals for "excellence" and "highest awards" were issued by the Sanitary, later Royal Sanitary, Institute, and reproduced on Frank Candy's letter headings, publications and advertisements. After some research, I found that the Institute had been renamed The Royal Society of Health in 1954 and whose librarian, Miss K.G.Jones provided me with copies of exhibition papers, discussion documents and advertisements covering the years 1880 - 1920, so bringing the "dark age" period to light.

8. The confidential file of letters between Frank Candy and Dr Thresh, as well as those between Frank Candy and the Reading Water Engineers, Mr Walker and his son, all provided information on the Polarite Chamber system installed in 1892-4 at Reading to uprate and purify the irony water before filtration through the English-type slow sand filters. Later, the Declor system of chlorination and de-chlorination was designed for the same authority and made Reading the first

Appendices

town to have this treatment. The letters also give much insight to the character and ability of Frank Candy and his son up to the Great War period.

9. The company financial reports for the 1920-1935 period indicated to me the foresight and enthusiasm of F.D.C.Allen and the practical designs of Pullen Candy who, with his new gravity filters and controls, chemical plant and pumps, put the company into a leading position. But the real interest of this period was the chlorine plant law-suit with Paterson and the acquisition of Candy's shares by Paterson. It was always thought by the Candy staff that the chlorinator case forced the sale of the shares, whereas throughout the negotiations Allen acted from a position of strength and disposed of the case very neatly.

10. Filter Floors.
Pullen Candy designed his nozzles and filter floor on the basis of 1 to 1.25 cu ft. free air per minute and an upwash rate of 5 to 6 gallons per sq. ft. per minute. At these rates the sand kept clean even though the raw water passed through very poor settling tanks compared to those developed some twenty years later. He was adamant that a higher upwash rate would separate the sand grains too much and that higher rates would be counter-productive. In talks and tenders he claimed that the system was superior to Paterson's with their higher wash rate and troughs and much superior to the high level wash system without air scour, used in American plants.

By the 1970's it was apparent that the earthenware pipe collection system was not economic and required re-designing. Also the nozzles were behaving erratically, because of higher upwash rates specified by some customers and the use of anthracite. So the necessity for a new system of collection, plus a new and thoroughly tested filter nozzle, using the same shape and having the same facilities as the original Pullen Candy design, became an urgent part of the research and development programme.

B Chapter 1. Notes

Chapter 1. Page 26
The Company had a nominal capital of £100,000 in £5 shares, and at the start, in addition to the £30,000 allocated as paid up by the Partners, £1,000 had also been subscribed or on call. The assets were valued at £30,000, a considerable sum in those days, which the Partners agreed would be converted into 6,000 £5 ordinary shares. These were allocated as follows:

George Marquis De Stacpoole	Gentleman	600
Frank Candy	Manufacturer and Geologist	2428
Dr Arthur Angell PhD.FIC	Analytical Chemist	1888
Leopold Nestor Frere	Civil Engineer	1080
John Daws Chew	Surveyor	1
Joseph Crewe	Land Agent	1
W B Hallett	Surveyor	1
Edward Stopford-Jones	Gentleman	1

Appendices

Chapter 1. Page 27
Extract from the paper entitled "The International System of Water and Sewage Purification" by Mr Henry Cadell B.Sc., FRSE, JP read before the Royal Scottish Society of Arts 1891, and for which he was awarded a silver medal:-

No system of water supply can be considered complete which does not embrace an equally adequate system of sewage disposal, and the question of getting the water out is often even more troublesome than that of getting it in. No scheme yet proposed fully satisfies all the conditions of this very pressing and perplexing problem, but advances are constantly being made and it is of the latest advance in this direction that I wish now to speak. Before however, going into the details of the latest methods, I shall briefly refer to some of the more important systems of sewage disposal in use at present, and point out their chief advantages or drawbacks.

For many years it was thought that sewage could be profitably disposed of by irrigation, but after long years of probation, it has been found that town sewage is not nearly such a valuable fertiliser as had been supposed and in several cases, farmers have even refused to use it when brought to their fields gratis. There are, it is true, many sewage farms and irrigation meadows still in existence, but very few of them are anything but financial failures, and the effluent water that flows from the field drains into the neighbouring streams has undergone but a slight improvement in sinking through the sodden ground.

To obviate some of the objections to ordinary sewage farming by irrigation, the system of intermittent downward filtration has been tried. In this case the sewage percolates intermittently down through specially prepared soil, and escapes by field drains, having parted with a large proportion of its suspended ingredients on the way. The ground thus fertilised yields good crops if the conditions are favourable, and the effluent is comparatively free from noxious matters. Of course, in cases where the soil is impervious and stiff, the conditions for the success of this system are a-wanting and in any case, a considerable area of land is required, which near a town is generally very valuable and difficult to be had for such purposes.

In the next class of sewage disposal systems, the question is treated from a chemical point of view and the desired end is sought to be gained by the use of precipitants of various kinds. These are mixed with the sewage and have the effect of causing the suspended and part of the dissolved matters to settle out in the form of sludge which sinks down, while the clarified liquid is drawn off above.

Now in all such systems the success depends on (1) the amount of purification effected, (2) in the quality of the sludge produced, and (3) on the relative cost as compared with other systems. What is wanted is the cheapest way of separating the pure water from its contents and at the same time producing sludge that will prove of some agricultural value and help to pay for the precipitate used in its extraction. Keeping these ends in view, many substances have been suggested as precipitants. In the old "ABC" or Alum, Blood, and Clay process, these materials were added and caused precipitation to take place. Instead of blood, charcoal or refuse from Prussiate of Potash is now added where the system is in use, but the chief objection is the great quantity of sludge produced and the excessive cost of producing it, which has led to it's being abandoned at several places where the system was in operation. Another favourite precipitant used at many places is lime, to which is sometimes added black ash waste, produced abundantly in alkali works. Lime gives a clear effluent, but one which contains much organic matter in solution, is liable to undergo rapid decomposition and when run into a stream, is apt to kill the fish in it. Moreover, it produces a large quantity of sludge to be got rid of and as lime has the power of setting free the combined ammonia, it both spoils the mineral value of the sludge and creates an intolerable nuisance by the fumes evolved. Where lime is used, the sludge produced is either sold at a merely nominal price, given away, dug into the ground, burned in a destructor, or its removal is paid for.

To produce a good result there must be not only a clear effluent, but the effluent must be innocuous and fit to turn into any river without destroying the fish or undergoing subsequent putrefaction. Like drinking water it must, in fact, be oxidised as much as possible and what is wanted is some plan that will, while producing a clear effluent, provide also a cheap supply of oxygen to attack the dangerous organic matters that may not be removed with the precipitate. There are at present, so far as I am aware, only two practical methods of obtaining a sufficient quantity of oxygen for this purpose. The first of these is the Webster process, in which electricity is used to decompose the fluid and set free by electrolysis some of the combined oxygen in the water. This very clever application of electricity to an unusual purpose has been attended in the experimental stage by satisfactory results. The second practical method is one about which there can no longer be any doubt as it has been sufficiently well tried to warrant a clear and satisfactory conclusion being formed as to it's working and merits, and I shall now devote the remainder of the paper to the International System of Sewage Purification.

After one of the most exhaustive enquiries that have been yet made as to the best method of sewage disposal, the Royal Commissioners on Metropolitan Sewage Discharge, who were appointed in June 1882, unanimously recommend in their report, dated November 27 1884, the system of precipitation and filtration. Precipitation and filtration had been used together or separately as we have seen, with more or less indifferent results and the great difficulty was to get the right materials to effect both these objects at the minimum of expense and maximum of efficiency. Happening to hear while on a visit to London in 1888 of a new process invented to meet the recommendations of the Commissioners, I paid a visit, in rather an incredulous mood, to Acton, a western suburb of the metropolis, where the 'International system' had been introduced more than a year previously to supersede the old ABC process, condemned on account of it's inefficiency and cost. I was both pleased and astonished at what I saw and on making enquiries as to its practical working, quickly changed my opinion as to the merits of new process. Three years have passed and I have had sundry opportunities of extending my investigations and watching it's operation and the more I have seen, the more I am convinced that from whatever aspect it is viewed, the 'International' is by far the best method of sewage purification that has yet been devised.

The system is characterised, not by any great novelty in it's mechanical principles, but by the nature of the materials it employs in the purification of the sewage. The precipitate known commercially as 'Ferrozone' is a black, magnetic preparation containing salts of iron, alumina and magnesia, as well as magnetic oxide of iron in a very spongy and absorbent condition, obtained as a bye-product in the manufacture of Polarite.

Appendices

From this analysis it will be seen that ferrous sulphate which acts as a powerful chemical disinfectant as well as a precipitant, enters largely into the composition of Ferrozone. The soluble salts of alumina, lime, and magnesia also assist in the decolourisation and precipitation of the sewage. The insoluble portion, consisting mainly of powdered Polarite, serves to oxidise the putrescible matter and to accelerate by its weight the subsidence of the precipitate. The rapidity of precipitation is hardly less important than it's completeness when large volumes of sewage have to be dealt with, as a speedy separation of the sludge from the supernatant fluid enables a much greater quantity to be treated in the same tanks than could be disposed of with a slowly working precipitant. The magnetic spongy iron has this further advantage, that it tends by its oxidising power to keep the sludge sweet during subsequent disposal, whether when being pressed or dried for manual purposes. This is an important consideration, as it prevents the proximity of the sewage works from being a public nuisance, such as is the case where lime enters into the composition of the precipitant. The absence of all disagreeable odour is not the least of the merits which are claimed by the 'International' system, and in the many visits I have paid to works on this system I have been much pleased and struck by this circumstance.

The value of sewage as a fertiliser has, as we have seen, not been found so great as was formerly supposed and this is one reason why sewage farming has been often abandoned. Sewage, it must be remembered, is a very indefinite term, and is very variable in composition. It is simply a name for all the liquid refuse of a populous place and may contain large quantities of chemical or other ingredients that have no agricultural value whatever.

Whatever the value of the manure from sewage may be, it is clearly the best principle in any system of precipitation to aim at turning this value to the best account. There is no use spending money, as in the ABC process, in practically putting in the fertiliser as a precipitant to take it out again along with the sediment from the sewage. Again, it is an equally wrong principle to leave out of view altogether this possible source of profit, as is done in the lime process which spoils the sludge as a fertiliser. What seems to be wanted is a precipitant that will throw down any valuable manure that the sewage may contain and produce a concentrated fertiliser that will find a market and help to pay the cost of its production. The sludge should be as small in quantity as is consistent with efficient purification, because, if it has any value at all, it is thus most concentrated and most valuable, and if it is worthless, then there is always the smallest quantity of get rid of. So far as my observations go, the sludge produced by Ferrozone satisfies these conditions as well as, or better than any other kind I have heard of. When pressed and dried at Acton it was selling as a garden fertiliser for 30s. per ton at the time of my visit three years ago, but I do not mean to assert that if large quantities were thrown on the market anything like this sum could be obtained from farmers generally. As to the cost of Ferrozone, it is found in practice that from 7 to 14 ppm are required to precipitate every gallon of sewage, the quantity varying according to the amount of impurity in the fluid. As Ferrozone costs about 3s. per cwt. if we take, say, 11 ppm as the average quantity used per gallon, we find that it costs about 30s.7.5d. to precipitate 1,000,000 gallons, or to reduce the scale, for something less than 3.5d 10,000 gallons of sewage can be effectually precipitated.

The International system can be used equally well by the smallest as well as the largest communities. At Acton the works are designed to meet the requirements of a population of some 20,000, and several of the large cities in England are making arrangements to follow the example

Appendices

of the smaller towns in which the system has proved a success. The following abstract of a report made last summer by Professor E. Frankland F.R.S., to Major Tulloch, the Chief Engineering Inspector of the Local Government Board, will show the high opinion which this eminent authority has formed, after investigating the working of the International system at Acton:-

"These results show that the raw sewage contained a very large proportion of highly polluted suspended matter and an unusually large amount of foul organic matter in solution and further, that the effluents from the subsidence tank and filter were derived from sewage of about equal polluting power as regards dissolved organic matter.

In the subsidence tank the suspended matter was reduced from 240 to 80 parts per 100,000 of tank effluent, whilst the effluent from the filter was free from suspended matter. It was clear and transparent. This is a satisfactory result. The effect upon the dissolved organic matter in the subsidence tank is very remarkable; its amount being reduced to little more that one-tenth of that present in the original sewage. In its subsequent passage through the filter, the dissolved organic matter is still further reduced to nearly one-sixteenth of that present in the original sewage. It is now in a state of purity greatly exceeding that prescribed by the standards of the Rivers Pollution Commissioners.

No chemical process of purifying sewage has ever, in my experience, approached this in efficacy and if the results obtained at Acton can be accomplished in other places, a most important advance will be made in the purification of the sewage of towns. I need scarcely add that the effluent from the filter is not only clear but inodorous and inoffensive. It is of course not fit for dietetic purposes, but it may be admitted in large volumes into running water without creating any nuisance."

Mr Carter Bell, ARSM., FIC., County Analyst for Chester, Salford & Co., also had occasion to analyse the crude sewage and effluent at Acton and the following is an extract from his report:-
"The effluent was flowing exactly like clear spring water, and when the sample was put into the bottle there was not the slightest odour of any kind, and it would have been impossible for anyone to have said, judging by the appearance, that it was not good drinking water. The analysis also shows that the reduction of the putrescent matter has been very great, and that such an effluent as this may be run into any stream with perfect safety. I am surprised to find that after more than three years working the filter beds can produce such a good effluent."

Two years ago the International system was introduced at Hendon, a district on the north of London with a population of 10,500, to supersede the lime process which had proved a complete failure. The existing precipitation tanks &c., were used for the Ferrozone, and Polarite filters were constructed at the outfall, instead of the earth filter beds intended to purify the lime effluents. The result of the change had been highly satisfactory. I visited the Hendon works in the beginning of this month and was very pleased at their success. In conclusion, the advantages of the International system may, I think, be summed up as follows:

1. A remarkably pure effluent is produced.
2. The process is very simple and easily worked.

Appendices

3. It is applicable on any scale.
4. It causes no public nuisance.
5. The minimum of area is required for the works.
6. The smallest quantity of sludge is produced.
7. The maximum value of the manure is obtained.
8. The working and first cost of the works are small.

I cannot but think it is to this system, or to something like it, that we must look for the successful disposal of the increasing volume of foul waters from our great cities and rural towns. Were the sewage of Glasgow collected at suitable points and treated in this way, the Clyde might again become a clear and wholesome flood. The south side of Edinburgh again might have all its sewage discharged as clear as crystal into the Powburn as is done into the Thames at Acton. It seems a pity to solve the problem by diverting the natural drainage of the land into sewers and pay compensation to millers for drying up the sources of our urban streams, when means have been invented of producing clean water at once quite pure enough to flow into any river. The cost of carrying out the International system is much less than that of laying miles of expensive sewers and the result is much better, for the sewers simply remove the nuisance to a distance and pollute the sea at their mouth, while the International system removes the nuisance altogether at its source, or, in other words, prevents the nuisance ever being formed. So soon as the foul water leaves the houses it is caught up, purified and run into the streams to find its way to the sea by the natural drainage channels of the country. Were this system adopted and the sewage of our towns concentrated at convenient places, purified and discharged into the nearest stream, the sludge being sold to the neighbouring farmers or market gardeners, a very great advance in practical sanitation would be made. Not only this, however; the land along our urban streams would increase in value, fish would again return to their old haunts, and life in the vicinity generally would be more worth living. There are, of course, some kinds of sewage, such as esparto liquor from paper mills, which, for chemical reasons may not be thus capable of purification, but I think I have said enough to show that as a means of purifying ordinary domestic sewage, which forms, as a rule, the great bulk of the liquid refuse of our cities, the International system has proved one of the most valuable aids to practical sanitation that has been invented within recent years."

Chapter 10 page 172
The following figures are of interest as they cover the period when Rabeneck was MD of PCI. Whilst the numbers appear very small, inflation would increase them by perhaps twenty-five times, suggesting that the business has grown very little over the years. The early profit figures are however, rather better than the industry normally achieves and were perhaps too high. The later figures illustrate the effect of the poorly controlled overheads in the late 1970s.

Year	Turnover £m	Trading Profit £m	Profit % T.O.
1968	2.37	0.12	4.98
1969	2.37	0.24	9.96
1970	3.07	0.21	6.94
1971	3.76	0.4	10.6

1972	6.47	0.66	10.11
1973	5.62	0.47	8.28
1974	6.07	0.38	6.26
1975	7.95	0.13	1.66
1976	10.44	0.38	3.64
1977	11.86	0.22	1.87

C Conversion Factors

mgd (Million Imperial gallons per day) = 4,546 m^3/day
1 US gallon = 0.832 Imperial gallons
ppm (parts per million) = mg/l (milligrams per litre)
1 foot = 304.8 mm
1 inch = 25.4 mm

D Glossary of technical terms

Activated sludge - a biological process in which the active (and beneficial) bacterial biomass is settled, part of it being discharged as sludge and the rest mixed back into the incoming biologically degradable material. One of the principal methods for treating sewage effluent.

Airscour - the use of low pressure air, distributed evenly over the base of the filter under the medium, to loosen the dirt retained by the filter, prior to or simultaneously with the backwash.

Alum (Aluminium sulphate) - a chemical commonly used as a coagulant to cause the suspended solids/turbidity/dissolved colour in untreated water to agglomerate (or flocculate) and separate from the water.

Anion - an atom or molecule (group of bonded atoms) with a negative electrical charge.

Backwash - the use of a reverse flow of water (usually treated water) to flush dirt from a filter.

Base-exchange - a process using ion-exchange resin to soften water by exchanging the hardness cations in the water (calcium and magnesium) for sodium ions temporarily held on the resin. The resin is periodically re-generated with strong sodium chloride (brine) and the accumulated hardness salts discharged to waste.

Biological filtration - the use of naturally occurring bacteria supported on a porous "bed" e.g. coke or clinker, to reduce the amount of biologically degradable material in a liquid effluent. (See Trickling filter).

Breakpoint chlorination - the process of dosing sufficient chlorine to oxidise ammonia in the water and to leave a residue to maintain disinfecting conditions in the distribution system. It is characterised by a rising curve, then a decline, then a final rise again in the "residual" level of chlorine as the chlorine is progressively added.

Cation - an atom or molecule with a positive electrical charge.

Chlorination - the application of chlorine or sodium hypochlorite to water in order to disinfect it.

Appendices

CIX - Continuous ion-exchange. A general name for ion-exchange processes where the resin(s) is moved continuously or semi-continuously to a separate regeneration unit while the main flow continues to be treated (in contrast to normal practice where the vessel containing the resin is taken out of service for regeneration).

Colour - the colour found in some untreated waters, which is not removed by simple filtration, usually caused by decayed vegetable matter such as peat.

Combined wash (sometimes called concurrent airscour wash) - a filter backwashing process in which the airscour and backwash are applied simultaneously.

Compound filter - a design which incorporates two or more filter beds of increasing fineness in a single vessel.

D-mixer - a mixing vessel in the shape of a "D" on its side, with slow speed paddles, used for lime slurries.

De-aeration - the use of steam or a vacuum to remove dissolved oxygen from boiler feed water.

De-chlorination - the removal of un-reacted or "free" chlorine from water by chemical re-action with a reducing agent, such as sulphur dioxide, sodium bi-sulphite, or by adsorption onto activated carbon.

De-gassing - the use of a counter current of air to remove dissolved gases (carbon dioxide, hydrogen sulphide etc.) from water.

Demineralisation - a process for removing the dissolved mineral ions from water.

Dissolved iron - iron which is in solution in the water. The iron is not visible until it oxidises due to contact with air etc. but then deposits a reddish brown precipitate.

Double regeneration - (ion exchange) - just that.

E-Coli - a bacterium identified by Theodore Escherich in 1885 which is used as an indicator of faecal pollution in water.

Electro-dialysis - a process which uses electricity to force the cations and anions dissolved in water through special membranes and so partially de-mineralise the water.

Filtration - a process for removing particulate matter from water (or other liquids) by passing the liquid through a porous medium e.g. a bed of sand, pre-coat, paper, textile, wire mesh etc.

Floatation (or flotation) - a process in which particulate material or flocculated material is caused to float by attachment of the material to micro-bubbles of air. The floated material can then be skimmed off the water.

Gravity filters - filters (usually in open tanks) which rely on the head of water within the filter vessel to force the water through the filter.

Head Loss - the total of the static and dynamic loss across a filter or other process device, usually measured in mm, m, inches or feet of water. (Synonymous with pressure loss).

Hydrogen ion exchange - the replacement of cations in water by hydrogen ions - see also Cation exchange.

Hydraulic scour - the use of rotating pressure jets impinging on the surface of the filter sand (or other medium) to loosen the accumulated dirt.

Ion - an ion is either an atom or molecule carrying an electrical charge.

Ion-exchange - The process of exchanging ions dissolved in water for ions temporarily held on special resins. The resins need to be re-generated periodically to remove the ions extracted from the water and re-charge the resins with the ions to be exchanged for them. The process is used for demineralising water.

Iron removal - a process for removing dissolved iron or iron combined with organic matter, from water.

Appendices

Kieselguhr - the naturally occurring skeletal remains of marine organisms (diatoms), usually in the form of a very fine white powder which is used as a pre-coat or filter cake for candle or textile filters.

Lime/soda softening - a process which uses either lime alone to precipitate bicarbonate ("temporary") hardness or in combination with soda ash (sodium carbonate) or sometimes caustic soda to precipitate both temporary and permanent hardness, to soften the water.

Magnesite - Candy's name for naturally occurring magnesium salts used for neutralising excess acidity (carbon dioxide) in water. The material replaces or supplements sand as the medium in the filter and dissolves as it reacts with carbon dioxide.

Marginal chlorination - the process of dosing just sufficient chlorine to leave a finite residual of chlorine.

Mixed bed - a demineraliser using mixed cation and anion resins in the same vessel. The device is capable of producing almost pure water. Ammonia if present will be converted to monochloramine.

Nano-filtration - a membrane process similar to Reverse Osmosis but which is designed to remove only part of the dissolved minerals in the water. (The rejection efficiency against ions and soluble molecules is between that of reverse osmosis and ultrafiltration).

Ozone - an unstable but very vigorous form of oxygen, used in the water industry as an oxidising agent. It has to be produced on site and cannot be stored.

Polarite - a catalyst used in iron/manganese removing filters. See Chapter 1 for an analysis of Candy's original material which was not the same as the present day Polarite which is manganese dioxide. Although the name was registered by Candy it has become generic for this type of catalyst.

Plumbo-solvency - the action of certain waters on lead piping.

Pre-coat filtration - a type of filtration where a powder such as Kieselguhr is deposited on a relatively coarse screen and then acts as a very fine filter. The powder is discarded when clogged, and is replaced.

Pressure filters - filters which operate without breaking the hydraulic head e.g. in a pipeline.

Rake filters - filters which used mechanical rakes to agitate the filter sand to loosen the accumulated dirt.

Resin - in the context of this story resin means a synthetic ion-exchange medium.

Reverse osmosis - a process which uses a semi-permeable membrane to separate dissolved minerals and organic molecules from water. A method of desalinating or de-mineralising water.

Sodium exchange - the replacement of calcium and magnesium ions in water by sodium ions - see also Base exchange.

Slow sand filters - sand beds which clean water by biological purification, developed by James Simpson and Robert Thom independently in the 1820s. The filters operate at a very low rate per unit area (about one fiftieth) compared with gravity or pressure filters but will remove organic and biological matter without the use of a coagulant whereas the "rapid" filters generally remove only particulate or coagulated matter.

Settlement (or clarification) - the process of separating particulate and flocculated matter from water (or other liquids) by settling the material in a suitable tank. (An alternative to floatation).

Sludge blanket - a zone of accumulated, concentrated sludge held in a settling tank or clarifier, through which the incoming water flows. With some designs the sludge may be recirculated and mixed with the incoming water.

Appendices

Trickling filters - shallow beds of porous material such as coke on which benevolent bacteria grow. The effluent is distributed over the surface by rotating or travelling sprinklers at a rate sufficient to prevent flooding of the filter medium and permit natural circulation of air. The bacteria destroy the bulk of the incoming biological pollution by aerobic oxidation.

E Sources

1. My main source is Bob Williams' rough draft, written in the early 80s and I have not attempted to verify the many claims for "firsts", "inventions" etc., and freely accept that some of these may be unfounded. Williams' early text covering the period up to the second war provides a fascinating insight to the company in those early days and as far as I know, is the only account available. His later text covered a period too fresh in his mind and I have discarded much of the detail and augmented his account with material from my contemporaries and company records to balance my own recollections. The photo of Bob looking uncharacteristically serious is by courtesy of his daughter, Mrs Susan Sergeant.

2. I am most grateful to my close friends from PCI who have patiently read and commented on my drafts. In particular, I thank John Armstrong for the overview of the industry and the company's part in it during the 60s and 70s. John Cheetham kindly checked the technical statements relating to the period 1963 to 1996, and David Stevenson the Glossary. David Banfield advised on the overall structure and balance as well as providing an overview of the company politics during the period 1970 to 1996. Doug Bird and John Farrer provided me with additional detail on the Permutit story, and Peter Jackson and Ken Piddington background on Boby's. David Carslaw gave help with the Stellar Filter story and Dave Burton with regard to the recent Rand Water Board works. I am grateful to John Sheffield for his assistance with the period of the merger of Paterson's with Candy's.

Unfortunately, no-one who knew any of the companies (in a senior position) prior to about 1950 is still alive so we must take much of the early part of the story on trust.

Most of the photos are culled from old company publications as the records are patchy. Paterson's kept excellent photographic records up to about 1955 and these have survived largely intact. Candy's records up to the early 60s were very poor and few originals remain. The records from the 60s and 70s were well organised and comprehensive but unfortunately are now a mess resulting from the interregnum prior to the sale to Black and Veatch. The same fate has affected the Permutit records and the few Boby records that survived the sale to Permutit. Perhaps curiously, I have found almost no photos of the founders and assume that they regarded photos of their plants as being more important!

3. The chapter on Permutit is based upon B.G.W.Balster's excellent booklet "Permutit-Boby, a History of Twentieth Century Water Treatment" which, although written with the company's commercial interest in mind, nonetheless provides a fascinating account of its achievements. The comments covering the more recent years are mine.

Appendices

4. I have not attempted to cover the substantial and impressive record of the various overseas subsidiaries, except in passing. Each merits its own record but this is a task for others.

5. The paragraphs on Bell's and Boby's are based largely on old brochures and detail from Boby pensioners and do not pretend to do more than skate over their stories. I am grateful to Mrs Frances Boby for copies of the family photos.

6. I am indebted to Yvonne Hewett who patiently edited my drafts and gave much encouragement.

7. Bob Williams acknowledged a number of sources for his text and the following is a brief list. Regrettably, many of the individuals mentioned are no longer alive.

The Scottish Royal Society of Arts

The Photographic Society of Great Britain

Museums and Universities
    The Ironbridge Museum Trust
    Welsh Industrial and Maritime Museum, Cardiff
    Vivian Art Gallery and Museum, Swansea
    Breckock Museum, Brecon
    South Wales Miners Library, Swansea
    University College of Swansea
    Department of Victorian Studies, Leicester University
    The Open University
    Imperial College of Science and Technology, London
    The President, Girard College, Philadelphia, USA

Newspapers
    Torbay Times
    South Wales Evening Post

Royal Establishments
    Estate Commissioner, Balmoral Castle
    Archives Department, Windsor Castle

Overseas Engineers
    J. Aage Huse, General manager, Copenhagen Water Supply

Central Libraries at
    Bath, Exeter, Newton Abbot, Torquay, Bristol, Ealing, Lyme Regis

Water Authorities
    South West Water Offices at Exeter, Paignton, Truro
    Wessex Water at Chippenham, Bridgewater, Taunton

Appendices

    Southern Water at Hastings
    North Surrey Water at Staines
    Welsh Water at Newport

Government Departments
    Capital House Company Records - Cardiff
    Capital House Company Records - Kew
    Registrar Births and Deaths - London
    The Patent Office, London

Technical Publications
    Water Services
    The Engineer
    Radio Times, Hulton Picture Library

Institutes
    Chartered Municipal Engineers Library
    Royal Society of Health, records
    Institute of Public Health Engineers, records
    Royal Sanitary Institute, records
    The Geological Society, London

Candy Family relatives
    Mrs P Robinson, New York, daughter of Frank Pullen Candy
    Mrs Jane Lloyd, New York, daughter of Mrs Robinson
    Mrs Jill Peters, Perth, Australia, daughter of Burville Candy
    Mrs Joyce Forster, Hythe, Hants., formerly Mrs Burville Candy
    Mrs Vivienne Bridges, Winchelsea, step-daughter of Frank Pullen Candy
    Peter Candy at Manor and Styrtingdale Farms, Bath

Candy Tile Company (now BCT) Heathfield Works, Newton Abbot

In Bath
    The Secretary, King Edward School
    H.E.J. Morris, Auctioneers and Surveyors
    Stothert & Pitt, Engineers

Candy Pensioners
    L.W.Smith, Erector and Hanwell Stores Manager
    A.C.Gough, Erector, son of E.Gough, Erector 1900-1927
    K.E.Rose, Draughtsman from 1922
    L.Leighton, son of George Leighton, Chief Draughtsman from 1920

Bell Pensioner
    John Porter

Appendices

Paterson Pensioner
> Horace Coulson, Director

Jewell & Paterson Pensioner
> Sydney Burrells, Director

F List of illustrations

Page	Name	Nearest town/ county	Country	Plant supplier/ photo source
4	River Itchen Scheme	Portsmouth	England	PCH
5	Bob Williams			Family
6	Ilkeston	Derbyshire	England	Reeves
7	Ransome continuous filter		England	Ransome-verMehr Machinery Co
8	Company logos			
9	Standerton Inauguration	Standerton	South Africa	Candy
10	Anderson's Purifier		England	Anderson Filters
11	Candy advert 1910			Co. archive
12	Patent filter		England	Mather and Platt
13	Clarkston Paper Mill	Glasgow	Scotland	Bell Brothers
14	Table Useful Data			Co. archive
15	Beware unfiltered Water!			Metafiltration Co
16	Native Well			Co. archive
17	Turnover Filters	Belfast	N. Ireland	Turnover Filters Ltd
18	Omdurman	Omdurman	Sudan	Co. archive
20	Frank Candy	Chippenham, Wiltshire	England	Co. archive
21	Candy medals			Co. archive
22	Great Western Pottery Brick and Tile Works	Devon	England	Candy & Co. Ltd
23	Partnership agreement extract, dated June 1887		England	Public Records Office, Kew
24	Polarite analysis			Co. archive

Appendices

25	Ferrozone analysis			Co. archive
25	Advert from "Water" 1904		England	Co. archive
26	Extract from "The Sanitary Record"		England	Co. archive
27	Patent oxidising filter		England	Candy, "Water"
28	Reading Corporation report extract September 1894	Reading	England	Co. archive
29	Brede 1902	Hastings	England	Candy
30	Holne filters	Paignton	England	Candy
31	Certificate issued by Leighton Buzzard UDC 1901	Leighton Buzzard	England	Co. archive
32	Port Elizabeth filters by train	Port Elizabeth	South Africa	Candy
33	Traction Engine		South Africa	Candy
33	Ox train		South Africa	Candy
34	King Williams Town filters, in course of erection.	King Williams Town	South Africa	Candy
35	Bell drawing			Co. archive
35	Bell 16 HP Phaeton		England	Beaulieu Motor Museum
36	BA type pressure filter		England	Bell Brothers
36	Cartoon			Bell Brothers
37	Morley	Yorkshire	England	Reeves
37	Cartoon			Bell Brothers
38	Cartoon			Bell Brothers
38	Birkenhead	Merseyside	England	Bell Brothers
39	Low Turbine type doser		England	Bell Brothers
39	Cartoon			Bell Brothers
40	Denton Workshop	Manchester	England	Bell Brothers
40	William Boby			Family
41	Vincent Boby			Family

Appendices

41	Gwalior triumphal arch		India	William Boby
41	Boby feedwater heater	Ipswich	England	William Boby
42	Michael Boby			Family
42	Dry softener on test		England	Co. archive
43	Blackbirds STP	Hertfordshire	England	William Boby
43	Railway lime softener	Coulsden	England	William Boby
44	Bankside Power Station	S.London	England	William Boby
44	Benghazi ED plant		Libya	William Boby
45	BP Baglan Bay	Port Talbot	Wales	William Boby
45	Lorry mounted unit		England	Lassen-Hjort
46	Lassen-Hjort auto-dosing apparatus		England	Co. archive
47	Lassen-Hjort lime-soda softener.		England	Co. archive
47	Horse-drawn treatment unit			UWS
48	Prenton softeners	Birkenhead	England	UWS
49	Pullen Candy			Co. archive
50	Patent 6126			Co. archive
50	Patent 6088			Co. archive
51	Extract from Patent 9179			Co. archive
52	Candy-Whittaker drainage tile.			Co. archive
52	Coventry STP	Coventry	England	Candy
53	Newport	Newport	Wales	Candy
54	Candy logo			Co. archive
54	Hastings, Brede 1903	Hastings	England	Candy
55	Harrogate testimonial			Co. archive
56	Candy VS pump			Co. archive
57	Declor Filters, Windsor	Windsor	England	Candy
57	Declor trademark			Co. archive
58	Newspaper extracts			Co. archive

Appendices

59	Candy Compound filter			Co. archive
60	Truro	Cornwall	England	Candy
60	Christchurch 1913	Hampshire	England	Candy
61	Cross section of Bi-flow filter			Candy
62	Ministry of munitions Avonmouth	Bristol	England	Candy
63	Talybont chemical pumps	Talybont	Wales	Candy
65	Gravity Doser			Candy
67	William Paterson aged about 80.			Co. archive
68	Paterson Osilameter			Co. archive
68	Royal Arsenal College, Tokyo	Tokyo	Japan	Paterson
69	Rowntree's, diagram	York	England	Paterson
70	Clydebank	Glasgow	Scotland	Paterson
70	Clydebank chemical plant	Glasgow	Scotland	Paterson
71	Kempton Park chlorinators.	W.London	England	Paterson
71	Paterson Chlorograph			Co. archive
72	Paterson Accentrifloc			Co. archive
72	Filter control table.			Paterson
73	Paterson type-G controller			Co. archive
74	Kempton Park	W.London	England	Paterson
74	Rand Water Board	Vereeniging	South Africa	Paterson
74	Kobe filter house	Kobe	Japan	Paterson
75	Tallin		Estonia	Paterson
75	Sandfields	South Staffs	England	Paterson
76	Langford cross section	Essex	England	Paterson
76	Huntington ozone	Liverpool	England	Paterson
77	Chellow Heights	Bradford	England	Paterson
77	MWB Green Lanes	London	England	Paterson

Appendices

78	Rio de Cobre		Brazil	Paterson
78	Fayoum plant.		Egypt	Paterson
79	Paterson logo			Co. archive
79	Whitacre	Birmingham	England	Paterson
80	Filter diagram			Paterson archive
81	St Annes Board Mill	Bristol	England	Paterson
81	Steenbras	Cape Town	South Africa	Paterson
82	King George opening the filters at Clydebank	Glasgow	Scotland	Co. archive
83	Chiquinquira		Colombia	Candy
84	Type-A floor			Co. archive
85	Laying floors, Kobe	Kobe	Japan	Candy
86	Tipper lime doser			Candy archive
87	Waitakere NZ		New Zealand	Candy
88	Diagram Candy type-A control system			Co. archive
89	Candy Module			Co. archive
90	Tuborg	Copenhagen	Denmark	Candy
91	Candy's slow-start controller			Co. archive
92	Kloof Nek	Cape Town	South Africa	Candy
92	Cheltenham Dowdeswell	Gloucestershire	England	Candy
93	Chlorine demand curves			Paterson "Blue Book"
94	Detail of venturi proportioning			Candy archive
95	Warwick Dufour			Family
96	Auckland, Ardmore	Auckland	New Zealand	Candy
97	Griffiths			Co. archive
98	Medium hand type Alumina doser			Candy archive
99	Diagram of hopper tank			Co. archive
100	Type-B floor			Co. archive

Appendices

101	Extract from board minutes			Co. archive
102	MWB Walton	W.London	England	Candy
103	R.W.Aitken			Co. archive
103	Density controller	Hurleston	England	Candy
104	Simmons' M pump			Candy
104	Autominor			Candy
105	Venturi proportioning apparatus			Candy, Co. archive
106	G pumps Mosswood	Consett	England	PCI
107	Extract of codes			Candy, Co. archive
108	Extract from Peacock's treatise			British Museum
109	Cork	Cork	Ireland	Candy
110	Candy M chlorinator			Co. archive
111	Candy's patented PRV			Co. archive
112	Weir type proportioning system			Candy, Co. archive
113	Pile of pipes and inscription			Co. archive
114	Adjustable V-notch weir			Candy, Co. archive
115	UWS logo			Co. archive
115	Permutit logo			Co. archive
115	Lassen-Hjort logo			Co. archive
116	L-H lime-soda softener with train	Castlethorpe, Bucks	England	Lassen-Hjort
117	SD softener		England	Co. archive
117	R.T.Pemberton			Co. archive
118	A.J.R.Walter			Co. archive
118	Early UWS softener		England	UWS
119	W.A.Low			Co. archive
120	Type-C pump		England	Permutit
121	Mehalla Kubra		Egypt	Permutit

Appendices

121	Barcelona	Barcelona	Spain	Permutit
122	Demineraliser 1937	Guildford	England	Co. archive
122	Sulphonated coal			Co. archive
123	Extract from roll of honour			Co. archive
124	Mixed bed demineraliser. RAF		England	Permutit
125	Emergency pack		England	Permutit
125	Shell Haven	Essex	England	Permutit
126	George Sansom			Co. archive
127	Uranium plant SA		South Africa	Permutit
128	Suomen Sokeri		Finland	Permutit
128	Anic Gela		Sicily	Permutit
129	Norsk Hydro		Norway	Permutit
129	Inverkip	Greenock	Scotland	Permutit
130	Fescol		England	Permutit
130	Spiractor, Kingston PS	Surrey	England	Permutit
131	Permex diagram			Permutit
131	Metafilters, S&N Edinburgh	Edinburgh	Scotland	SMF
132	Stella Filters Drakelow	Kidderminster	England	Permutit
133	Military NBC unit		England	SMF
134	Varivoid filters, British Steel	Newport	Wales	Permutit
134	North Sea desalinator			Permutit
135	Bayswater RO train	NSW	Australia	Permutit (Australia)
136	F.C.Blight			Co. archive
137	Second war Military water set		England	Paterson
138	J.A.Pickard			Co. archive
138	Stellar element			Co. archive
139	New Consolidated Goldfields Ltd		South Africa	PCI (South Africa)
140	Autopact diagram			Co. archive

Appendices

141	Anderson shelter		England	Imperial War Museum
142	Kampala	Kampala	Uganda	Candy
143	Flow meters, Torquay	Devon	England	Co. archive
144	Tees Valley, Broken Scar	Middlesborough	England	Paterson
145	Strensham sequencer	Coventry	England	Candy
146	Caithness		Scotland	Candy
147	Bukit Nanas	Kuala Lumpur	Malaysia	Paterson
147	Tsun Wan		Hong Kong	Paterson
148	RWB No.2 station	Vereeniging	South Africa	Candy
149	Orange Free State Goldfields	Balkfontein	South Africa	Candy
149	Sandford Mill	Essex	England	Candy
150	Diddington, batch weighers	Huntingdon	England	Candy
150	Weir Wood	East Sussex	England	Candy
151	Pitsford pumphouse	Northampton	England	Candy
152	Diddington, "Blobins"	Huntingdon	England	Candy
153	Paterson siphon diagram			Co. archive
154	Maundown	Taunton	England	Candy
154	RTB	Port Talbot	Wales	Candy
155	Appleby Frodingham	Scunthorpe	England	Paterson
155	Guandu signing	Rio de Janeiro	Brazil	Co. archive
156	Guandu	Rio de Janeiro	Brazil	Paterson
157	Hanningfield	Essex	England	Paterson
158	The Stack controller			Paterson
159	River Dove	York	England	Paterson
159	Kerrison et al			Co. archive
160	Small Clorocel			Paterson
161	Centrifugal Balancer	Torquay	England	Candy
162	"Yesterday"			Co. archive
163	Netley Mills	Leatherhead	England	Candy
164	Tewkesbury	Gloucestershire	England	Candy

Appendices

164	Shek Pik		Hong Kong	Paterson
165	Huntington	Liverpool	England	Paterson
165	ICI Severnside	Bristol	England	Candy
166	MWB Coppermills	N.London	England	PCI
167	Elvington	Sheffield	England	Candy
168	Ind Coope	Wrexham	England	Candy
169	Diddington control panel	Huntingdon	England	PCI
170	Diddington filter gallery	Huntingdon	England	PCI
171	PCI logo			Co. archive
171	Church Wilne	Nottingham	England	PCI
171	Llandegfedd control room	Cardiff	Wales	Candy
172	Loch Eck		Scotland	PCI
172	Mosswood	Consett	England	PCI
173	Clatto	Dundee	Scotland	PCI
173	Leo Rabeneck			Co. archive
174	Bough Beech	Sevenoaks	England	PCI
175	Glendevon	Perth	Scotland	PC-H
176	Barcombe Mills chemical house	Lewes	England	PCI
176	Purton	Bristol	England	PCI
177	Suva		Fiji	PCI
177	Native children getting water			Co. archive
178	Waterman			PCI
179	Sha Tin		Hong Kong	Paterson
179	CP plant		West Africa	PCI
180	Cartoon			Co. archive
181	B1 Module			PCI
182	Stora Nymolla		Sweden	PCI Membranes Ltd
183	Strathclyde, Afton		Scotland	PCI
184	British Steel	Port Talbot	Wales	Permutit

Appendices

185	NZ Ammonia		New Zealand	PCI (New Zealand)
186	Tilbury	E.London	England	PCI
187	Permak	Devon	England	Permutit
188	FB clarifier diagram			PCI, Co. archive
189	Sludge cones			PCI, Co. archive
190	Melbourne, Sugarloaf	Victoria	Australia	Boby (Australia)
191	Oshogbo-Ede	Oyo State	Nigeria	PCI
192	Ankara		Turkey	PCI
193	K-filter isometric			PCI, Co. archive
194	K-filter under construction			PCI, Co. archive
195	Karkh panoramic	Baghdad	Iraq	PCI
196	Karkh filters	Baghdad	Iraq	PCI
196	Karkh pumphouse	Baghdad	Iraq	PCI
196	Karkh pre-sedimentation. tanks	Baghdad	Iraq	PCI
197	Benue before		Nigeria	PCI
197	Benue after		Nigeria	PCI
198	LA Aqueduct Scheme	Los Angeles	USA	PCI
199	Walton	W.London	England	PWT Projects
199	Damanhur		Egypt	PCI
200	Jebel Ali		Dubai	PWT Projects
200	CoCo DAF diagram			PWT, Co. archive
201	Izmit	Izmit	Turkey	PWT Projects
202	Sharjah		UAE	Paterson Candy Ltd
202	Silchester	Berkshire	England	PWT Projects
203	Panjrapur	Bombay	India	PWT Projects
203	PCL logo			Paterson Candy Ltd
204	Simly		Pakistan	PWT Projects
204	East Hyde digester	Luton	England	Paterson Candy Ltd
205	BNFL	Cumbria	England	Paterson Candy Ltd
205	Labourer			Co. archive

Index

ABC process 27
Abercrave works 24,26
Activated carbon 57,200
Activated sludge 13
Acton sewage treatment works 26,27,28
Airscour 49,63,102
Aitken, R.W. 103
Allen, F.D.C. 85,86,**93**,94,102,110,111
Amalgamation 111
Amberley Mews 62,86
Anderson, Sir John 68
-shelter 140
Angell, Dr A. 28,30,32,53
Ankara 192
Auckland 95,146
Automatic plants 145,149,150,152,154,165,166,169,189
Autopact 140
B1 Reverse Osmosis Module 181
Backwash
-combined 49,83,100,146
-separate 63,83
Bacterial Water Treatment Co. Ltd 54
Bankruptcy 30
Barcelona 120,121
Bayswater power station 129,135
BEAMA formula 175
Bell Brothers 5,12,14,35,53,74,113,138
-1927 38
-Domestic 39,184
Bell Cars 35
Benue 197
Binnie and Partners 98,170
Biological filter 50
-filter tiles 51,**52**
Biwater 16
Black and Veatch 14,18,203
Bleaching powder 58,61
Bloemfontein 102
Boby
-Michael 42
-Vincent 41
-William Boby Ltd 5,14,40,59,116,135,184
-William Boby (Australia) 177
-William 5,42
Boiler feed water 35,40
Bournemouth Water Co. 73,147
Brazil 53,180
Brentford (Commerce Rd) 126
British Berkefeld 14,145
British Steel 134
Broadside 145
Broken Scar 144,189
Cadagua 179,186

Cadell, H 27,28
Caink 49
Calabar 197
Candy
-Burville 96,186
-Candy Filter Co. Ltd 6,12,53,74,83,138,143,171
-Candy Filters (India) Ltd 97,111,177
-Candy Filters (NZ) 158,178
-Candy-Whittaker 51
-Edgar Ralph 21,33
-Frank 5,9,11,13,21,24,30,53,54,61,71,85,86
-Frank Pullen 6,21,24,29,33,49,54,61,96,104,109,14
Canton 92
Carbon in pulp process 140
Cash worries 183
Catterick camp 61
Centrifuges, Pitsford 150
Chiswick works 120,126,129
Chlorinators
-Candy type-M 110
-Chloronome 71
-lawsuit 109
-pressure 70,86,92,152
-vacuum 92,152
Chlorination 9,166
-break-point 11,93
-de-chlorination 47,58,92
-for algal growths 71
-marginal 11,92,115
-super 47,58
Chlorination Equipment Ltd (Portacel) 152,158
Christchurch 31,60
Chudleigh 22
Church Wilne 98,169
Compagnie Internationale des Eaux 180
Clarifiers 12
-Accentrifloc (Accelator) 72,73,101,187
-Candy hopper tank 97,**99**,188
-CP 197
-Centrifloc 195
-Flat-bottom (FB) 100,187,**188**
-horizontal 73
-Pulsator 100,187
Clark, R 77,**120**
Clorocel 160
CoCo DAF 200
Consulting Engineers 15
Condensate polishing 121
Continuous ion-exchange 41
Contractors 15,16,17,166,175,201
Copenhagen 59
Cork 109
Coulson, H 79,159,**160**
Counter-current regeneration 43

231

Index

Counties Public Health Laboratories 32
Court Farm 120,177
Coventry sewage works 137
-Strensham 145
Crown Agents 143
Croydon 9,52
De-Acidite 126
De-aerators 41
De-tartriser 40
Declared contracts 174
Declor 11,55,**56**,61,62
Deep Shaft process 186
Degremont-Laing 16,165,176
Deminrolit 124
Density controller 103
Denton works 37,39,40,170,186
Dewplan 42,184
Diddington 150,152,169
Dosing pumps 86
-Autominor 104
-Candy G 106
-Metering Pumps Ltd 105,152,170
-Minor 104,170
Drakelow power station 121
Dufour, W.F.H.D. 93,**94**,111,112,142,159,171
Dunlop, John Boyd 49
Ealing site 129,152,170
Earthquakes 198
Eastchurch aerodrome 61
Egypt 101
El Car Paterson Candy Italiana 179,186
Electro-chlorine 41
Electro-dialysis 44,133
-membranes 44
Elvington 12,150,**167**
Enabling programme, Thames 200
Envirex 186
Fayoum Water Grid Scheme 78
Ferrous sulphate 25
Ferrybridge power station 122
Ferrozone 23,24,26
Field-Reid, E. 160
Filming, alum. 30,54
Filters
-air space 29
-anthracite 154
-bi-flow 59,86
-biological 24
-carbon 57
-compound 37
-gravity 11,13,64,69,87,88,145
-horizontal 59,85
-hydraulic scour 59,63,87
-Metafilter 139

-neutralising 56
-oxidising 27,55
-pre-coat 131
-pressure 12,29,37
-rake 12,36,54,102
-rapid gravity see gravity filters
-Stellar 131,138,139,144
-tertiary 13,43,146
-upflow 59
-Varivoid 134
Filter floor
-plenum 190
-Candy type-A 63,83,**84**,85,87,189,190
-Candy type-B 83,100
-PCI type-K 83,85,191,**193**,194,198
Filter nozzle 49,63,83,87,100
Floatation 13,187,200
Filter flow controllers
-Infilco venturi 72
-Candy "Module" flow controller 86,**89**
-Paterson "Stack" controller 158
France 179
Gans ion-exchange material 46,116
Gold mines 131,139
Gongola State 197
Graver 42,184,194
Greensand 116
Griffiths, J.H.T. **97**,165,169
Guandu, Brazil 155,156
Guernsey, St Saviours 137
Halifax 101
Ham Baker Ltd 53
Hanningfield 75,157
Hanwell (Church Road) works 92,95,101,111,152
Harlow Hill 55
Harrogate 55
Hastings 24,29,55,63,64,85
-Brede 29
-Filsham 29,87
Heart disease 13
Hegro 133
Helsingfors 76
Hipol 134
Holroyd and Healy 122
Holst 16,174
Houseman and Thompson 132
Howard Filtration Ltd 54
Howick Place 62,86,94
Ion-exchange (demineralisation) 46,116,126,128,168
Ion-Exchange (India) Ltd 129
Immedium filter 42,45,59,146
Infilco 72,73
International Water and Sewage Purification Co. Ltd 26,49

Index

International Purification Syndicate 30
Iron removal 30,63,87
Irvine (Clydebank) 64,70,87
-King George V 82
Izmit 194,**201**
Japan 92
Jarvis, A. 33,53,62,90
Jewell Filters 14,53,54,74,113,177
Karkh 78,**195**
Kempton park 71,73,101
Kennet river 29
Kerrison, O.C. 79,94,111,112,140,156,**159**,171
Kingston-on-Thames 52
Kingston, Jamaica 137
Kingsway 158,162
Langford 75,76
Lassen J.J. 48
Lassen-Hjort 45,47,115
Launceston 95,143
Laverstoke 172,179
-Investment Trust 157
Lawsuit 109
Lincoln 57
Lockheed valve actuators 104,153
Longham 109,147
Longmore camp 61
Los Angeles Aqueduct Scheme 198
Low, W.A. 119
Luton Sewage Works 60,146,204
Magnesite 55,**56**
Maidstone Water Co. Boxley 76
Malaya 178
Manston aerodrome 61
Maundown, Taunton 154
Mather and Platt 36,53,147
Mehalla Kubra, Egypt 120,121
Metafiltration Co. Ltd 14,138
Metering Pumps Ltd see Dosing pumps
Metropolitan Water Board (MWB) 11,32,70,73
Milton J.G. 77,**120**
Ministry of Munitions 61,70
Mixed bed 41,121,**124**,125
Mobile (Military) treatment units 45,47,131,138
Nanofiltration 13,181
National Rivers Authority (NRA) 11,168
New Works Engineer 164,166
New Zealand 111
Nuclear power stations 128
Ornstein 109
Oxidium 24,32,54
Ozone 13,58,76,79,189,192
Paignton 56
Paper mills 77,144
Partnership 23

Patent Automatic Distributors Ltd 50
Patents 21,24,49,79
Paterson Candy International Ltd (PCI) 6,14,15,42,164,**170**,176,185
-South Africa 178
Paterson Candy Holst Ltd (PC-H) 16,175,176
Paterson Candy Ltd 18,201,203
Paterson
-buys Bells, Candy's and Jewell Filters 74
-knighthood 140
-Paterson Engineering Co. Ltd (P.E.Co.) 6,12,**67**,138,144
-Paterson Engineering Co. (India) Ltd 70,177,178
-William 5,13,**67**,79,94,109,112,156
PCI see Paterson Candy International
PCI Membranes Ltd 173,**180**
Peel Harvey 59,90
Pemberton, R.T. 117
Permak (Permex) 130
Permutit 5,6,14,42,**115**,183
-AG Berlin 117
-Australia 129
-domestic softeners 126
-New York 117
-Service Dept. 125
-South Africa 120
-trademark 117
Phillips et Pain 117
Pickard, Prof.J.A. 138
Pitsford 12,150,**151**
Plumbo-solvency (Plumbism) 30,56
Polarite 11,23,24,25,26,30,30,86
Poona 70
Pontypridd 63
Port Elizabeth 32
Portals 14,80,117,127,**132**,135,144,155,156,171,183,199
Privatisation 11,16,17,199,202
Profit sharing scheme 101
Proportioning devices 38,63
-Bell's low turbine 39
-Centrifugal Balancer 63,**161**
-Lassen-Hjort 46
-Paterson Osilameter 68
-Weir-type "Clorstop" 112
Peuch-Chabal 53
PWT Projects Ltd 6,14,18,**199**
Rabeneck, L. 107,171,**173**,179,190
Railways 115,118,119
Rand Water Board 77,100,103,**148**
Reading 11,24,28,30,55,57
Re-carbonation 202
Red Book (Paterson) 68
Reeves Filters 6,36
Regional Water Authorities 10,11,15,164,176,185
Reigate sewage works 52

Index

Resins (anion, cation) 43,122,125,127
Reverse Osmosis 133,139,181
-B1 module 181
Revolving Purifier (Anderson's patent) 10
Riedal J.D. 117
River balancing reservoirs 12,164
River Boards 10,11,167
Rotterdam 78
Royce, J.G. 138
SAFe submerged aeration filters 202
Salisbury Plain camp 61
St Anne's Board Mill 77,81
Sandford Mill, Chelmsford 149
Sansom, G.W. 126
Saudi Arabia 180
Scion 135
Sea water demineralisers 124
Septic tanks 9
Settling tanks see clarifiers
Sewage treatment/disposal 9,10,11,13,25,28,50,130, 186,202
Shanghai City Waterworks 91
Shell Haven refinery 125
Simmons, G. 101,**104**
Simon-Hartley Ltd 202
Siphons 153
Slow sand filters 9,10,23,29,54,69
Slow start 72,90,**91**
Sludge blanket 99
Sludge cones, "Gravitrol" 189
Smalley, W. 79,159
Sofnol 46
Softening
-base-exchange 41,46,47,116
-hot 46,122
-lime 12,13,46,75,98,99,149,165
-precipitation see lime softening
South Africa 53,103,147
Southall works 173
South Staffs. Water Co. 73
-Huntington 76,165
-Sandfields 75
-Seedy Mill 144
South Wales factory 126,130
South West Suburban Water Co. 31
Split contracts 175
Sprinklers (distributors) 28,50,51
Statutory Water Companies 11
Steelworks 154,155,184
Stella-Meta Filters Ltd 131,132,173
Strood 56
Sulphonated coal 121
Swimming pools 36,145
Talybont 63,100

Tar Roads Syndicate 49
Tewkesbury 64,**69**,87,164,189
Thames Water 14,132,182,199
Thomas W.D.J. **106**,168
Thresh, Dr J. 32,57,62
Torquay, Tottiford 59,143,161
TNO 44
Trickling filters 13,24,28,49
Tripol 134
Truro 60
Turnover Filters 17
Turn-key contracts 16,174,177
Typhoid 9,55,56
UKAEA 45,180
United Filters Ltd. 42
United Water Softeners Ltd (UWS) 6,7,46,**47**,77,110, 115,116
Uranium recovery 120,**127**
Utilities 16
Wallace and Tiernan 11,92,115,152
Walter, A.J.R. 117,**118**,122
Wanson 179
Wars
-Boer 47,61
-1st World (WW1) 45,47,61
-2nd World (WW2) 122,137,141,
-Gulf 200
Water Softeners Ltd 48
Water Treatment Advisory Services Ltd 32
Water Act 1945 10
Weardale and Consett Water Board 69
Webster 27
West Africa 143,178
West Hants Water Board 59
Weir Group 42,43
Whittaker 49
Wind of Change 177
Williams, W.G.(Bob) 5,103,184,rear cover flap
Whitechapel works 23,26
Wolverhampton 54
York 54
Zambia 147
Zeo-Karb 126
Zeolite 46,124
Zerolit 117,127
Zimbabwe 147
Zinc precipitation process 139

THE FAMILY TREE

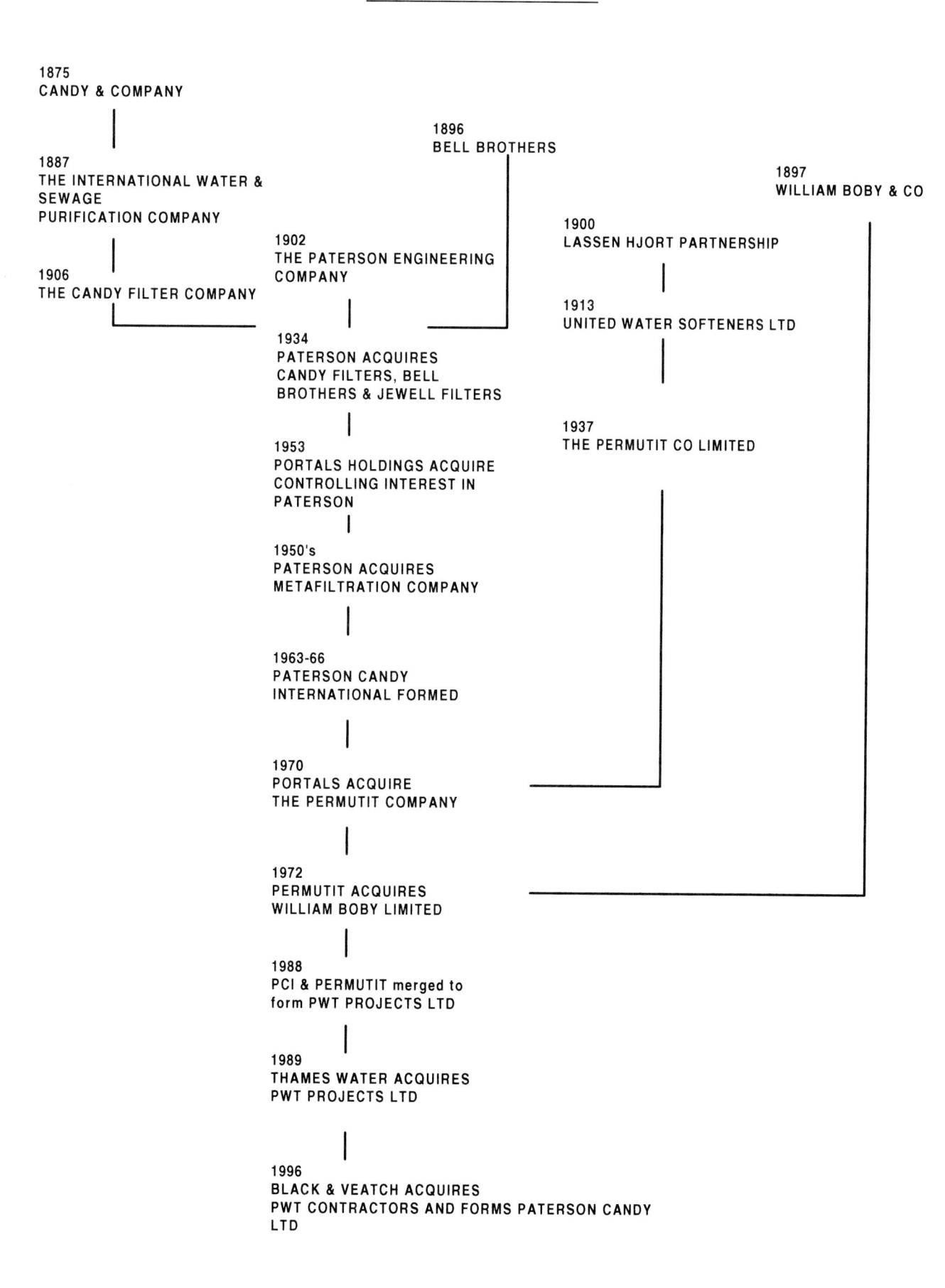

1875
CANDY & COMPANY

1887
THE INTERNATIONAL WATER & SEWAGE PURIFICATION COMPANY

1896
BELL BROTHERS

1897
WILLIAM BOBY & CO

1900
LASSEN HJORT PARTNERSHIP

1906
THE CANDY FILTER COMPANY

1902
THE PATERSON ENGINEERING COMPANY

1913
UNITED WATER SOFTENERS LTD

1934
PATERSON ACQUIRES CANDY FILTERS, BELL BROTHERS & JEWELL FILTERS

1937
THE PERMUTIT CO LIMITED

1953
PORTALS HOLDINGS ACQUIRE CONTROLLING INTEREST IN PATERSON

1950's
PATERSON ACQUIRES METAFILTRATION COMPANY

1963-66
PATERSON CANDY INTERNATIONAL FORMED

1970
PORTALS ACQUIRE THE PERMUTIT COMPANY

1972
PERMUTIT ACQUIRES WILLIAM BOBY LIMITED

1988
PCI & PERMUTIT merged to form PWT PROJECTS LTD

1989
THAMES WATER ACQUIRES PWT PROJECTS LTD

1996
BLACK & VEATCH ACQUIRES PWT CONTRACTORS AND FORMS PATERSON CANDY LTD